Here is a selection of the best poems written in English by Canadians, from the beginning of the nineteenth century to the present time—250 poems by 76 authors. The first poem included in the anthology was published in 1825, the last in 1943. Both the old and the modern schools of poetry are well represented.

In his Introduction Mr. Smith gives an interesting sketch of the development of Canadian poetry. The selections of the contributing authors are preceded by critical notes varying in length from a single paragraph to three pages. The emphasis, however, is not upon Canadian literary history or social background but on the poetry itself.

"In a sense this book is an act of faith. The compiler believes that here is an increasingly significant body of verse, at its best cogent, intense, and finely shaped, and that it may be presented as a not unworthy expression of Canada's self-awareness."—*Introduction.*

THE BOOK OF
CANADIAN POETRY

A Critical and Historical Anthology

Edited with an Introduction and Notes by
A. J. M. SMITH

THE UNIVERSITY OF CHICAGO PRESS
CHICAGO · ILLINOIS

In Canada
W. J. GAGE & CO., LIMITED, TORONTO

THE UNIVERSITY OF CHICAGO PRESS · CHICAGO

Agent: THE CAMBRIDGE UNIVERSITY PRESS · LONDON

PREFACE

I HOPE that this book will give pleasure to the general reader both in Canada and in the United States and that it contains enough information and criticism to make it useful to the student of Canadian literature. I have tried to present a more balanced view of the development of Canadian poetry as a whole than can be obtained from other anthologies, and to this end I have placed rather less emphasis upon the poets of the school of Carman and Roberts than has been customary in Canada. But in compensation there is a fuller treatment of some of the older poets, particularly Heavysege, Sangster, and the two remarkable poets of the eighties, Isabella Valancy Crawford and George Frederick Cameron; while the younger poets of the modern revival are generously represented for the first time.

Every anthology is conditioned by a contemporary bias, the results of which are seen in the selections from the poets of the past as well as from those of the present. This is inevitable and natural, and I have made no attempt to avoid it. One omission, however, will strike every reader. I have not tried to illustrate the fine poetic literature of the French-Canadians. To do so adequately would have doubled the size of this book and would, in any case, have been beyond my abilities.

That there are no errors of fact or judgment I cannot presume to hope, and that there are not more is due in great part to the kindness of many authorities and many friends. I wish to thank particularly for their advice and encouragement Dr. Pelham Edgar, dean of Canadian critics; Dr. E. J. Pratt and Mr. Northrop Frye, of Victoria University, Toronto; Dr. Duncan Campbell Scott, of Ottawa; Professor R. S. Knox, Professor A. S. P. Woodhouse, and other members of the English Department at University College, Toronto; Captain Earle Birney and Lieutenant Ernest Sirluck, of Toronto; and Professor F. R. Scott, of McGill University, Montreal. All of these have read the Introduction and many of the notes and in every case have given me generous help. Professor Roy Daniells, of the University of Manitoba, read the manuscript at a late stage of its preparation, and his careful and detailed criticism has been of the utmost value. I am indebted to Professor Frank H. Underhill, of the University of Toronto, for a note on Howe and on the rebellions of 1837. Mr. Arthur S. Bourinot, of Ottawa, and Mr. Ralph Gustafson, of New York, lent me books I could not easily obtain elsewhere. Dr. Leon Edel, of New York, Professor E. K. Brown, of Cornell University, and Mr. L. A. Mackay, of the University of British Columbia, have all assisted me with suggestions and encouragement. Lieutenant Paul Corbett, formerly of W. J. Gage & Co. Limited, Toronto, has shown me many kindnesses. I wish to thank Professor A. S. P. Woodhouse, editor of the *University of Toronto Quarterly*, for allowing me to reprint a part of the Introduction that appeared in that journal.

My greatest debt of gratitude is to the Trustees of the John Simon Guggenheim Memorial Foundation, of New York, whose award of a fellowship during the year 1941–42 made this work possible. I owe thanks also to the Michigan State Board of Agriculture, which granted me a leave of absence from my duties in the English Department at the Michigan State College of Agriculture and Applied Science. I cannot conclude without acknowledging the help afforded by my wife, whose critical judgment and discriminating taste have been invaluable.

A. J. M. S.

East Lansing, Michigan
February 1943

ACKNOWLEDGMENTS

THE editor makes grateful acknowledgments to the following publishers, magazines, authors, and holders of copyright for permission to reprint poems contained in this volume. Every effort has been made to find the owners of copyright material; if anyone has been overlooked, the compiler extends his apologies and regrets.

Adelphi: for a poem by A. J. M. Smith.

Marcus Adeney: for a passage from *Mansong*.

Margaret Avison: for four poems.

Alfred G. Bailey: for two unpublished poems.

Behrman's Jewish Book House, New York: for selections from *Hath Not a Jew,* by Abraham M. Klein.

Arthur S. Bourinot: for a poem from *What Far Kingdom* (Toronto, 1941).

Charles Bruce: for three poems published originally in the *Canadian Poetry Magazine.*

Canadian Forum: for poems by Patrick Anderson, Alfred G. Bailey, Robert Finch, Ralph Gustafson, Ronald Hambleton, Raymond Knister, L. A. Mackay, P. K. Page, and James Wreford.

Canadian Review of Music and Art: for a poem by Dorothy Livesay.

Carol Coates Cassidy: for a selection from *Poems* (Toronto, 1941).

Contemporary Verse: A Canadian Quarterly: for poems by Ronald Hambleton, Dorothy Livesay, Floris Clark McLaren, P. K. Page, A. J. M. Smith, and James Wreford.

Coward-McCann, Inc.: for selections from *Songs of the Coast Dwellers,* by Constance Lindsay Skinner. Copyright 1930 by Coward-McCann, Inc., New York.

Leo Cox: for a poem from *North Star.*

Dodd, Mead and Company: for "Low Tide on Grand Pré" and "A Northern Vigil," by Bliss Carman, and "The Shooting of Dan McGrew," by Robert W. Service. Reprinted by permission of the publishers, Dodd, Mead and Company, New York.

Robert Finch: for poems.

Hermia Harris Fraser: for selections from "Totem Town Vignettes" published originally in the *Canadian Poetry Magazine*.

Ralph Gustafson: for poems from *Epithalamium in Time of War* (1941) and *Lyrics Unromantic* (1942).

Katherine Hale (Mrs. John Garvin): for a selection from *The Island and Other Poems*.

Leo Kennedy: for poems from *The Shrouding*.

A. M. Klein: for an unpublished poem.

Frederick E. Laight: for a poem published originally in the *Canadian Poetry Magazine*.

Dorothy Livesay: for a poem from *Signposts*.

McClelland and Stewart, Limited: for selections from *Dr. Drummond's Complete Poems*, *Bliss Carman's Poems*, *The Poems of Duncan Campbell Scott*, and *The Complete Poems of Marjorie Pickthall*. Reprinted by permission of the copyright owners, McClelland and Stewart, Limited, Toronto.

Floris Clark McLaren: for an unpublished poem.

Macmillan Company of Canada, Limited: for selections from *Dream Tapestries*, by Louise Morey Bowman; *A Dryad in Nanaimo*, by Audrey Alexandra Brown; *Halt and Parley*, by George Herbert Clarke; and *Titans*, *The Fable of the Goats and Other Poems*, and *Dunkirk*, by E. J. Pratt. Reprinted by permission of the publishers, Macmillan Company of Canada, Limited, Toronto.

Menorah Journal: for a poem by Abraham M. Klein.

Musson Book Company, Limited, and Hodder and Stoughton, Limited (Canada): for a poem from *Flint and Feather*, by E. Pauline Johnson.

Nation: for a poem by A. J. M. Smith.

L. C. Page and Company: for three poems from *Pipes of Pan*, by Bliss Carman, and for seven poems from *Poems*, by Charles G. D. Roberts. Reprinted by permission of the publishers, L. C. Page and Company, Inc., Boston.

Partisan Review: for a poem by Ronald Hambleton.

Poetry: A Magazine of Verse: for poems by Patrick Anderson, Robert Finch, Abraham M. Klein, Dorothy Livesay, P. K. Page, E. J. Pratt, W. W. E. Ross, and F. R. Scott.

Preview: for poems by Patrick Anderson and P. K. Page.

Providence Sunday Journal: for a poem by Ronald Hambleton.

Queen's Quarterly: for a poem by E. J. Pratt.

Ryerson Press: for selections from *David and Other Poems*, by Earle Birney; *The Collected Poems of Wilfred Campbell*; *Pipes of Pan*, by Bliss Carman; *Songs and Sonnets*, by Helena Coleman; *For This Freedom Too*, by Mary Elizabeth Colman; *Sheepfold*, by Leo Cox; *Lilies and Leopards*, by Annie

C. Dalton; *Lyrics of Earth*, by Archibald Lampman; *By Stubborn Stars*, by Kenneth Leslie; *In Flanders Fields and Other Poems*, by John McCrae; *West by East and Other Poems*, by J. E. H. MacDonald; *The Complete Poems of Tom MacInnes; Viper's Bugloss*, by John Smalacombe (L. A. Mackay); *Tecumseh: A Drama, and Canadian Poems*, by Charles Mair; *The Wind Our Enemy* and *Salt Marsh and Other Poems*, by Anne Marriott; *Selected Poems of Sir Charles G. D. Roberts; I Sing of Life*, by Lloyd Roberts; *The Leather Bottle*, by Theodore Goodridge Roberts; *Collected Verse*, by Robert W. Service; and *The Complete Poems of Francis Sherman*. Reprinted by permission of the publishers, Ryerson Press, Toronto.

Saturday Night: for a poem by Audrey Alexandra Brown.

Duncan Campbell Scott: for "At Delos."

Archdeacon Frederick George Scott: for selections from *Poems*.

F. R. Scott: for poems, including one from *New Provinces*.

Sewanee Review: for poems by Ralph Gustafson.

Arthur Stringer: for three poems.

Neil Tracy: for selections from *The Rain It Raineth*.

Vice-Versa: for a poem by A. J. M. Smith.

Voices: for poems by Patrick Anderson, Ralph Gustafson, Ronald Hambleton, and P. K. Page.

TABLE OF CONTENTS

PART III. THE NEW NATIONALISM: "THE GOLDEN AGE"

PART IV. VARIETIES OF ROMANTIC
SENSIBILITY

PART V. MODERN POETRY: THE NATIVE TRADITION

PART VI. MODERN POETRY: THE COS-MOPOLITAN TRADITION

INTRODUCTION

INTRODUCTION

I

AT A TIME when Canadian poetry is entering a period of renewed vitality it is good to look back over the span of a century and a half during which people living in Canada have tried to interpret the life around them through the medium of verse. It will help us to appreciate the poetry of the present if we can see it beside that of the past. Thus we shall come to understand the essential unity of spirit that animates good work in whatever age it is produced and in whatever style it is written.

The main purpose of this collection is to illustrate in the light of a contemporary and cosmopolitan literary consciousness the broad development of English-Canadian poetry from its beginnings at the end of the eighteenth century to its renewal of power in the revolutionary world of today. The emphasis, however, is not upon literary history or social background but on the poetry itself. Poetry is primarily an art, and it is most revealing when it is most itself. What it tells us about society is something we have to catch as an overtone from what it tells us about an individual. No extended effort, therefore, has been made to focus a direct beam upon the social, political, or economic background. Yet if the reader is not helped to understand that background a little more clearly by the indirect evidence afforded even by "pure" poetry, this book will have fallen short of complete success.

Whatever can be hoped for, however, the editor has been encouraged by the conviction, growing as the work progressed, that a catholic hospitality toward every period of Canadian literature and every type of poetry, traditional and experimental, ambitious and homely, does not demand the adoption of any ambiguous standard of excellence. The true standard, after all, is one of degree, not kind.

We shall, as Mr. W. H. Auden has reminded us, "do poetry a great disservice if we confine it only to the major experiences of life." In seeking to arrive at a just estimate of Canadian poetry we would do well to remember this dictum. Some of the best of the verse has been concerned with the homelier aspects of life, and its value often lies in a spirit of unpretentious sweetness that lasts well—sometimes long after much more imposing material has gone sour. William Henry Drummond's tender and humorous evocations of the olden times in French Canada are a classic instance of the preservative value of humility, humanity, and good sense.

It is when our poets have gathered their singing robes about them to hymn the mysteries of Life and the grandeurs of Empire that they have tended to become a little tiresome. There will be found here no prejudice in favor of "high seriousness." The significant tests are sincerity and vitality rather than loftiness of aim or solemnity of treatment. After we have made sure that we know what the poet is saying, we must ask: Does the poet mean what he says? Is his poem alive? We must impose, that is, a standard determined by the *pressure* under which experience has been realized, not by any preconception in favor of the kind of experience we are accustomed to label "poetic." Such an attitude makes it possible not only to take delight in the newer, and very accomplished, experimental poetry of today but—what is more difficult—at the same time to find pleasure in the verse of Canada's earliest period, which is sometimes vigorous, or curious, or even merely historically interesting, without being excellent as poetry.

Yet it is, in the long run, as excellent poetry that the greater part of the sequence of verses here presented must justify its claim to serious attention. In a sense this book is an act of faith. The compiler believes that here is an increasingly significant body of verse, at its best cogent, intense, and finely shaped, and that it may be presented as a not unworthy expression of the growth of Canada's self-awareness.

II

Canadian poetry, indeed, is the record of life in Canada as it takes on significance when all the resources of sensibility, intelligence, and spirit are employed in experiencing it or in understanding it. Some of the poets have concentrated on what is individual and unique in Canadian life and others upon what it has in common with life everywhere. The one group has attempted to describe and interpret whatever is essentially and distinctively Canadian and thus come to terms with an environment that is only now ceasing to be colonial. The other, from the very beginning, has made a heroic effort to transcend colonialism by entering into the universal, civilizing culture of ideas.

To trace this twofold purpose back to the beginning of Canadian literature would involve an examination of the rather mediocre verse produced in the various British North American colonies in the last two or three decades of the eighteenth century and the first two or three of the nineteenth. What might be called the "extra-Canadian" tradition arose first. It could be illustrated in the hymns of Henry Alline and the rather angular poetry of Puritan piety, which was brought into Nova Scotia by schoolmasters, ministers, and judges educated at Harvard College. Under the impact of the Revolutionary War and the influx of the United Empire Loyalists, this poetry of religious ejaculation gave way to political satire leveled at republican "treason." The poets of the Loyalist tradition, of whom Jonathan Odell was perhaps the bitterest and the best, were disappointed Tories, who used the couplet of Pope and Churchill in a conventional and not very competent way. When they essayed the formal patriotic ode, the results were seldom happy.

Neither the Puritans nor the Tories seem to have found any compelling subject of poetry in the challenge of the new land to the sanguine and hardy settlers from Europe. But this was a subject that the Canadian poet could not avoid, though the lateness of its appearance is rather surprising. It testifies, perhaps, to the hardness of the conditions. The first poet who attempted such a subject on an ambitious scale was Oliver Goldsmith, grandnephew and namesake of the famous poet, who was born at Annapolis, Nova Scotia, in 1781. In 1825 he published *The Rising Village*, a kind of sequel to his granduncle's finest poem, and here, instead of the slow decay of a village of the Old World, he described the rise of a happy community of Loyalist settlers in the Acadian wilderness of the new. The poem has some touches of convincing realism and some instances of sincere feeling, but for the most part it is a rather conventional essay in late-eighteenth-century sentimentalism. The diction is familiar without being memorable, the heroic couplets are smooth and monotonous, and the native element is largely in the author's intention.

No poet of outstanding ability, indeed, was to appear until after the nineteenth century had reached the halfway mark. The task of subduing the wilderness absorbed all the energies of a young people. As the new century began, British North America consisted of a number of busy communities—Loyalist, French, and Scottish—in the Maritimes, Lower Canada, and Upper Canada; but they had little to do with one another and, in the words of Professor Baker, "nothing in common but a sense of isolation." It took events like the War of 1812 and the rebellions of 1837 to awaken a lively sense of the need for unity, and it was not until the fifties and sixties that the national ideal began to take shape in reality or to find expression in genuine poetry. Then, if not in the old-fashioned, high-spirited verses of Howe, in the sincerely felt lyrics of Sangster and the descriptive poems of Mair, Canadian poetry began little by little to individualize itself.

III

The Honorable Joseph Howe was a busy man of affairs, proprietor and editor of the most influential newspaper in Nova Scotia, a politician and, indeed, a statesman, for many years the leader of a sort of Nova Scotian nationalism that caused him to oppose Confederation, though he was finally won round to its support. As a poet he was an elegant amateur, whose descriptive couplets and gaily tender lyrics were quite in the eighteenth-century manner. He wrote light verse, sophisticated and sentimental, and sometimes, as in his own peculiar version of the Noble Savage, the delightful "Song of the Micmac," at once ridiculous and charming. The theme of his more serious work was the dangers and ardors of life in the new land, and his most ambitious poem, the unfinished "Acadia," represented an advance along the lines that had been laid down by the younger Goldsmith, but no important change. It is one of those long descriptive poems written in smooth couplets, filled with passages of moralizing and relieved by anecdote and narrative, which were so much in fashion in the eighteenth century. Yet the poem is not without interest, for Howe was closer to his subject than European sentimentalists. His diction and his moralizing are conventional, but he paints the hardships, and indeed the terrors, of the settlers' life with a moving honesty.

When Howe's "literary remains" were published in 1874, a year after his death, they must have seemed like the product of a century earlier, for by this time the Romantic movement had long made itself felt. The Canadian poet who first came under its spell and who attempted to breathe its spirit into his pictures of the scene around him was Charles Sangster. Like Howe, Sangster was to a great extent a literary poet, but the shades that hang about him are not those of the eighteenth century. It is Lord Byron, Tom Moore, Wordsworth, Poe, and the early Tennyson that we sometimes feel through his poems. Sangster's two books, *The St. Lawrence and the Saguenay* (1856) and *Hesperus* (1860), have been long out of print, and he is

remembered now only for a few pieces preserved in the standard anthologies. This is unfortunate, for the greater number of
the selections do little more than tempt the unguarded reader
to a casual glance and a patronizing smile. But to dismiss a
man capable of the music of lines like

> "Love is swift as hawk or hind,
>   Chamois-like in fleetness,
> None are lost that love can find,"
>   Sang the maid, with sweetness.

or the gnomic strength of

> Ye whose souls are strong and firm,
> In whom love's electric germ

> Has been fanned into a flame
> At the mention of a name;
> Ye whose souls are still the same
> As when first the Victor came,

> Stinging every nerve to life,
> In the beatific strife,

> Till the man's divinest part
> Ruled triumphant in the heart,
> And, with shrinking, sudden start,
> The bleak old world stood apart,

> Periling the wild Ideal
> By the presence of the Real . . . .

is to dismiss a poet of unusual sensibility and of no mean power.
Sangster has been praised as the first Canadian poet who made
a successful attempt to express a personal reaction to experi-
ence in terms of his native landscape and his northern weather.
Yet he is not exclusively, or even mainly, a "Canadian" poet.
His finest lyrics are not his patriotic pieces, like the elegy on
Brock (though this is not without considerable merit), or his
descriptions of typical Canadian scenes, like "Chaudière
Falls" or "The Rapid," but poems quite free from nationalism
or provincialism, lyrics like "Mariline" or "An Autumn
Change," in which a pure and elegant music rises out of
thought and feeling and is expressed with a kind of stubborn
self-taught solidity of language that is worth a good deal more

than the fluidity and glibness of some of the more accomplished
poets of a later generation.

Eight years after Sangster's second, and last, volume there
appeared in Montreal the first book of a writer who sought to
realize the poetic possibilities in purely Canadian themes.
This was *Dreamland and Other Poems* (1868), by Charles Mair.
Mair was himself to take an active part in the opening of the
West and to make an adventurous escape from death at the
hands of Louis Riel during the first Red River rebellion. The
vast wilderness of prairie, the Indian hunter, and his prey—the
rapidly vanishing bison—touched Mair's imagination, and in
his most characteristic poems and his chronicle play, *Tecumseh*
(1886), he tried to do justice to the drama of the white man's
pushing westward amid all the romantic aspects of the Canadian wilds. Unfortunately, his verse suffers from the load of
poetic diction carried over from his reading of the popular
English and American poets—Byron, Tennyson, Poe, and
Bryant—and it is very uneven in quality. One is astonished by
lapses[1] that do, however, serve to throw into bold relief the
lines and stanzas that are melodious and the images that are
just. Indeed, although few of Mair's poems are satisfactory in
their entirety, their best passages afford some delightfully precise close-ups of the Canadian woodlands and their flowers,
animals, and insects, caught as they are under the parching
sun of August or in the drenching moonlight of spring, and reveal in Mair an eye for the tiny realities of nature that many
better poets might envy. Here and there, too, Mair shows a
sensitiveness to strange states of feeling, which, in the best
stanzas of "Dreamland" and a few other early poems, seems to
promise an imaginative poetry that he was, perhaps wilfully,

---

[1] Such, for example, as the following quatrain preserved in Wilfred Campbell's *The Oxford Book of Canadian Verse* (Toronto, 1913):

> "Beneath her sloping neck
> Her bosom-gourds swelled chastely, white as spray,
>   Wind-tost—without a fleck—
> The air which heaved them was less pure than they."

to turn away from. Yet if he could have gone on to write as
sensitively and as powerfully as this:

> The silent shadows lay about the land,
> In aching solitude, as if they dreamed;
> And a low wind was ever close at hand,
> And, though no rain-drops fell, yet always seemed
> The rustle of the leaves like falling rain . . . .

he might—in spite of the lingering echoes of Tennyson—have
deserved the eulogy his modern editor pronounced upon him.[2]

The greatest poet of the pre-Confederation period, however,
has not received from succeeding generations of Canadians the
high praise that once was accorded him by American and
English men of letters into whose hands his astonishing dramatic poem *Saul* had come. Charles Heavysege came to Montreal from England in middle life and settled down to his trade
of cabinetmaker and carpenter. A great reader of Shakespeare
and the Bible, he took the themes of his ambitious poetry from
the histories of the Jews or elaborated them in a world of
Elizabethan sensibility. He made no effort to be a national
poet or to describe the flora and fauna of his new home, and
this, in part, accounts for the grudging recognition of his significance in the handbooks of Canadian literature. In these,
the fact that he came to Canada late in life outweighs the fact
that he settled there permanently and wrote his poems there.
The universality of his themes is made a reproach that they are
not "Canadian," and the originality of their conception and
execution is remarked upon only to explain that he had little
influence on the development of Canadian poetry. What ap-
pealed, however, to such admirers of *Saul* as Hawthorne,
Emerson, Coventry Patmore, Longfellow, and Bayard Taylor
was the richness and comprehensiveness of the intellectual and
moral experience out of which the poem arose.

Saul was published in 1857, and in two subsequent editions
(1859 and 1869) it was revised and improved. It is a mam-

---

[2] Robert Norwood, who wrote in his Introduction to the Radisson Society's
edition of Mair's complete works (1926): "Charles Mair is our greatest Canadian
poet by every count."

moth drama, anticipating in form and machinery, as well perhaps as in its fine gloom, *The Dynasts* of Thomas Hardy. The play is in three parts, each of five acts, and altogether it is about ten thousand lines long. The third edition is a volume of over four hundred closely printed pages. *Saul* is a moral drama, conceived with psychological insight and with a richness of imagination that is expressed in a grandiloquent and sometimes grand rhetoric. What Heavysege lacked was not the ability to write moving and majestic lines but the power to construct an orderly narrative or a cumulatively intensifying drama. The play is episodic, and the spacings of its languid sections and its climaxes often seem haphazard. Yet the magnificence of the finest passages, such as the slaughter of the Amalekites and the ironic comments of the Demons conducting the souls of the slain to Hell, commands the highest admiration. So does the sensitiveness and power with which the King's madness is developed. In personifying the spirit of Saul's affliction as the vacillating agent of evil, the fallen angel Malzah, Heavysege has created a figure as original and convincing as an Ariel or a Caliban.

The other works of the author of *Saul* have not the scope and power of that poem, yet they are, in their way, remarkable enough. *Count Filippo, or The Unequal Marriage* (1860) is a brilliantly written and well-constructed problem play, very much in the manner of Beaumont and Fletcher. It analyzes with a good deal of subtlety and a refreshing absence of squeamishness the moral risks involved in a marriage between youth and age. It is one of those rare things—a successful imitation of the Elizabethans—and, because of its poetry and its characterization, it is still good reading. A more conventional work and one which, despite its prolixity, has been more highly praised, is Heavysege's third and last major contribution to Canadian literature, the blank-verse narrative, *Jephtha's Daughter* (1865). With it was published a selection of the strange and somber "sonnets" that the poet had written earlier and that he now revised and carefully pruned. These reveal in little the strength and originality that make *Saul* a significant interpretation of the moral world.

IV

None of these poets of Canada before Confederation had succeeded in creating a poetry that was clearly and definitely "Canadian" in the sense that it differed from the poetry of England as the flowers and foliage, the lakes and rivers, and the mountains and the very air itself of Canada differed from those of the mother-country. From the beginning it had been expected that a national poet would arise to celebrate the wild nobility of the scenery and to voice the aspirations of the colonists to become the citizens of a strong, united nation. Standish O'Grady, a disgruntled Irishman, who published in 1842 the first and only canto of *The Emigrant: A Poem, in Four Cantos*, was expressing a common thought when he wrote in the Preface:

> This expanded and noble continent will no doubt furnish fit matter for the Muse. The diversity of climate, the richness of soil, the endearing qualities of a genial atmosphere must no doubt furnish a just excitement to the poetic mind, and arouse that energy correspondent with a richness of scenery, which the contemplative mind will studiously portray. . . . .

Some twenty years later Dr. Henry J. Morgan, in his valuable *Sketches of Celebrated Canadians and Persons Connected with Canada* (1865), translated this thought into the present tense and applied it to "Mr. Sangster, the Poet":

> We in Canada are unfortunate enough not to have had many persons entitled to the distinction of being marked as poets, though possessing every facility that a grand and romantic scenic country presents, capable of exciting the proper inspiration and spirit of poetry. . . . . The gentleman whose name heads this notice stands in the first rank of our Canadian poets.

The same implication, namely, that the whole duty of the poet in Canada is to be "Canadian," had already been made in the Introduction to our first anthology, the Reverend Edward Hartley Dewart's *Selections from Canadian Poets* (1864), and here also it was Sangster who had been designated first of Canadian poets:

Indeed, in the variety of subjects selected from the scenery, seasons, and past history of this country and in the success and originality with which he has treated them, he has no competitor whatever. His genius is more truly Canadian than that of any other poet of distinction in this Province.

Sangster was not—though perhaps he wanted to be—a Canadian poet of this type. Dr. Dewart and Dr. Morgan were indulging in wishful thinking. The test is the quality of the poetry. Sangster's best work is literary, and it is English. The pretty passage included here from *The St. Lawrence and the Saguenay* has the quaint charm of a Bartlett print, and it is written throughout in the language of *The Lady of the Lake*. The village where Mariline dwells is the village of Tennyson's May Queen; but out of it, in the strange final section at least, Sangster creates his most impressive poetry.

Mair makes a more consistent effort to become a national poet; but, although he has excellent powers of observation, their expression is defeated by a ruminating and undistinguished mind. His treatment of nature—apart from the language—is still that of Thomson and Cowper. In contrast to Lampman and the romantic nature poets who were soon to arise, he is impersonal, conventional, and calm—accurate enough as an observer but not vivid enough as a writer. He is reflective and sentimental, not imaginative or intellectual.

But there was one poet, a predecessor of Roberts, Lampman, and Carman—a young woman who died almost unrecognized at the age of thirty-seven—whose poetry had the exciting vitality that Mair's lacked. Vivid, energetic, imaginative, intellectual—these were the qualities of the best poems in a crudely bound paper-covered volume with the clumsy title *Old Spookses' Pass, Malcolm's Katie, and Other Poems* that Isabella Valancy Crawford published at her own expense—and at a dead loss—in 1884. Although the book was praised in a number of literary journals in England as well as in Canada and by such distinguished persons as the Marquis of Lorne and the Earl of Dufferin, it was not until a collected edition of her poems was published in 1905 that Miss Crawford's real stature

came to be generally recognized in Canada. Some of her lyrics
—she wrote copiously for the newspapers in order to live—are
conventional and sentimental in the peculiarly awful manner
of Victorian album verse. But where her imagination catches
fire, as it does in her poems of the Canadian wilderness, she
writes cleanly and vigorously, with a rushing sweep of energy
and with a boldness of imagery unapproached in Canadian
poetry until we come to the contemporary work of E. J. Pratt.
In "Malcolm's Katie" and "The Canoe" the spirit of the
northern woods under the impact of the changing seasons has
passed into the imagery and rhythm of the verse. If there is a
Canadian poetry that exists as something distinct from English
poetry, this—and this almost alone—is it.

With the work of Isabella Valancy Crawford we must link
that of George Frederick Cameron. Cameron, a brilliant student at Queen's University, sometime resident of Boston, later
a newspaper editor in Kingston, died at the age of thirty-one
and left behind him a body of poetry as individual and powerful in its very different way as that of Miss Crawford. A selection of his poems was published in 1887 under the accurate title
Lyrics on Freedom, Love, and Death. Cameron was a classical
scholar, an internationalist, and a cosmopolitan. Clarity,
strength, and suavity are the distinguishing features of his style.
We are told that he had read Virgil and Cicero in the original
before his fourteenth year, and this discipline left its mark on
his tightly packed, cleanly constructed stanzas.

One has little difficulty in setting the work of Cameron apart
from the dominant tradition of Canadian verse as it was developing in the late eighties and nineties into a school of descriptive nature poetry. There is no effort in him to do justice to
any aspect of national scenery. His themes are political, personal, and universal. They rise out of an intense love of justice
and a hatred of tyranny, a passionate desire for the woman he
loves, and an inescapable preoccupation with the idea of death.
His command of form and of metrics is admirable, and he has
the rare gift of taking a somewhat artificial style and infusing

into it a tone that is energetic, convincing, and almost colloquial. There are literary echoes here and there—of Poe in
the earlier poems and sometimes of Swinburne; and the influence of *Maud* can be felt in the background of the remarkable
lyrical monodrama "Ysolte." Yet this is of little importance,
for the literary influences are generally well assimilated. The
individual quality of Cameron's best poetry is an energy that
rises out of the clash of wit and intelligence with the forces of
sense and passion. In a romantic age he maintained some of
the classical virtues. Passionate yet resigned, and enthusiastic
yet disillusioned, he was able, in the last month of his life, under the shadow of death, to write:

> For we shall rest; the brain that planned,
> That thought or wrought or well or ill,
> At gaze like Joshua's moon shall stand,
> Not working any work or will,
> While eye and lip and heart and hand
> Shall all be still—shall all be still!

V

In 1880 Charles G. D. Roberts published *Orion and Other
Poems*, and a scholarly young undergraduate at Trinity College, Toronto, Archibald Lampman—ignorant as yet of the
poetry of Isabella Valancy Crawford and George Frederick
Cameron—hailed the book with a significant sense of libera-
tion and pride. Wrote Lampman:

Like most of the young fellows about me I had been under the depressing
conviction that we were situated hopelessly on the outskirts of civilization,
where no art and no literature could be, and that it was useless to expect
that anything great could be done by any of our companions, still more
useless to expect that we could do it ourselves. I sat up most of the night
reading and re-reading *Orion* in a state of the wildest excitement. . . . . It
seemed to me a wonderful thing that such work could be done by a Canadian, by a young man, one of ourselves.

Lampman's own first volume, *Among the Millet*, appeared in
1888, and in 1893 came that of his friend and fellow civil
servant, Duncan Campbell Scott. The same year, too, brought
Bliss Carman's *Low Tide on Grand Pré*. Thus it was that the

work of four friends, all born between 1860 and 1862, in-
augurated a movement that produced in Canada a body of
descriptive nature poetry which, though it was sometimes indebted in style or inspiration to Keats, Tennyson, Arnold, or
Swinburne, was at its best sincere and original, the expression
of genuine feeling and accurate observation. Moreover, these
poets had a command of technique, surer and less spasmodic
than that of their predecessors, which lifted them above the
rank of mere imitators of the great Victorians.

Of the four, Lampman, though he died a comparatively
young man at the very height of his powers, left the most completely satisfying body of work. His reputation has suffered a
little both from the injudicious zeal of his admirers among the
older critics, who have tried to present him as an important
philosophical poet, which he was not, and from the disparage-
ment of younger men, who have charged him with living in an
ivory tower on the banks of the Ottawa, unmindful of the
pulsing industrialization of Canadian life. But the truth is that
the greatness of Lampman lies in the purity and sweetness of
his response to nature and in his fine painter's eye for the details of landscape. Sensitive, and indeed passionate, observation upon which the artist has imposed the formal elegance of
a strict but never inert control gives to poems like "Heat" or
the magnificent sonnet, "Winter Evening," a peculiar authen-
ticity much more significant in its vitality than any didactic
element, philosophical or social, that was or that might have
been injected into his work. There are, indeed, indications in
his correspondence and in such poems as "Midnight" and
"The City of the End of Things" that Lampman would
not have been satisfied to remain a poet of pure nature. Yet it
is as a poet of pure nature that he achieved his best and most
characteristic work, and to have been anything but what he
was by temperament would, one feels, have been to court failure. His best poems have a timeless and placeless significance
which, paradoxically enough, rises out of their faithfulness to
the local scene and to the specific experience. In them the

woods and streams and the changing seasons of Lampman's
beloved Ottawa Valley have been fixed forever in the life-giv-
ing permanence of art. The Canadian poet, he had once declared, "must depend solely upon himself and nature," and it
is because he recognized so clearly his powers and his limitations that Lampman commands so high a measure of our respect and affection.

With Bliss Carman the case is somewhat different. Carman
is probably the best known of all Canadian poets, and it is true
that the peculiar magic of his finest poems can transport their
willing victims into a strange realm of sensation and feeling
where pleasure and pain are curiously confused. There is a
heightened consciousness and a delightful shiver in lines like
these:

> Outside, a yellow maple tree
> Shifting upon the silvery blue
> With small, innumerable sounds,
> Rustles to let the sunlight through.
> . . . .
>
> Come, for the night is cold,
> The ghostly moonlight fills
> Hollow and rift and fold
> Of the eerie Ardise hills!
>
> The windows of my room
> Are dark with bitter frost,
> The stillness aches with doom
> Of something loved and lost.
>
> Outside, the great blue star
> Burns in the ghostland pale,
> Where giant Algebar
> Holds on the endless trail.

But this intensity is diffused too thinly through the body of
Carman's work, and sometimes it is produced by rather tawdry
stimuli or by no definite ones at all. Even the much-praised
"Low Tide on Grand Pré," after a magnificently resonant
opening chord, fades out into a vague and imperfectly realized
emotionalism. Too often Carman was the victim of his own
glibness—a glibness of feeling as well as of language. He in-

vited his soul in a spasm of perpetual vagrancy to travel hope-
fully toward a spiritual goal that was attractive mainly because
it was unattainable. Thus he affords an excellent, if minor,
example of Mr. Santayana's class of "Barbarian poets," the
two most distinguished members of which are Browning and
Whitman, both of whom were among Carman's particular
heroes.

Carman thought of himself as reacting against the effemi-
nate poets of the decadent nineties, and he sought in the school
of Stevenson, Henley, and his friend Hovey to sing the praises
of the strenuous life, the open road, and the call of the far
horizon. At the same time he attempted to express a kind of
national individuality in his imagery of maple, tamarack, and
pine. But the inescapable impression is that Carman, like so
many other red bloods of his generation, is in essence a *fin de
siècle* aesthete turned out of the overstuffed boudoir into the
almost equally overstuffed outdoors.[3]

Charles G. D. Roberts and Duncan Campbell Scott, the two
survivors of the group, have produced a large body of work
that stands somewhere between the lyrical fervor of Carman
and the contemplative precision of Lampman. They wrote
lyrics, descriptive idyls, and dramatic narratives that had for
their setting the forests and rivers of the Maritimes and the
Ottawa Valley and for their theme the emotional and spiritual
enrichment that the earth of the new land grants to the sympathetic dweller in harmony with nature. Of the two, Roberts
has been the more prolific and the more various. He has al-

[3] Because of the romantic beauty of his best work and because of the impressive bulk of his publications, Carman has suffered by being overpraised more
than any other Canadian poet, with the possible exception of Roberts. The wisest
judgment on Carman is that of Mr. L. A. Mackay, who wrote in the *Canadian
Forum* (February, 1933): "At times, at his best, to the very end of his work, he
retains what I think is his genuinely personal note; a sort of shy, awkward, half-
inarticulate adolescence, its quick fresh exuberance, the smooth-skinned, soft-
fleshed delicacy, and the graceful charm of one of Donatello's youths.

"It is the great mass of inferior work that hurts his reputation. Someday,
someone will make the right, judicious selection, and Carman will be rediscovered in his true place, as one of the most agreeable of the American minor
poets."

ways been an extremely competent craftsman, but his inspiration has been the most genuine in his simpler, less ambitious pieces. He began, in the book that so pleased Lampman, with classical idyls imitative of Keats, and then, after producing an elaborate elegy on the poet Shelley, he turned to a delicate and objective nature poetry which presented a restrained and subtle interpretation of his native New Brunswick. Such graceful and sensitive poems as "The Solitary Woodsman" and "In the Barn-Yard's Southerly Corner" and some of the sonnets in *Songs of the Common Day* (1893) shine with a sober veracity that gives them a high place in the regional art of Canada. These are Roberts' best contribution to the national literature, and they have a value far greater than that of his more pretentious work, which includes nearly all, if not quite all, of his erotic poems and most of his rather facile transcendental pieces.[4] Roberts has always been an active and powerful personality, and his variety of moods and unquestioned technical facility have enabled him to keep in the forward van of popular feeling. Upon the death of Bliss Carman he won wide recognition as the unofficial laureate of the Dominion.

Unlike Carman and Roberts, Duncan Campbell Scott has not received the full measure of admiration he deserves. This is regrettable, but it is not hard to understand. Like Lampman, Duncan Campbell Scott is a scholarly poet, a conscientious and unassuming artist. His talent is quieter than that of Carman or Roberts, yet he shows a deeper interest in human beings and in dramatic action, and he is more fastidious and accurate in feeling. If he does not rise to the heights that they occasionally attain, neither does he descend as they sometimes do to an obvious and swaggering lyricism. His interest in music and his refined and cultivated sensibility reveal themselves in many carefully wrought lyrics of love and nature. John

---

[4] For an excellent analysis of the irresponsibility of these see Professor James Cappon's *Roberts and the Influences of His Time* (Toronto, 1905), one of the classics of Canadian literary criticism.

Masefield has testified to the magical beauty of his long ballad "The Piper of Arll."

Dr. Scott's lifework as an administrator in the Department of Indian Affairs at Ottawa has provided him with the material for many remarkable poems of Indian life—from "The Half-breed Girl," in his first volume of 1893, to the tragic master-piece, "At Gull Lake: August, 1810," in the volume of later poems collected in 1936. As an interpreter of the Indian, Duncan Campbell Scott is deserving of more serious consideration than is the widely acclaimed poetess Pauline Johnson. But Miss Johnson had special advantages: she was a real Indian princess, a genuine half-breed girl.

Pauline Johnson, whose Indian name was "Tekahionwake," was born in 1862 on the Iroquois Reservation near Brantford, Ontario. Her father was a full-blooded Indian, chief of the Six Nations Confederacy, and her mother was an Englishwoman. The poetry of Miss Johnson was much admired in Canada, where the romantic fact of her Indian birth, played up by critics and journalists, was accepted as convincing proof that she spoke with the authentic voice of the red man. She had a vigorous personality and an excellent sense of the theater. Dressed in Indian costume, she read her verses with great effect to audiences in Canada, the United States, and England. Furthermore, she was enthusiastically praised by a fashionable London critic. Theodore Watts-Dunton, who had been attracted to her poems in W. D. Lighthall's *Songs of the Great Dominion* (1889), hailed Miss Johnson as the accredited spokesman "of the great primeval race now so rapidly vanishing" and later wrote a rhapsodic introduction to her collected poems, *Flint and Feather*, which was published soon after her death in 1913.

The claim that this volume contains genuine primitive poetry or that it speaks with the true voice of the North American Indian will hardly be made by responsible criticism. Pauline Johnson's early home was not a primitive one, and she was reared in cultured surroundings. Her education was literary.

"She had read Scott, Longfellow, Byron, and Shakespeare," Professor Rhodenizer tells us, "before she was twelve years of age."[5] She must also have read Tennyson and Swinburne before she wrote her most characteristic lyrics. "Shadow Lake," "The Song My Paddle Sings," and "In the Shadows"—her best-known pieces—are decorous imitations of "Airy, Fairy Lillian" and "Sweet and Low." They have a graceful and easy-flowing cadence, which presents admirably vague impressions of pellucid waters and shadowy depths, but they are as empty of content as any devotee of pure poetry could wish. There is nothing primitive about them, nothing characteristic of the Indian or of Canada. They are minor Victorian escape poems, and their music is that of the waters of Putney and the gently flowing Cam. When Miss Johnson tried to portray more directly and more dramatically the feelings of the aborigines, she became, in such poems as "A Cry from an Indian Wife," "As Red Men Die," and "The Pilot of the Plains," theatrical and crude. The rhythm is heavy, the imagery conventional, and the language melodramatic and forced. Her best work is to be found not in her Indian poetry at all but in one or two pretty and very artificial little lyrics.

Two other poets of the same generation remain to be mentioned. One of them, Wilfred Campbell, was closely associated with the four friends whose work has already been discussed. The other, Archdeacon Frederick George Scott, of Quebec, stands somewhat apart.

Frederick George Scott is not, like the others, primarily a nature poet, nor is there much in his work of a national savor. He is frankly and unmistakably in the English tradition of Tennyson, Matthew Arnold, and Robert Bridges. In his best poems noble and sometimes profound thoughts have been expressed in simple, moving language in a style that is sometimes both elegant and strong. His themes are the universal ones—nature, love, hope, the transmutations of time, the mystery of death—but they are presented with a serenity and sureness

[5] V. B. Rhodenizer, *A Handbook of Canadian Literature* (Ottawa, 1930), p. 196.

that bear witness to the consistency and discipline of the poet's world view, which is that of Anglican Christianity. In contrast to the dominant romantic school of Carman and Roberts, Scott's poetry seems calm, if not cold; but it is the expression of an orderly world view, not of adventurous gropings into the half-world of cosmic fancy. It is a measure of the poet's personality, not an exhibition of it.[6]

Wilfred Campbell perhaps had greater gifts than F. G. Scott, but he squandered them recklessly. Both in voluminousness and in loftiness of theme, Campbell's work testified to his seriousness of intention, but the solemnity of his self-dedication as a poet betrayed him into grandiosity and triviality. He lacked the ability to write well enough for long enough, and the large emotional abstractions he concerned himself with in his odelike celebrations of Mother England and Vaster Britain seem now rather threadbare and tawdry. The same is true, in the main, of his mordant philosophical poems and his crowded Tennysonian dramas. Occasionally, however, as in the remarkable "Lazarus," he produced a striking and original poem, though he was too careless of form and too generous with padding to do it often. His best work is his earliest, the descriptive poems that evoke the vast emptiness of the northern lake country, which were published in *Lake Lyrics* (1889).

Turning now from these poets as individuals, we must try to make some judgment of their accomplishment as a whole, particularly that of the four leaders—Roberts, Carman, Lampman, and D. C. Scott. Orthodox critical opinion in Canada holds that their poetry represents the most complete and satisfying body of work in the whole range of Canadian literature and is perhaps Canada's most significant artistic and spiritual achievement. These poets are the Parnassians,

---

[6] This judgment, it must be recorded, is to be reserved for the best of Archdeacon Scott's poetry—that in the *Collected Poems* of 1910. His patriotic verse, in which he has expressed the vigorous faith of a British imperialist, has enjoyed wide popularity in the Dominion and is not without its value in wartime, but it lacks the authority of his earlier scholarly poetry and his religious lyrics.

and the nineties, when their finest work was appearing, is
Canada's "Golden Age." Undeniably, their prolific output
was astonishing in a country as careless of culture as Canada
was then. But more impressive than the generous bulk of their
"collected works"—or the fact that many of their books bore
the imprint of London or Boston—was the unmistakable polish, the genuine literary aura, and the high conception of the
responsibilities and privileges of their craft which testified to
the seriousness of their ambition. Amid the enthusiasm this
flowering evoked, it seemed as if the patriotic hopes of Dr. Morgan and Dr. Dewart had been more than fulfilled, and that
Canada, within a quarter of a century of Confederation, had
produced not one national poet but four!

It was harder to realize that the concentration upon personal
emotion and upon nature, while it made for an easier success,
meant a serious narrowing of range and sometimes a thinning
of substance. Delicate sensibility and often accurate feeling
went along with a good deal of rather commonplace thinking
and conventional moralizing. The supreme values were placed
in whatever touched the heart and spirit in the beauty of
nature.

The claim of this poetry to be truly national, adequately sustained in the field of scenery and climate, must, on the whole,
be denied to a body of work which ignored on principle the
coarse bustle of humanity in the hurly-burly business of the
developing nation. It was an awareness of a lack of complete
relevancy that led the most acute of our older critics, the late
Professor James Cappon, of Queen's University, to observe
that "perhaps our best Canadian poets have devoted themselves too much to an almost abstract form of nature poetry
which has too little savour of the national life and the national
sentiment about it and is more dependent on literary tradition
than they seem to be aware of."[7]

[7] *Op. cit.*, p. 84. Literary criticism in Canada, which is firmly rooted in romanticism, has not often presented this point of view. Mr. W. E. Collin, in a
valuable essay on Lampman in *The White Savannahs* (Toronto, 1936), and Mr.
L. A. Mackay, in several brilliant articles in the *Canadian Forum* during 1932 and

But this is not the last word on these poets. It defines their limitations, but it does not state their value. This can be done briefly. In one respect their dependence upon literary tradition is not a defect, for it was more fundamental than any mere surface imitation. It arose out of a belief in the continuity of culture, and in their best work it was a preserving and civilizing force. They have, it is true, except in their second-rate work, no message and no philosophy; but, if their theme was narrow, it was an important one, and they presented it with great variety, charm, and precision. In general terms, it was nothing less than the impingement of nature in Canada upon the human spirit.

VI

The powerful influence of Roberts, Carman, and Lampman was both an inspiration and a handicap to their successors for at least two generations. In the often moving though slighter work of Marjorie Pickthall, Francis Sherman, and, more recently, Audrey Alexandra Brown, the tradition of romantic nature poetry became brittle and glazed, and its imagery, which in the older poets had been genuinely local, tended to harden into convention. The Pre-Raphaelite movement and the Celtic Twilight were influences from Europe that weakened rather than strengthened the poetry of the interim. To Marjorie Pickthall, the most gifted poet of her generation, they provided the framework of a dream world in which she created a graceful and nostalgic poetry, from which at the end of her life she wanted to escape into reality. And she succeeded, in one or two of her last lyrics, in fusing an intense awareness of the beauty and transcience of life with the mystic's adoration of God. The beautiful "Resurgam" and the strange little poem "Quiet" are as striking in their way as the finest lyrics of Christina Rossetti.

1933, have laid the groundwork for a modern approach. They were anticipated in some respects by Gordon Waldron, a disciple of Goldwin Smith, who published in the *Canadian Magazine* for December, 1896, a forceful attack on the school of Roberts as poets of mere scenery.

But the writer of this generation who came most strongly under the domination of the Pre-Raphaelites was the New Brunswick poet, Francis Sherman. An ardent admirer of William Morris and a follower of Carman, Sherman produced a small body of carefully wrought poems in the best of which nature is interpreted through feelings that become dramatic because of their intensity and mercurial responsiveness. But the colorful monotony of the background and what is intended to be a pregnant vagueness of the whole emotional situation impose a richly decorated but opaque screen between the reader and reality.

A personality stronger than Miss Pickthall or Sherman—strong enough, indeed, if not to escape the prevailing romantic influences at least to find them in new sources and to transmit them in an original way—was the westerner, Tom MacInnes, whose *Rhymes of a Rounder* (1913) is one of the most engaging volumes in Canadian literature. MacInnes' originality consists in the gusto and skill with which he has used the Old French forms—ballade, villanelle, and rondeau—for the expression of a genial and intelligent bohemianism.

At its base MacInnes' philosophy is as dark as Thomas Hardy's, but, like Dr. Johnson's friend Edwards, the poet finds "cheerfulness is always breaking in," and he is saved from the despair that is the natural goal of a thoroughgoing materialism by an obstinate faith, the sources of which are human sympathy, sheer sensuous joy of living, and a feeling for artistic form. "God must be fascinated with matter," he wrote with conscious ambiguity, "seeing he has made so much of it." MacInnes is a philosopher in the popular sense: he is concerned with the problem of how to live as well as we can under the limiting conditions of circumstance and natural depravity. "I mean well, but I mean to live," he remarks quietly, and he has found words for the inarticulate wisdom of countless millions. He is willing to accept life as an eternal struggle in which the joyous and the strong survive, and here he speaks with the composite voice of the generation of Jack London and Teddy

Roosevelt. "We who are all in the mud together," he writes in
a "Ballade of Virtues," "make too much of right and wrong:
Three virtues sum it all—Courage, Cleanliness, Charity." He
utters a curse against all meddlers—"ministers, medicals,
meddlesome wives"—and finds a good word for one kind of
meddling only, the helping hand to the down-and-out:

> Whether at sea or whether on shore,
> Or at the job or over the wine,
> Whether on two legs, whether on four—
> All good fellows are friends of mine.

The same salty honesty with which MacInnes celebrates the
less heroic pleasures compels him to recognize the pain and
cruelty at the heart of life, and in "The Tiger of Desire" he
looks, with a Blake-like candor, at the truth that "fair and foul
are close of kin."

Bohemianism, of course, had had its exponents in Canadian
poetry before MacInnes. Carman and the American poet,
Richard Hovey, had done well by it in their three series of
Songs from Vagabondia (1894, 1896, 1901), mainly because they
took it lightheartedly. But Roberts (and Carman in his later
work) had been at some pains to dignify as a cosmic awareness
or a spiritual responsiveness what was really only an ethical
instability. MacInnes did not make this mistake; nor did another poet, a much more popular writer, whose sensibility was
strong and crude and whose ideas were elementary. This was
the poet of the Yukon, Robert W. Service.

Service has been read with delight by many who never read
poetry. His work represents the lowest common denominator
of the muscular dynamism, stemming from Nietzsche, that
found various forms of expression in Kipling, Theodore Roosevelt, and Jack London. A strong, brutal realism, frankly melodramatic themes, and a heavy, clanging rhythm have attracted many readers, while repelling others. The ethics of existence are simplified into a justification of the strong, who, in
the very nature of things, are bound to survive. But the harsh-

ness of this determinism is mitigated by a sentimental insistence upon a primitive code of honor. Much of his verse is trash, but in one or two robust ballads, of which the best is "The Shooting of Dan McGrew," Service has caught the spirit of folk poetry of low life—a poetry which blends violence, suffering, and high-spirited humor.

None of these poets who explored the varieties of individual romanticisms provides any link between the poets of the nineties and the younger experimentalists of the world between the wars. Such a link, because of the intensity, boldness, and variety of his work and because his sympathetic understanding is given to both the old and the new, is found in the narrative poet, E. J. Pratt. Indeed, it is from the publication in the *Canadian Forum* in 1925 of "The Cachalot," the first of Pratt's "little epics," that we must date the modern revival. Pratt, a Newfoundlander with salt and iron in his blood, has revealed himself as a poet of generous scope; and he is at his best when he has plenty of room, as he has in the fine series of heroic narratives, of which the latest is *Dunkirk* (1941).

Whether Pratt writes of the struggles of primordial monsters ("The Great Feud" [1926]) or of civilized man's battle with the elemental sea (*The Roosevelt and the Antinoe* [1930]; *The Titanic* [1935]), it is always courage and the lust for life that are at the center of his theme. Though MacInnes and Service are both poets of the rough humors of the strenuous life and both are worshipers of strength and bravado, Pratt is a much more serious poet than they. In him, activity, however strong or brave, is not admired for its own sake. Heroic action is action directed toward an end and aimed at an ulterior good. Perhaps the outstanding feature of Pratt's career has been the consistency of his preoccupation with the heroic and the sureness of his development in the direction of reality and moral seriousness. This development has brought him in his most ambitious poem, *Brébeuf and His Brethren* (1940), not only closer to a significant moral theme but closer to a truly national one. Yet when he lets his muse out on holiday in a world of pure fan-

tasy, as he did in *The Witches' Brew* (1925), he is unexcelled
for high spirits and sheer boisterous fun.

Pratt is the greatest of contemporary Canadian poets, for he
is the only one who has created boldly and on a large scale.
His work is popular in the sense that it is never obscure, or even
difficult, but it does not ignore or flout the intellect. In the
richness and variety of his diction and in his willingness to ex-
periment with new forms, Pratt points to the work of some of
his younger contemporaries. But he has had little direct influence on them. Indeed, the very expansiveness of his good nature and the exuberance of his energy serve as something of a
barrier, for the younger men are divided and complex, and,
whatever virtues they possess, geniality and heartiness are not
among them.

In place of the liberal humanitarianism that underlies the
work of Pratt, they are more likely to find a congenial philosophy in communism, or humanism, or in the irony and despair of an aesthetic detachment. They feel that the tradition
of romantic nature poetry which arose with Sangster and Mair
and came to its finest flower in Isabella Valancy Crawford,
Archibald Lampman, and Duncan Campbell Scott has finally
played itself out. What, indeed, the poets of today are bringing back to Canadian verse is an intellectualism unknown
since Heavysege and a merging of personality into a classicism
of form that might find its exemplar in Cameron.

VII

The modern revival began in the twenties with a simplification of technique. Following the lead of the "new poets" in the
United States and the Georgians in England, Canadian poets
turned against rhetoric, sought a sharper, more objective imagery, and limited themselves as far as possible to the language
of everyday and the rhythms of speech. These reforms were
largely the work of younger poets whose outlook was native
rather than cosmopolitan and whose aims were those of real-

ism. These poets sought to render with a new faithfulness much
that had been passed over as "unpoetic" by previous genera-
tions. Some of the lyrics of Dorothy Livesay, the farm poems of
Raymond Knister, Charles Bruce's stirring "Words Are Never
Enough," the cadenced "laconics" of W. W. E. Ross, and
Anne Marriott's fine example of proletarian poetry, *The Wind
Our Enemy* (1939), are representative of this aspect of the mod-
ern movement.

But it was not in the simplification of style and the emphasis
upon the harsher aspects of reality that the new poets made the
most significant departure from the school of Roberts, Carman, and Lampman. The older masters had sought a spiritual
nourishment in the beauty of their natural surroundings. For
them, the challenge of environment strengthened both the
moral virtues and the aesthetic sensibilities and led ultimately
to a powerful feeling of communion with the Divine Spirit,
more or less pantheistically conceived. The poets of today, in-
heritors of what I. A. Richards has called the "neutralisation of
nature," have turned away from all this. They have sought in
man's own mental and social world for a subject matter they
can no longer find in the beauty of nature—a beauty that
seems either deceptive or irrelevant. Their early simplicity,
assumed in reaction to the overloaded diction of much Victorian
verse, has been replaced by a variety of individual and subtle
rhetorics derived in part from Pound or Eliot, the later Yeats,
or the seventeenth-century metaphysicals. Generally speaking,
it is the poetry of ideas, of social criticism, of wit and satire,
that has replaced the descriptive or contemplative poetry of
the nineteenth century.

The new poetry is rich and various; and, contrary to a good
deal of popular misconception, it is neither untraditional nor
formless. Most Canadians have yet to get used to verse that
has freed itself from the fetish of the exalted subject and the
romantic cliché, so that when one of our younger poets draws
upon the versification of a Jacobean dramatist to write a poem
about a salmon, the ulterior theme of which is man's economic

rape of nature, critic and anthologist are needed to testify to
its value.

> Hung like a murderer with stretched-out neck,
> Prepared for dissection, absorption, use, ...
> In gaunt symmetry lies the wonder fish;
> The trip from the egg to the waterfall,
> Leaping lively or lying sunned,
> The spawning, the schooling, the quick increase,
> Are value and profit and capital.
> No natural course is dissatisfied,
> No function corrupted, there is no waste.
> Use has been served up with vinegar, ...
> All harmony, because all enmity
> Has logically come to stay; . . . .
> For man and fish find purest pleasure
> In their prostituting mutual sight.

This is the language of the intelligence. The verse is traditional, unassuming, and brilliant; the poetry rises out of the
assimilative powers of the mind and achieves its purpose by
harmonizing apparently incompatible features of reality. Allusiveness of imagery and directness of language are characteristic features of metaphysical poetry, and they can be discerned
in a fairly large number of poems in the later pages of this
book. Kenneth Leslie's "The silver herring throbbed thick in
my seine," Earle Birney's "Dusk on English Bay," Robert
Finch's "The Sisters," Margaret Avison's "Neverness" and
"The Butterfly," Ralph Gustafson's "Final Spring," Patrick
Anderson's "Capital Square," and Patricia Page's "The Ste-
nographers," with its vivid concluding image—

> In their eyes I have seen
> the pin-men of madness in marathon trim
> race round the track of the stadium pupil—

all testify to the success with which the younger Canadian
poets have entered into the metaphysical tradition, which both
in England and in the United States is now firmly established.

When to the qualities of the poets named we add the packed
classical richness and penetrating satire of L. A. Mackay, the
irony and social consciousness of F. R. Scott, the macabre

lyricism of Leo Kennedy, and the passionate Jewish intellectualism of Abraham Klein, one begins to appreciate the variety and high level of accomplishment that distinguish the modern revival. The intelligence that this poetry reveals and the scope and power of the experiences it masters are the measure of a maturity reached before in Canadian poetry only by isolated masters—Heavysege, Crawford, Cameron, Duncan Campbell Scott, and Lampman.

Whether this new poetry is distinctively national is a question that our writers are not much concerned with. It is not that they have recoiled from the somewhat blatant nationalism of the 1900's into a disillusioned indifference but that they have grown interested in the world-wide revolutionary movement of modern times, in the new developments in psychology and anthropology, and in the elaborate techniques and abstruse theories of American and European writers unknown to Canadian philistinism. They are Canadian poets because they are importing something very much needed in their homeland. They are no longer in the exporting business, for maple sugar is a sickly and cloying commodity—especially in a world where, as a few recent war poems make clear, it is again possible to feel the tragic emotion and the sense of duty as a purifying and poetic force.

PART I

INDIAN POETRY AND FRENCH-CANADIAN FOLK SONGS

Translated by HERMIA HARRIS FRASER

SONGS OF THE HAIDA

69909

THESE songs are adaptations, rather than translations, of genuine primitive poetry. They are the fruit of a number of years of study and research among the Indians of the British Columbia coast. "Haida" is the popular name for the Skittagetan Indians of Queen Charlotte Islands, where they have lived for many generations, developing in isolation a remarkable and individual culture. They are noted as the most skilful carvers of totem poles. The earliest account of them is that of Juan Perez, 1774, and interesting reports are to be found in the journals of various early explorers, such as Captain Torrens. For a firsthand account of life among the Haidas in recent times see *Klee Wyck* by the Victoria painter, Emily Carr, perhaps the most vivid and artistically satisfying interpretation of native life in the whole range of Canadian literature.

SONG OF WELCOME

Ai, ai, my small red man,
Why do you weep on my bosom,
Here in the Hut of the Newborn,
Fresh from the beak of the Raven,
He who made earth from the rain clouds,
He who made Queen Charlotte Islands,
He who made men from the clam mounds?

Long did you lie in a hammock
Swung near the Hanging Horizons,
Trailing your feathers of swansdown
Blown through the masks of Divine Ones,
Hearing the Whistlers, the spirits,
Pierce the dense blueness of Starland;

Lost, until my heart called to you,
Lost until my body bore you.
Wah, ah wah, my small red man,
Welcome, the journey is ended!

35

CHANT TO A WERE-BEAR

Were-bear, why are you not in hell?
Are you too evil for Het-gwau-la-na?
On my neck is this amulet—See it well!
A great bear's tooth to charm you away.

Ai! If you follow my faithful squaw,
Twins she may have, if she sees you now;
In this Laughing Goose Month she must hide away
In the Newborn hut by the willow bough.

I shall paint my face with a red bear paw
And dance in the light of the flowing flame,
If thou art but sent by High Sha-la-na—
Morning and night I shall call thy name!

SONG TO THE WANDERER

I cannot stay, I cannot stay!
I must take my canoe and fight the waves,
For the Wanderer spirit is seeking me.

The beating of great, black wings on the sun,
The Raven has stolen the ball of the sun,
From the Kingdom of Light he has stolen the sun.

I cannot stay, I cannot stay!
The Raven has stolen the Child of the Chief,
Of the Highest Chief in the Kingdom of Light.

The Slave Wife born from the first clam shell
Is in love with the boy who was stolen away,
The lovers have taken the Raven's fire.

The Slave who was born from the first clam shell
Has made love to the wife who was born from the shell,
This Slave man has stolen her treasures away.

He is the Wanderer spirit who calls me,
He is the One who has charge of the birds,
He is the One who loves plants, beasts, and fish.

I am the one who loves the wild woods,
I am the one who embraces the sea.
I must take my canoe and escape tonight!

THE ROUSING CANOE SONG

Hide not, hide not,
Deer in lowlands,
Elk in meadows,
Goats on crag-lands.
Hide not brown bear,
Island black bear,
Lynx and cougar,
Mink and beaver.

Safe the marten,
Safe the raccoon,
Now we hunt not
Wolf and cougar,
Brant nor swan
Nor wild geese soaring,
Porpoise, whale
Nor cod nor herring.
Nor bald eagles
From the snow peaks
Curving where the bay is misty.

Lo! we hunt the female otter!
With our spears
We shall surround her.
He who slays her triumphs doubly,
Double prize shall be his portion.

Lo! we hunt the red witch-woman,
Who with magic tricks has harmed us
Even seizing our Great Copper!

Hide not, hide not,
Game in caverns,
Only hide *thee*, Lost Enchantress!

NOTES

Some of the references to Haida mythology in these poems require
elucidation. The following notes have been supplied by Mrs. Fraser:

SONG OF WELCOME

The Raven was a spirit of creation. The Haidas believed in a great spirit
of light, *Sha-la-na*, and a mighty, evil spirit, *Het-gwau-la-na*. At first, the
Raven was a go-between, but for his deceit he was finally barred from the

kingdom of light. Having no place to go, the Raven beat spray from his cloudy nest. The spray melted to rocks and became the Queen Charlotte Islands. From a clam mound, the Raven made the first man and woman.

CHANT TO A WERE-BEAR

A prospective father, guarding a hut of the Newborn, wore charms and a mask to drive away the Were-Bear, whose presence might cause the mother to have twins. But if twins did arrive, the father, trying to appear delighted, danced and sang. This would please the Grizzly Spirit, who then became guardian and nursemaid to the little ones. The *Laughing Goose Month* was the month of March. The Haidas had charming names for months. The *Chae Kung-as* was November, literally, when bears paw ground for roots.

SONG TO THE WANDERER

The Raven, like the Greek Prometheus, was daring and cunning. He not only stole the sun to light the earth he had made but also stole a divine child. He dropped the child into the sea, but it was saved by a fish. The divine child married the original clam woman. The clam man took their treasures and wandered away, to become a great nature spirit who will care for plant and animal life until the end of time.

Translated by CONSTANCE LINDSAY SKINNER

SONGS OF THE COAST DWELLERS

~~~~~~

THE songs translated and adapted by Constance Lindsay Skinner are also from the folk poetry of the Haida tribes. The late Miss Skinner was born and reared in the wilderness of northern British Columbia, where her father was a Hudson Bay Company factor. At the age of sixteen she began contributing short stories and sketches to the newspapers, and shortly afterward she took up newspaper work in Los Angeles and later in Chicago. She has written plays, novels, and tales for children. In 1913 and 1914 her Indian poems won important prizes offered by the London *Bookman* and *Poetry* (Chicago). Her best poems were collected in 1930 and published in New York under the title, *Songs of the Coast Dwellers*.

~~~~~~

SONG OF WHIP-PLAITING

In the dawn I gathered cedar-boughs
For the plaiting of thy whip.
They were wet with sweet drops;
They still thought of the night.
All alone I shredded cedar-boughs,
Green boughs in the pale light,
Where the morning meets the sea,
And the great mountain stops.

Earth was very still.

I heard no sound but the whisper of my knife,
My black flint knife.
It whispered among the white strands of the cedar,
Whispered in parting the sweet cords for thy whip.
O sweet-smelling juice of cedar—
Life-ooze of love!
My knife drips:
Its whisper is the only sound in all the world!

Finer than young sea-lions' hairs
Are my cedar-strands:

39

They are fine as little roots deep down.
(O little roots of cedar
Far, far under the bosom of Tsa-Kumts!—
They have plaited her through with love.)
Now, into my love-gift
Closely, strongly, I will weave them—
Little strands of pain!
Since I saw thee
Standing with thy torch in my doorway,
Their little roots are deep in me.

In the dawn I gathered cedar-boughs:
Sweet, sweet was their odor,
They were wet with tears—
The sweetness will not leave my hands,
No, not in salt sea-washings.
Tears will not wash away sweetness.
I shall have sweet hands for thy service.

(Ah—sometimes—thou wilt be gentle?
Little roots of pain are deep, deep in me
Since I saw thee standing in my doorway.)
I have quenched thy torch—
I have plaited thy whip.
I am thy Woman!

THE CHIEF'S PRAYER AFTER THE
SALMON CATCH

O Kia-Kunæ, praise!
Thou hast opened thy hand among the stars,
And sprinkled the sea with food;
The catch is great; thy children will live.
See, on the roofs of the villages, the red meat drying;
Another year thou hast encompassed us with life.
Praise! Praise! Kunæ!
O Father, we have waited with shut mouths,
With hearts silent, and hands quiet,
Waited the time of prayer;
Lest with fears we should beset thee,
And pray the unholy prayer of asking.
We waited silently; and thou gavest life.

Oh, praise! Praise! Praise!

Open the silent mouths, the shut hearts, my tribe:
Sing high the prayer of Thanksgiving,
The prayer He taught in the beginning to the Kwakiutl—
The good rejoicing prayer of thanks.
As the sea sings on the wet shore, when the ice thunders back,
And the blue water floats again, warm, shining, living,
So break thy ice-bound heart, and the cold lip's silence—
Praise Kunæ for life, as wings up-flying, as eagles to the sun.
Praise! Praise! Praise!

SONG OF THE FULL CATCH

Here's good wind, here's sweet wind,
Here's good wind and my woman calls me!
Straight she stands there by the pine-tree,
Faithful waits she by the cedar,
She will smile and reach her hands
When she sees my thousand salmon!
Here's good wind and my woman calls me.

Here's clear water, here's swift water,
Here's bright water and my woman waits me!
She will call me from the sea's mouth—
Sweet her pine-bed when the morning
Lights my canoe and the river ends!
Here's good wind, here's swift water,
Strong as love when my woman calls me!

Translated by CHARLES G. LELAND

WABANAKI SONG

THE following lines are a simple and direct rendering of aboriginal poetry. They are reprinted from W. D. Lighthall's *Songs of the Great Dominion* (1889). It is interesting to compare them with Duncan Campbell Scott's well-known poem, "The Forsaken," which treats a similar situation more elaborately but equally powerfully.

WABANAKI SONG

Now I am left on this lonely island to die—
No one to hear the sound of my voice.
Who will bury me when I die?
Who will sing my death-song for me?
My false friends leave me here to die alone;
Like a wild beast, I am left on this island to die.
I wish the wind spirit would carry my cry to my love!
My love is as swift as the deer; he would speed through the
   forest to find me;
Now I am left on this lonely island to die.
I wish the spirit of air would carry my breath to my love.
My love's canoe, like the sunlight, would shoot through the
   water to my side;
But I am left on this lonely island to die, with no one to
   pity me but the little birds.
My love is brave and strong; but, when he hears my fate,
   his stout heart will break;
And I am on this lonely island to die.
Now the night comes on, and all is silent but the owl. He
   sings a mournful song to his mate, in pity for me.
I will try to sleep. I wish the night spirit to hear my song;
   he will tell my love of my fate; and when I awake, I shall
   see the one I love.
I am on this lonely island to die.

Translated by WILLIAM MCLENNAN

SONGS OF OLD CANADA

THESE translations of French-Canadian folk songs are from a pioneer work in the field, William McLennan's *Songs of Old Canada* (1886). McLennan, who lived from 1856 to 1904, was born in Montreal and educated at the High School there and at McGill University, from which he graduated in law in 1880. He practiced with distinction in Montreal. Besides his translations of the old chansons, his literary work consists of a picaresque adventure novel, *Spanish John* (1898); a historical novel, *The Span of Life* (1899), written in collaboration with Jean McIlwraith; and a series of short stories interpreting with much humor and pathos the lives of the French-Canadian habitant. McLennan's tales rank with those in Duncan Campbell Scott's *In the Village of Viger* and with the poems of Drummond as masterpieces of the local-color school.

McLennan's Preface to his little book of verse translations indicates something of his aims and his method. In 1885 he wrote:

Many of these translations were published during the course of the present year in the column of *Ephemerides* in the Montreal *Gazette*, and were written in response to an enquiry for English translations of the old Canadian songs. The object of the translator has been to present, in an English dress and in a form that will allow of their being sung to the airs which most of us have heard with delight, a few of the more popular and striking of those songs of Old France, so wonderfully preserved by our song-loving countrymen. Of these, many have disappeared in their mother-country, and in nearly all of them changes and corruptions have debased either the words or the air. It is also to be feared, alas! that even in the Province of Quebec, which has been their ark of safety for so long, some of them are being forgotten.

This fear may today be fairly safely dispelled, for there are now a large number of works on French-Canadian folk poetry. It will be useful to list some of the best of these:

ERNEST GAGNON, *Les Chansons populaires du Canada*. 2d ed. Quebec, 1880.

Forty-four French Folk Songs and Variants from Canada, Normandy, and Brittany. Collected and harmonized by JULIEN TIERSOT; English translations by HENRY GRAFTON CHAPMAN. New York, 1904.

MARIUS BARBEAU and EDWARD SAPIR, *Folk-Songs of French Canada*. New Haven, 1925.

J. MURRAY GIBBON, *Canadian Folk Songs* (*Old and New*). London and Toronto, 1927.

MARIUS BARBEAU, *Folk-Songs of Old Quebec*. Song translations by REGINA L. SHOOLMAN. National Museum of Canada Bull. 75. "Anthropological Series," No. 16. Ottawa.

Two smaller but very interesting works are *National Ballads of Canada*, imitated and translated from the originals by "Allid" (George T. Lanigan) (Montreal, 1865), and *Songs of French Canada*, selected and arranged by Lawrence J. Burpee (Toronto, 1909)—a small anthology of translations by Lanigan, McLennan, Lighthall, and others.

EN ROULANT MA BOULE

Behind the Manor lies the mere,
En roulant ma boule;
Three ducks bathe in its water clear,
En roulant ma boule.
Rouli, roulant, ma boule roulant,
En roulant ma boule roulant,
En roulant ma boule.

Three fairy ducks swim without fear:
The Prince goes hunting far and near.

The Prince at last draws near the lake:
He bears his gun of magic make.

With magic gun of silver bright,
He sights the Black but kills the White.

He sights the Black but kills the White:
Ah! cruel Prince, my heart you smite.

Ah! cruel Prince, my heart you break,
In killing thus my snow-white Drake.

My snow-white Drake, my Love, my King;
The crimson life-blood stains his wing.

His life-blood falls in rubies bright,
His diamond eyes have lost their light.

The cruel ball has found its quest,
His golden bill sinks on his breast.

His golden bill sinks on his breast,
His plumes go floating East and West.

Far, far they're borne to distant lands,
Till gathered by fair maidens' hands;

Till gathered by fair maidens' hands;
And form at last a soldier's bed.

And form at last a soldier's bed,
  En roulant ma boule;
Sweet refuge for the wanderer's head,
  En roulant ma boule.
    Rouli, roulant, ma boule roulant,
    En roulant ma boule roulant,
      En roulant ma boule.

MALBROUCK

Malbrouck has gone a-fighting,
  Mironton, mironton, mirontaine,
Malbrouck has gone a-fighting
But when will he return?

Perchance he'll come at Easter
Or else at Trinity Term.

But Trinity Term is over
And Malbrouck comes not yet.

My Lady climbs her watch tower
As high as she can get.

She sees her page approaching
All clad in sable hue:

"Ah page, brave page, what tidings
From my true lord bring you?"

"The news I bring, fair Lady,
Will make your tears run down;

"Put off your rose-red dress so fine
And doff your satin gown.

"Monsieur Malbrouck is dead, alas!
And buried too, for aye;

"I saw four officers who bore
His mighty corse away.

"One bore his cuirass, and his friend
His shield of iron wrought;

"The third his mighty sabre bore,
And the fourth—he carried nought.

"And at the corners of his tomb
They planted rose-marie;

"And from their tops the nightingale
Rings out her carol free.

"We saw, above the laurels,
His soul fly forth amain;

"And each one fell upon his face
And then rose up again.

"And so we sang the glories
For which great Malbrouck bled;

"And when the whole was ended
Each one went off to bed.

"I say no more, my Lady,
    Mironton, mironton, mirontaine,
I say no more, my Lady,
As nought more can be said."

LE POMMIER DOUX

An apple tree there groweth,
    Fly away, my heart, away;
An apple tree there groweth
Within my father's close;
    So sweet,
Within my father's close.

Oh, bright is every leaf thereon,
    Fly away, my heart, away;
Oh, bright is every leaf thereon
And sweet the fruit that grows
    So sweet,
And sweet the fruit that grows.

The King's three lovely daughters,
    Fly away, my heart, away;
The King's three lovely daughters
Beneath its branches lay,
    So sweet,
Beneath its branches lay.

The youngest wakens lightly,
    Fly away, my heart, away;
The youngest wakens lightly:
My sister, here is day!
    So sweet,
My sister, here is day!

'Tis but a star that's gilding,
    Fly away, my heart, away;
'Tis but a star that's gilding
With its sweet light our love,
    So sweet,
With its sweet light our love.

Our lovers ride to battle,
    Fly away, my heart, away;
Our lovers ride to battle
Their love for us to prove,
    So sweet,
Their love for us to prove.

And if they gain the battle,
    Fly away, my heart, away;
And if they gain the battle,
Our love shall crown the day,
    So sweet,
Our love shall crown the day.

Oh, let them win or let them fail,
    Fly away, my heart, away;
Oh, let them win or let them fail,
Our love is theirs alway,
    So sweet,
Our love is theirs alway.

MARIANSON

"Ah, Marianson, my beauteous dame,
Where is your lord and master gone?"

"My lord rides to the battle-plain,
I know not if he'll come again."

"Ah, Marianson, my lady fair,
Lend me your rings of gold so rare."

"In the iron chest beside my bed,
You'll find the rings," she sweetly said.

"Now, Goldsmith, fashion me with care
Three golden rings of metal rare.

Three golden rings of fashion rare,
Like those that Marianson doth wear."

When he receives his golden rings
Upon his steed he lightly springs.

The first he meets upon the road
Is Marianson's haughty lord.

"Fair greeting now, bold cavalier,
What tidings do you bring me here?"

"Of tidings new I bring you none,
Save of the Lady Marianson."

"Ah, Marianson, my lady fair!
She's faithful aye, I'll boldly swear."

"I say not 'yes,'—I say not 'no,'
But see—the rings from her hands of snow."

"You lie! you lie! bold cavalier:
My wife is faithful, far or near."

His wife stood on the ramparts high:
She saw her lord ride wildly by.

Her heart stood still with a sudden fear
When she marked his face as he drew anear.

"Now, mother, show our new-born child,
Its grace will calm his anger wild."

"My son, behold your son and heir:
What name wilt thou give the babe to bear?"

He cried, "I'll give the child a name
That will fill its mother's life with shame."

He has seized the infant in its mirth,
And thrice has dashed it to the earth.

And Marianson, that lady fair,
He has tied to his horse by her golden hair.

Three days, three nights, he rode like wind,
And never cast a look behind.

Till, at close of the third long night,
He turned and looked on that awful sight.

"Ah, Marianson, my lady fair,
Where are your golden rings so rare?"

"In the iron chest, beside my bed,
You'll find the rings," she sadly said.

He has ta'en the keys with an evil grace,
And has found the rings in their hiding place.

"Ah, Marianson, my lady fair,
You shall have the best chirurgeon's care."

"The best chirurgeon I would crave
Is a fine white sheet for my quiet grave."

"Ah, Marianson, my beauteous dame,
Will God e'er pardon all my shame?"

"My death is pardoned now," she smiled,
"But never that of our helpless child."

PART II
PIONEER AND EMIGRANT
THE RISE OF A NATIVE
TRADITION

OLIVER GOLDSMITH (1781-1861)

OLIVER GOLDSMITH, a grandnephew and namesake of the author of *The Deserted Village*, was born at Annapolis, Nova Scotia, in 1781. His father was a son of the first Oliver Goldsmith's brother Henry, to whom *The Traveller* had been dedicated, and had served in the British army during the Revolutionary War. The Canadian Oliver Goldsmith entered government service and eventually became commissary-general of Nova Scotia. In his later years he moved to England and died in Liverpool in 1861.

The author of some passable occasional verse and some artificial lyrics of sentiment, the younger Oliver Goldsmith is remembered for the historical interest which attaches to his poem *The Rising Village* (1825). This was an imitation of his granduncle's best-known poem, an attempt to sketch in a companion piece the rise of a happy community of Loyalist settlers in the Acadian wilderness. The work is a somewhat pedestrian essay in late-eighteenth-century sentimentalism, and the diction is familiar without being memorable. Howe's unfinished "Acadia" is a more successful application of the same traditional methods to a kindred theme. A second edition of *The Rising Village*, to which was added some shorter pieces, was published in 1834.

From THE RISING VILLAGE

I

What noble courage must their hearts have fired,
How great the ardor which their souls inspired,
Who, leaving far behind their native plain,
Have sought a home beyond the western main;
And braved the terrors of the stormy seas,
In search of wealth, of freedom, and of ease!
Oh! none can tell but they who sadly share
The bosom's anguish, and its wild despair,

53

What dire distress awaits the hardy bands
That venture first on bleak and desert lands;
How great the pain, the danger, and the toil
Which mark the first rude culture of the soil.
When, looking round, the lonely settler sees
His home amid a wilderness of trees:
How sinks his heart in those deep solitudes,
Where not a voice upon his ear intrudes;
Where solemn silence all the waste pervades,
Heightening the horror of its gloomy shades.

II

Not fifty summers yet have passed thy clime—
How short a period in the page of time—
Since savage tribes, with terror in their train,
Rushed o'er thy fields, and ravaged all thy plain.
But some few years have rolled in haste away
Since, through thy vales, the fearless beast of prey,
With dismal yell and loud appalling cry,
Proclaimed his midnight reign of terror nigh.
And now how changed the scene! the first afar
Have fled to wilds beneath the northern star;
The last has learned to shun man's dreaded eye,
And, in his turn, to distant regions fly.
While the poor peasant, whose laborious care
Scarce from the soil could wring his scanty fare,
Now in the peaceful arts of culture skilled,
Sees his wide barn with ample treasures filled;
Now finds his dwelling, as the year goes round,
Beyond his hopes, with joy and plenty crowned.

III

The wandering Pedlar, who undaunted traced
His lonely footsteps o'er the silent waste;
Who traversed once the cold and snow-clad plain,
Reckless of danger, trouble, or of pain,
To find a market for his little wares,
The source of all his hopes and all his cares,
Established here, his settled home maintains,
And soon a merchant's higher title gains.
Around his store, on spacious shelves arrayed,
Behold his great and various stock in trade!

Here, nails and blankets side by side are seen;
There, horses' collars, and a large tureen;
Buttons and tumblers, fish-hooks, spoons and knives,
Shawls for young damsels, flannel for old wives;
Woolcards and stockings, hats for men and boys,
Mill-saws and fenders, silks, and children's toys;
All useful things, and joined with many more,
Compose the well-assorted country store.

IV

How sweet it is, at first approach of morn,
Before the silvery dew has left the lawn,
When warring winds are sleeping yet on high,
Or breathe as softly as the bosom's sigh,
To gain some easy hill's ascending height
Where all the landscape brightens with delight,
And boundless prospects stretched on every side
Proclaim the country's industry and pride.
Here the broad marsh extends its open plain,
Until its limits touch the distant main;
There verdant meads along the uplands spring,
And grateful odors to the breezes fling;
Here crops of grain in rich luxuriance rise,
And wave their golden riches to the skies;
There smiling orchards interrupt the scene
Of gardens bounded by some fence of green;
The farmer's cottage, bosomed 'mong the trees,
Whose spreading branches shelter from the breeze;
The winding stream that turns the busy mill,
Whose clanking echoes o'er the distant hill;
The neat white church beside whose wall are spread
The grass-clad hillocks of the sacred dead,
Where rude-cut stones or painted tablets tell,
In labored verse, how youth and beauty fell;
How worth and hope were hurried to the grave,
And torn from those who had no power to save.

GEORGE J. MOUNTAIN (1789–1863)

THE Reverend George Jehoshaphat Mountain was born at Norwich, England, in 1789 and came to Canada in 1793. He was educated in England and took orders. On returning to Canada, he served as a missionary in the Northwest Territories, and while in the Northwest he wrote the verses that were published in London, England, in 1846 under the title, *Songs of the Wilderness*. He became Anglican bishop of Quebec and died at Quebec City in 1863. Humanitarianism and missionary zeal hardly add up in the following representative sonnet to significant poetry, but the sonnet is an early expression of the feeling, later to be more eloquently presented in Mair's *Tecumseh*, that the Indian had suffered injustice and cruelty at the hands of the white man.

THE INDIAN'S GRAVE

Bright are the heavens, the narrow bay serene;
No sound is heard within the shelter'd place,
Save some sweet whisper of the pines,—nor seen
Of restless man, or of his works, a trace:
I stray, through bushes low, a little space:
Unlook'd-for sight their parted leaves disclose:
Restless no more, lo! one of Indian race;
His bones beneath that roof of bark repose.

Poor savage! in such bark through deepening snows
Once did'st thou dwell—in this through rivers move;
Frail house, frail skiff, frail man! Of him who knows
His Master's will, not thine the doom shall prove:
What will be yours, ye powerful, wealthy, wise,
By whom the heathen unregarded dies?

STANDISH O'GRADY

THE author of *The Emigrant, A Poem, In Four Cantos*, the first and only canto of which was privately published in Montreal in 1842, was born in Ireland and educated at Trinity College, Dublin. He was graduated B.A. in the same class as the patriot, Robert Emmet. An impoverished Protestant clergyman, unable to collect his tithes and revenues, "disgusted with the government, and unable to exist at home, [he] sailed for America, with a small competency, and abandoned the tithe question altogether." He landed at Quebec in 1836 and took up a homestead near Sorel, on the south bank of the St. Lawrence where the Richelieu flows into it. He suffered severely from the cold—"a Canadian stud horse with one miserable cow," he tells us, "were the only remnants of my stock which survived the winter"—and disliked the French-Canadians. Nevertheless, he declares in a Preface addressed to "the Population of the Province of Canada" that he is not an enemy to immigration. He goes on to say:

This Lower Province, however, is not calculated to afford happiness to the European settler; the cold is excessive, and its winters are too long; those best innured to the climate, and the soil, are its best inhabitants,—I mean the French Canadians, who agree well among each other, and best subsist on a tolerable diet. The Upper Province is by far a more desirable emporium for our redundant population; a corresponding scenery, a mutual intercourse and fellow feeling for each other, will at all times render them more familiar, and less estranged, in a country so similar to their own.

The poem consists of over a thousand heroic couplets. The writing is often amateurish and faulty, but here and there O'Grady's native wit and vigorous personality give a toughness and reality to his verse that is not found in the smooth gentility of Goldsmith's *The Rising Village* or Howe's "Acadia." The canto is followed by sixty pages of notes that are both entertaining and instructive. "Old Nick in Sorel" is one of several pieces of light verse scattered among the notes.

From THE EMIGRANT

[*WINTER IN LOWER CANADA*]

Thou barren waste; unprofitable strand,
Where hemlocks brood on unproductive land,
Whose frozen air on one bleak winter's night
Can metamorphose *dark brown hares to white!*

Here forests crowd, unprofitable lumber,
O'er fruitless lands indefinite as number;
Where birds scarce light, and with the north winds veer
On wings of wind, and quickly disappear,
Here the rough Bear subsists his winter year,
And licks his paw and finds *no better fare* . . . .

One month we hear birds, shrill and loud and harsh,
The plaintive bittern sounding from the marsh;
The next we see the fleet-winged swallow,
The duck, the woodcock, and the ice-birds follow;
Then comes, drear clime, the lakes all stagnant grow,
And the wild wilderness is rapt in snow.

The lank Canadian eager trims his fire,
And all around their simpering stoves retire;
With fur clad friends their progenies abound,
And thus regale their buffaloes around;
Unlettered race, how few the number tells,
Their only pride a *cariole and bells!*
To mirth or mourning, thus by folly led,
To mix in pleasure or to chaunt the dead!
To seek the chapel prostrate to adore,
Or leave their fathers' coffins at the door!
Perchance they revel; still around they creep,
And talk, and smoke, and spit, and drink, and sleep!
. . . .

With sanguine sash and eke with Indian's mogs,
Let Frenchmen feed on fricassees or frogs;
Brave Greenland winters, seven long months to freeze,
With naught of verdure save their Greenland trees;
Bright veiled amid the drap'ry of night,
In Ice-wrought tapestry of gorgeous white,
No matter here in this sad soil who delves;

Still leave their *lower province* to themselves.
Let patriots flourish, other deeds displace,
Let adverse men new politics embrace;
Yet come it will when wisdom may control,
And one sound policy conduct the whole.

[*OLD NICK IN SOREL*]

Old Nick took a fancy, as many men tell,
To come for a winter to live in Sorel.
Yet the snow fell so deep as he came in his sleigh,
That his fingers and toes were frost-nipt on the way.

In truth, saith the demon, who'd ever suppose,
I must go back again with the loss of all those;
In either extreme, sure it matters me not,
If I freeze upon earth or at home I'm too hot;

So he put back his sleigh, for he thought it amiss,
His clime to compare to a climate like this;
And now 'tis resolved that this frightful new-comer
Will winter in hell and be here in the summer.

SUSANNA MOODIE (1803-85)

SUSANNA STRICKLAND, one of the three literary Strickland sisters, was born at Reydon Hall, Suffolk, England, in 1803. She was married in 1831 to J. W. Dunbar Moodie, a British army officer, and with her sister, Catherine (Mrs. Traill), emigrated to British North America, where their husbands had been granted land in the backwoods of Upper Canada. During several years they experienced hardships that their early training had done little to fit them for, but which energy and strength of character enabled them to triumph over. The Moodies bought a farm near Port Hope, but they left it after a short time to settle on four hundred acres of unbroken wilderness to the north of Peterborough. Here Mrs. Moodie and her family were left to manage alone when her husband was recalled to the colors to help suppress the rebellion in 1837. Later Major Moodie became sheriff of Hastings County, and the family moved to Belleville. Mrs. Moodie died in 1885.

The poems included here are taken from Mrs. Moodie's masterpiece, *Roughing It in the Bush* (1853), a prose account of her experiences as a settler's wife. The book contains a number of descriptive lyrics that are not without some historical interest, though the conventionality of most of the verse is in sharp contrast to the vigorous, witty, and homely prose. Mrs. Moodie is very much the cultured Englishwoman—superior, strong-minded, humorous, energetic, and, when necessary, courageous. Her book, because of these qualities, is the most vivid and authentic account we have of the conditions under which the English settlers opened up the frontier in Upper Canada.

There is an informative essay on Mrs. Moodie in Lawrence J. Burpee's *A Little Book of Canadian Essays* (1909).

THE CANADIAN HERD-BOY

[A SONG OF THE BACKWOODS]

Through the deep woods, at peep of day,
The careless herd-boy wends his way,
By piny ridge and forest stream,
To summon home his roving team:
Cobos! Cobos! from distant dell
Sly echo wafts the cattle-bell.

A blithe reply he whistles back,
And follows out the devious track,
O'er fallen tree and mossy stone,
A path to all save him unknown:
Cobos! Cobos! far down the dell
More faintly falls the cattle-bell.

See, the dark swamp before him throws
A tangled maze of cedar boughs;
On all around deep silence broods
In Nature's boundless solitudes:
Cobos! Cobos! the breezes swell
As nearer floats the cattle-bell.

He sees them now; beneath yon trees
His motley herd recline at ease;
With lazy pace and sullen stare
They slowly leave their shady lair:
Cobos! Cobos! far up the dell
Quick jingling comes the cattle-bell.

THE FISHERMAN'S LIGHT

The air is still,—the night is dark,—
No ripple breaks the dusky tide;
From isle to isle the fisher's bark,
Like fairy meteor, seems to glide,—
Now lost in shade,—now flashing bright;
On sleeping wave and forest tree,
We hail with joy the ruddy light,
Which far into the darksome night
Shines red and cheerily.

With spear high poised, and steady hand,
The centre of that fiery ray,

Behold the skilful fisher stand,
Prepared to strike the finny prey;
"Now, now!" the shaft has sped below,—
Transfixed the shining prize we see;
On swiftly glides the birch canoe,
The woods send back the long halloo
In echoes loud and cheerily!

Around yon bluff, whose pine crest hides
The noisy rapids from our sight,
Another bark, another glides,—
Red spirits of the murky night,—
The bosom of the silent stream
With mimic stars is dotted free;
The tall woods lighten in the beam,
Through darkness shining cheerily.

JOSEPH HOWE (1804-73)

JOSEPH HOWE'S father was a New England editor who sided with the British in the Revolutionary War. He brought his printing press—that of the *News-Letter*, the first newspaper printed in New England—to Halifax. The boy, who was born in that city in 1804, left school at the age of thirteen and entered his father's printing office. Ten years later he bought a partnership in a weekly newspaper and soon made a name for himself as an energetic and fearless editor. He employed intelligence and wit in the cause of a free press and a moderate liberalism. The *Novascotian*, which he edited from 1828 to 1841, became the leading journal in the colony. In 1835 he defended himself in the Halifax courts against the charge of libeling the city magistrates and won a victory that established the freedom of the press in British North America. He was elected to the assembly the next year and soon took the lead in the struggle for responsible government—a struggle that was won for Nova Scotia in 1848.

"What made Howe significant," writes Professor Frank H. Underhill, "was that, in both his politics and his literary writing, he gave expression to a sort of Nova Scotia nationalism. Nova Scotia had the oldest settled English-speaking society of the British colonies; its economy was flourishing, with fish, coal, and shipping; and it developed an incipient national feeling of its own, which made it very reluctant to join the new Canadian nation. Howe delivered some speeches on British-American union in the 50's, but was the outstanding opponent of the Confederation scheme when it came in 1864."

Howe served on many important commissions and was made premier of Nova Scotia in 1860. He finally became a supporter of Confederation, and in 1873, only a few days before his death, he was honored with the lieutenant-governorship of his province.

A volume of Howe's "literary remains" was published by his family in 1874. As the brief Introduction indicates, "these selections embrace a number of short poems on various subjects, many of which were written in early life, some portions of an unfinished poem entitled 'Acadia,' together with the essay read on the tercentenary of Shakespeare in Halifax in 1864 . . . . and several other essays."

63

As a poet, Howe belonged to the eighteenth-century school of
Goldsmith. Though he lacks originality, he is saved by his own high
spirits and sturdy common sense from being swamped by the artifi-
cialities of the late-eighteenth-century poetic style. That this style
was not incompatible with realism can be seen by the passage from
"Acadia" given here.

THE FLAG OF OLD ENGLAND

*(A Centenary Song, written for the one hundredth anniversary
of the landing of Lord Cornwallis at Halifax.)*

All hail to the day when the Britons came over,
    And planted their standard, with sea-foam still wet,
Around and above us their spirits will hover,
    Rejoicing to mark how we honor it yet.
Beneath it the emblems they cherished are waving,
    The Rose of Old England the roadside perfumes;
The Shamrock and Thistle the north winds are braving,
    Securely the Mayflower* blushes and blooms.

Chorus

Hail to the day when the Britons came over,
    And planted their standard with sea-foam still wet,
Around and above us their spirits will hover,
    Rejoicing to mark how we honor it yet.
      We'll honor it yet, we'll honor it yet,
      The flag of Old England! we'll honor it yet.

In the temples they founded, their faith is maintained,
    Every foot of the soil they bequeathed is still ours,
The graves where they moulder, no foe has profaned,
    But we wreathe them with verdure, and strew them with
      flowers!
The blood of no brother, in civil strife pour'd,
    In this hour of rejoicing, encumbers our souls!
The frontier's the field for the Patriot's sword,
    And curs'd be the weapon that Faction controls!

Chorus—Hail to the day, &c.

* The Mayflower is the emblem of the Province of Nova Scotia.

Then hail to the day! 'tis with memories crowded,
  Delightful to trace 'midst the mists of the past,
Like the features of Beauty, bewitchingly shrouded,
  They shine through the shadows Time o'er them has cast.
As travellers track to its source in the mountains,
  The stream, which far swelling, expands o'er the plains,
Our hearts, on this day, fondly turn to the fountains
  Whence flow the warm currents that bound in our veins.

  Chorus—Hail to the day, &c.

And proudly we trace them: No warrior flying
  From city assaulted, and fanes overthrown,
With the last of his race on the battlements dying,
  And weary with wandering, founded our own.
From the Queen of the Islands, then famous in story,
  A century since, our brave forefathers came,
And our kindred yet fill the wide world with her glory,
  Enlarging her Empire, and spreading her name.

  Chorus—Hail to the day, &c.

Ev'ry flash of her genius our pathway enlightens—
  Ev'ry field she explores we are beckoned to tread,
Each laurel she gathers, our future day brightens—
  We joy with her living, and mourn for her dead.
Then hail to the day when the Britons came over,
  And planted their standard, with sea-foam still wet,
Above and around us their spirits shall hover,
  Rejoicing to mark how we honor it yet.

  Chorus—Hail to the day, &c.

THE SONG OF THE MICMAC

Oh! who on the mountain, the plain, or the wave,
  With the arm of the Micmac will dare to contend?
Who can hurl the keen spear with the sons of the brave
  Or who can the bow with such energy bend?

Who can follow the Moose, or the wild Cariboo,
  With a footstep as light and unwearied as he?
Who can bring down the Loon with an arrow so true,
  Or paddle his bark o'er as stormy a sea?

Who can traverse the mountain or swim the broad lake?
Who can hunger and thirst with such fortitude bear?
Or who can the Beaver as skilfully take?
Or the Salmon so nimbly transfix with his spear?

And if the wild war whoop ascends on the gale,
Who can with the Micmac the tomahawk wield?
Oh! when was he known in the combat to quail?
Whoe'er saw him fly from the red battle field?

Free sons of the forest, then peal forth the song,
Till each valley and rock shall of victory tell,
And the ghosts of our heroes, while flitting along
With triumph shall smile on the spots where they fell.

From "ACADIA"

[THE INDIAN MASSACRE]

*(A family of settlers in the early days of Acadia retire to sleep
at nightfall in their log cabin in the wilderness.)*

For them no stately canopy is spread:
Dried fern and withered leaves compose their bed—
Rough couch—but still their waning strength it cheers,
For Labour sweetens it, and Love endears.
How oft Ambition, on his softest down,
Implores the God of Sleep his cares to drown;
How oft the anxious child of Commerce tries
To calm his thoughts and close his sleepless eyes,
While Slumber mocks his unavailing prayer,
And seeks the hut to strew its poppies there.

Why starts the mother from that soft repose?
What means the horror that her looks disclose?
Why are her children clasped with eager care,
While Hope seems wildly struggling with Despair?
Why has the father seized the axe and knife,
Like one resolved to combat Death for Life,
And yield no vantage that his arm can hold
Though hungry wolves assail his gentle fold?
Hark to that horrid and soul-piercing yell
That seems the war-cry of a fiend from Hell;
That starts the raven from the lofty pine
On which he closed his wing at day's decline,

And echoing back from the surrounding hills,
The beating hearts in that lone cottage chills;
For Hate, Revenge, and Murder's deepest tone,
Tell them the Micmac's toils are round them thrown.

From the wild covert of the forest shade,
By stealthy march their slow approach was made,
Now, by the spreading foliage concealed,
Now, by some sudden op'ning half revealed,
As to the settler's dwelling they drew nigh,
And gazed upon it with malignant eye.
'Twas yet high noon when it appeared in sight,
But for his work the Indian loves the night.
In patient ambush scattered round they lay,
Content to linger ere they seized their prey.
They marked the settler at his weary moil,
And smiled to think how they'd repay his toil;
Saw him partake the draught his boy would bring
To cheer his labor, from the crystal spring,
And vow'd, e'er morning's dawn, their souls should laugh,
While the parch'd earth his blood should freely quaff;
And when he sought his home at eventide,
To taste the pleasures of his dear fireside,
With ears attentive—footsteps light and true,
And treacherous hearts, around the eaves they drew,
Listen'd the song the mother sung her child,
Heard the light converse that the hours beguiled,
And joyed to think the time would not be long
Ere midnight's cries would follow evening's song.

When sleep had closed the weary cottar's eyes,
They sought to take the slumberers by surprise—
Essay'd the door, and then the window tried
With gentle pressure, studiously applied,
Nor knew how light a doting mother sleeps,
When near her babes its watch the spirit keeps.
The first faint whisper of alarm within,
Convinced them force, not fraud, their prey must win.
'Twas then their shout of fierce defiance rose,
While fast and vehement their heavy blows
On door and shutter diligently fell,
Each followed by a wild tumultuous yell;
Nor are the inmates idle—logs of wood,

Trunks, cribs, what'er can make defences good,
Are piled against the bars that still are true,
Despite the efforts of the howling crew.
This done, the gun is seized—the Father fires,
Chance guides—a groan—one bleeding wretch expires.
Again he loads, again a savage dies—
Again the yells upon the welkin rise,
Hope half persuades that till the dawn of day
The fierce besiegers may be kept at bay.
What scene so dark, what stroke of fate so rude,
That Hope cannot a moment's space intrude?
But soon he flies, for now an Indian flings
Himself upon the roof, which loudly rings
To every stroke the polished hatchet lends;
The bark which bears him, to the pressure bends,
It yields—it breaks—he falls upon the floor—
One blow—his fleeting term of life is o'er,
The settler's axe has dashed his reeking brain
Upon the hearth his soul had sworn to stain.
Fast through the breach two others downward leap,
But, ere they rise, a knife is planted deep
In one dark breast, by gentle Woman's hand,
Who, for her household, wields a household brand;
The axe has clove the other to the chin.
But now, *en masse*, the shrieking fiends leap in,
Till wounded, faint, o'erpowered, the Father falls
And hears the shout of triumph shake his walls.
The wretched Mother from her babe is torn,
Which on a red right hand aloft is borne,
Then dashed to earth before its Parent's eyes,
And, as its form, deform'd and quivering lies,
Life from its fragile tenement is trod,
And the bruised, senseless, and unsightly clod,
Is flung into the soft but bleeding breast
To which so late in smiling peace 'twas press'd.

Nor does the boy escape—the smouldering fire
Is stirred,—and, as its feeble flames aspire
In wanton cruelty they thrust his hands
Into the blaze, and on the reddening brands,
Like Montezuma bid him seek repose
As though his couch were but a perfumed rose.
Sated with blood, at length the scalps they tear

Ere life be yet extinct—for these, with care,
The Indian tribes, like precious coins, retain
To count their victories, and the victims slain.

Now plunder follows death—then one applies
Fire to the bed, from which the flames arise
Fiercely and fast, as anxious to efface
All record of so sad, so foul a place.
Around the cot the Indians form a ring,
And songs of joy and triumph wildly sing
With horrid gesture and demoniac strain,
Then plunge into the forest depths again.

Such are the scenes Acadia once display'd;
Such was the price our gallant Fathers paid
For this fair land, where now our footsteps rove
From lake to sea, from cliff to shady grove,
Uncheck'd by peril, unrestrained by fear
Of more unfriendly ambush lingering near
Than timid rabbits lurking in the fern
And peeping forth your worst intent to learn;
Or mottled squirrel, frisking round the pines
To seek the buds on which he lightly dines;
Or feather'd fav'rites, who, on ev'ry spray
Cheer and enchant with many a simple lay,
And though their plumage cannot boast the dyes
That deck the feather'd tribe 'neath milder skies,
Their ev'ning songs can sweeter strains impart
To charm the list'ning ear, or touch the heart.

C. D. SHANLY (1811-75)

CHARLES DAWSON SHANLY was born in Dublin in 1811 and came to Canada as a young man. He became well known in journalistic circles and for some years was editor of *Punch in Canada*. Later he went to New York, where he won distinction as an art critic. His best poem, the effective ballad included here, was originally published in the *Atlantic Monthly*. Shanly's fugitive verses have never been collected. He died in Florida in 1875 and is buried near London, Ontario, where he had made his home in Canada.

THE WALKER OF THE SNOW

Speed on, speed on, good Master!
  The camp lies far away;
We must cross the haunted valley
  Before the close of day.

How the snow-blight came upon me
  I will tell you as we go,
The blight of the Shadow-hunter
  Who walks the midnight snow.

To the cold December heaven
  Came the pale moon and the stars,
As the yellow sun was sinking
  Behind the purple bars.

The snow was deeply drifted
  Upon the ridges drear
That lay for miles between me
  And the camp for which we steer.

'Twas silent on the hill-side
  And by the sombre wood,
No sound of life or motion
  To break the solitude,

Save the wailing of the moose-bird
  With a plaintive note and low,
And the skating of the red leaf
  Upon the frozen snow.

And I said, "Though dark is falling
  And far the camp must be,
Yet my heart it would be lightsome
  If I had but company."

And then I sang and shouted,
  Keeping measure as I sped,
To the harp-twang of the snowshoe
  As it sprang beneath my tread.

Nor far into the valley
  Had I dipped upon my way
When a dusky figure joined me,
  In a capuchon of grey,

Bending upon the snowshoes
  With a long and limber stride;
And I hailed the dusky stranger
  As we travelled side by side.

But no token of communion
  Gave he by word or look,
And the fear-chill fell upon me
  At the crossing of the brook.

For I saw by the sickly moonlight,
  As I followed, bending low,
That the walking of the stranger
  Left no footmarks on the snow.

Then the fear-chill gathered o'er me
  Like a shroud around me cast,
As I sank upon the snow-drift
  Where the Shadow-hunter passed.

And the otter-trappers found me
  Before the break of day,
With my dark hair blanched and whitened
  As the snow in which I lay.

But they spoke not as they raised me;
  For they knew that in the night
I had seen the Shadow-hunter,
  And had withered in his blight.

Sancta Maria, speed us!
  The sun is falling low,—
Before us lies the valley
  Of the Walker of the Snow!

CHARLES HEAVYSEGE (1816-76)

CHARLES HEAVYSEGE was born in Huddersfield, England, in 1816, and came to Montreal in 1853, where he worked as a cabinetmaker and carpenter and occasionally engaged in journalism. The poet published his first book, the inconsequential *Revolt of Tartarus*, in 1852, just before coming to Canada, but it was with the publication of *Saul* (Montreal, 1857) that his remarkable powers were first revealed. Two other editions appeared, the second in Montreal (1859), and the third, revised and greatly strengthened, in Boston (1869). Passages that were prolix or vague were carefully pruned, the language in many places made more familiar and vivid, and a number of lines of outstanding merit added.

One of the best descriptions and justest appreciations of Heavysege's masterpiece remains the review of the first edition which appeared in an article on "The Modern British Drama" in the *North British Review*, August, 1858. Dr. L. J. Burpee, whose monograph on Heavysege (*Transactions of the Royal Society of Canada* [1901]) is the most complete and enlightened study of the poet, quotes the authority of Richard Garnett for ascribing this review to Coventry Patmore. Here are some interesting passages:

> *Saul* is in three parts, each of five acts, and altogether about ten thousand lines long. It is the greatest subject, in the whole range of history, for a drama, and has been treated with a poetical power and a depth of psychological knowledge which are often quite startling. . . . .
>
> The author proves that he knows the Bible and human nature. Shakespeare he also knows far better than most men know him; for he has discerned and adopted his method as no other dramatist has done. He takes not virtue and morality, and their opposites *generally*, as other dramatists do, but these under the single aspect of their dependence upon *spiritual influences*, of whatever kind: the direct influence of the Divine Spirit; and the influence of good spirits; and of the principalities and powers of darkness; and even the mysterious influences of music, the weather, etc., upon the moral state of the soul. Like most of Shakespeare's plays, this drama has the appearance of being strangely chaotic. There are hundreds of passages for the existence of which we cannot account until the moral clew is found, and it would never be found by a careless and unreflecting reader; yet the

work is exceedingly artistic, and there are few things in recent poetry so praiseworthy as the quiet and unobtrusive way in which the theme is treated. . . . . We are not far from the writer's intention, when we say, that in Saul he represents a man who is *eminently* the creature of spiritual influences; who is of the happiest sensitive and perceptive constitution, but lacks the one thing needful, the principle of *faith*, which would have given the will to submit himself to the good influence and resist the bad. "Faith wanting, all his works fell short," is the only *explicit* statement in the whole poem of this idea; but the whole poem indirectly implies it. This view of Saul's character, which is amply justified by Scripture history, is carried out and illustrated with an elaborate subtlety. . . . .

Heavysege's next work was a five-act tragedy, *Count Filippo, or The Unequal Marriage*, privately printed in Montreal (1860). This problem play develops its theme of incompatibility in marriage between youth and age with a refreshingly Elizabethan boldness. The frankness of the play and the curiously intuitive understanding of evil it revealed did not recommend it to the critics or the public. It is a tragedy of intrigue and revenge; the climax is adultery, and the denouement remorse and renunciation. Although *Filippo* lacks the majesty and power of *Saul*, it shows no falling-off in characterization or versification.

In his third and last book Heavysege turned from the drama to the dramatic poem and produced in *Jephtha's Daughter* a blank-verse narrative about 1,250 lines in length. The book was published in London in 1865. It tells the familiar biblical story of Jephtha's rash vow and the resulting sacrifice of his only daughter. Heavysege, as Burpee pointed out, is pre-eminently an interpreter of moral impulses. "He is never so successful as when dealing with a subtle moral situation or tracing the development of character," and in *Jephtha's Daughter* this power is triumphantly demonstrated in the dramatization of the growth of the young girl's soul as she moves from the first natural weakness of fear and resentment to her final exalted acquiescence in the divine decree. The weakness of the poem is its prolixity in the early and middle scenes, but the power of the language as the tragedy moves to its climax is worthy of high praise.

The selections from *Saul* that follow present the character of Malzah, Heavysege's most original creative triumph. The article in the *North British Review* contained an excellent account of the philosophical drama implied in the poet's presentation of this supernatural creature who yet can feel human passion and remorse.

The evil spirit of the King is brought personally, under the name of Malzah, upon the stage; and we are made to understand Saul's nature, and the nature of all who are the more or less passive slaves of natural and spiritual influences *ab extra*, by the exaggeration of this character in the spirit himself, who is depicted with an imaginative veracity which we do not exaggerate in saying has not been equalled in our language by any but the creator of Caliban and Ariel. Malzah is decidedly "well disposed," like many another evil spirit, human or otherwise; he knows his faults; is almost changed, for the moment, into a good spirit by artistic influences, especially music; he has attained to be a deep philosopher through the habitual observation of himself; and does not at all like the evil work of destroying the soul of Saul,—a work which he undertook voluntarily, and to which he returns as the fit takes him. The following passages will carry out what we have said, and will illustrate the oddity, subtlety, and originality of this writer's language. Malzah tries to exonerate himself, in soliloquy, from the guilt of destroying Saul:—

> I've had no part in this. I'm sorry, too,
> (Like thee, O King,) that ever I came to thee.
> Zounds! why, I ought to have strong penance set me,
> Or else be branded with some sign of shame
> For having volunteered for his undoing.
> There's no essential honor nor good i' the world,
> But a pure selfishness is all in all.
> Nay, I could curse my demonhood, and wish
> Myself to be thrice lost for that behavior;—
> But I believe I am a very mean-souled spirit.

Even finer than this flippant, imbecile, and impotent penitence of Malzah is the . . . . song ["There was a devil and his name was I"], which seems to us to be scarcely short of Shakespearean. . . . .

In this poem, for the first time, spirits have been represented in a manner which fully justifies the boldness involved in representing them at all. Malzah is a living character, as true to supernature as Hamlet or Falstaff are to nature; and, by this continuation, as it were, of humanity into new circumstances, and another world, we are taught to look upon humanity itself from a fresh point of view, and we seem to obtain new and startling impressions of the awful character of the influences by which we are beset. Seldom has art so well performed the office of handmaiden to religion as in this extraordinary character of Malzah, in whom we have the disembodiment of the soul of the faithless, sophistical, brave, and generously disposed king of Israel, and a most impressive poetical exposition of the awful truth, that he who is not wholly for God is against him.

This is perhaps an old-fashioned kind of criticism, but it is none the worse for that. Its value is due to the fact that it supplies something better than a capricious or arbitrary explanation of the source of our interest in the characters of Malzah and Saul.

[*THE AGES OF MAN*]

Childhood alone is glad. With it time flees
In constant mimes and bright festivities.
It, like the ever-restless butterfly,
Or seeks or settles on some flower of joy.
Youth chases pleasure, but oft starteth pain;
And love, youth's birthright, oft is love in vain;
While manhood follows wealth, or woos ambition,
That are but courted cares; and, with transition
Insensible, he enters upon age;
Thence gliding like a spectre from life's stage,
E'en through the door of dotage. So he passes
To second childhood; but, as quickening gases,
Being fled, leave zestless a once cheering draught,
We grow not merry though the Dotard laughed.

[*THE DEAD*]

How great unto the living seem the dead!
How sacred, solemn; how heroic grown;
How vast and vague, as they obscurely tread
The shadowy confines of the dim unknown!—
For they have met the monster that we dread,
Have learned the secret not to mortal shown.
E'en as gigantic shadows on the wall
The spirit of the daunted child amaze,
So on us thoughts of the departed fall,
And with phantasma fill our gloomy gaze.
Awe and deep wonder lend the living lines,
And hope and ecstasy the borrowed beams;
While fitful fancy the full form divines,
And all is what imagination dreams.

[*THE WINTER GALAXY*]

The stars are glittering in the frosty sky,
Frequent as pebbles on a broad sea-coast;
And o'er the vault the cloud-like galaxy
Has marshalled its innumerable host.
Alive all heaven seems! with wondrous glow
Tenfold refulgent every star appears,
As if some wide, celestial gale did blow,

And thrice illume the ever-kindled spheres.
Orbs, with glad orbs rejoicing, burning, beam,
Ray-crowned, with lambent lustre in their zones,
Till o'er the blue, bespangled spaces seem
Angels and great archangels on their thrones;
A host divine, whose eyes are sparkling gems,
And forms more bright than diamond diadems.

[NIGHT]

'Tis solemn darkness; the sublime of shade;
Night, by no stars nor rising moon relieved;
The awful blank of nothingness arrayed,
O'er which my eyeballs roll in vain, deceived.
Upward, around, and downward I explore,
E'en to the frontiers of the ebon air;
But cannot, though I strive, discover more
Than what seems one huge cavern of despair.
Oh, Night, art thou so grim, when, black and bare
Of moonbeams, and no cloudlets to adorn,
Like a nude Ethiop 'twixt two houris fair,
Thou stand'st between the evening and the morn?
I took thee for an angel, but have wooed
A cacodæmon in mine ignorant mood.

From SAUL

[ZAPH DESCRIBES THE HAUNTS OF MALZAH]

The Jewish king now walks at large and sound,
Yet of our emissary Malzah hear we nothing:
Go now, sweet spirit, and, if need be, seek
This world all over for him:—find him out,
Be he within the bounds of earth and hell.
He is a most erratic spirit, so
May give thee trouble (as I give thee time)
To find him, for he may be now diminished,
And at the bottom of some silken flower,
Wherein, I know, he loves, when evening comes,
To creep, and lie all night, encanopied
Beneath the manifold and scented petals;

Fancying, he says, he bids the world adieu,
And is again a slumberer in heaven:
Or, in some other vein, perchance thou'lt find him
Within the walls or dens of some famed city.
Give thou a general search, in open day,
I' the town and country's ample field; and next
Seek him in dusky cave, and in dim grot;
And in the shadow of the precipice,
Prone or supine extended motionless;
Or, in the twilight of o'erhanging leaves,
Swung at the nodding arm of some vast beech.
By moonlight seek him on the mount, at noon
In the translucent waters salt or fresh;
Or near the dank-marged fountain, or clear well,
Watching the tadpole thrive on suck of venom;
Or where the brook runs o'er the stones, and smooths
Their green locks with its current's crystal comb.
Seek him in rising vapors, and in clouds
Crimson or dun; and often on the edge
Of the gray morning and of tawny eve:
Search in the rocky alcove and woody bower;
And in the crows'-nest look, and into every
Pilgrim-crowd-drawing Idol, wherein he
Is wont to sit in darkness and be worshipped.
If thou shouldst find him not in these, search for him
By the lone melancholy tarns of bitterns;
And in the embosomed dells, whereunto maidens
Resort to bathe within the tepid pool.
Look specially there, and, if thou seest peeping
Satyr or fawn, give chase and call out "Malzah!"

[*MALZAH SPEAKS*]

Ah, weary! I am called the laughing devil.
Yet I walk up and down existence weeping.
But what when demons disbelieve their eyes,
And their false ears for jests take my bewailings? . . . .
—I do not know myself;
I have so many moods, that I know not
Which of them shows the veritable Malzah.
But this I know, my gladness always borders
Upon the doleful region of the dumps.—
Ah, me!

How like is man unto the fallen angels!
How many in my mood now walk this world!
Some sullen at their fellows, some at fate,—
From which there is no more escaping than
There is from our free wills; and some are sad
With envy at another's good, and some
With unfulfilled ambition; some with hate
Are sad, and some with love unlucky; some
With fear of missing heaven, some with dread
Of falling into hell; and many more
With curious worldly cares:—and here comes Saul
And Jonathan, and both of them dejected.
We were a mournful trio, should I join them:
Grave as three owls, as sober as three storks,
More gloomy than a trinity of ravens.

[MALZAH'S SONG]

There was a devil and his name was I;
From out Profundus he did cry:
He changed his note as he changed his coat,
And his coat was of a varying dye.
It had many a hue: in hell 'twas blue,
'Twas green i' the sea, and white i' the sky.
O, do not ask me, ask me why
'Twas green i' the sea, and white i' the sky;
Why from Profundus he did cry:
Suffice that he wailed with a chirruping note,
And quaintly cut was his motley coat.—

I have forgot the rest. Would I could sleep;
Would I could sleep away an age or so,
And let Saul work out his own weal or woe:
All that I ask is to be let alone.

O, to be let alone! to be let alone!
To laugh if I list; if I list to groan;
Despairing, yet knowing God's anger o'erblown.
O, why should God trouble me?
Why should he double my
Sorrow, pursuing me when he has thrown
Me out of his favor? O, why should he labor
Down lower ever thrusting me into hell's zone?
O let me alone! O let me alone!
O leave me, Creator, Tormentor, alone!

["*LO! I AM SAUL*"]

Creature, begone, nor harrow me with horror!
Thine eyes are stars; O, cover them, O, wrap
Them up within thy cloudy brows: stand off,
Contend not with me, but say who thou art.
Lo! I am Saul, the sad, demoniac king,
But who art thou, strange, yet familiar?
Methinks I know thee,—yes, thou art my demon;
Thou art the demon that torments my soul.
I charge thee say, mysterious visitant,
At whose behest thou comest, and for what
Offences deep of mine: nay, stand aloof:
Confess, malicious goblin, or else leave me;
Leave me, O goblin, till my hour is come:
I'll meet thee after death; appoint the place;
On Gilead, or beside the flowing Jordan;
Or, if parts gloomier suit thee, I'll repair
Down into Hinnom, or up to the top
Of Horeb in the wilderness, or to the cloud-
Concealéd height of Sinai ascend,
Or dwell with thee 'midst darkness in the grave.

ALEXANDER McLACHLAN (1818–96)

THE voice of the Scottish settler in the days of the pioneer makes itself heard in the homely poetry of Alexander McLachlan. The poet was born of poor parents near Glasgow in 1818 and after a rudimentary schooling was apprenticed to a tailor. In 1840 he immigrated to Upper Canada, where, not without enduring some hardships, he established himself on a small clearing near Guelph. He spent the greater part of his life in rural Ontario, though he returned to Britain in 1863 to lecture on the advantages of immigrating to Canada. By then the homesickness for the motherland which finds expression in his early poems had been replaced by an ardent love of his new home. He died in 1896.

The three volumes upon which McLachlan's reputation is based are *Lyrics* (1858), *The Emigrant, and Other Poems* (1861), and *Poems and Songs* (1874). A collected edition, with a "Memoir" by Rev. Hartley Dewart, was published in 1900.

McLachlan was an admirer and imitator of Burns. Dr. Dewart, the first Canadian anthologist, in his *Selections from Canadian Poets* (1864), spoke of the qualities that McLachlan shares with his master—his strong human sympathy, his subtle appreciation of character, his deep natural pathos—and praised his power of commanding "those gushes of noble and manly feeling which awaken the responsive echoes of every true heart."

The reader today will be more conscious of McLachlan's sentimentality and crudeness than of his virtues. The faults in his work are due to a lack of culture and self-criticism. Some of his poems are facile in sentiment and rather too folksy in their humor, and the intention to create a serious or tender mood is often defeated by too obvious a rhythm and an overemphatic use of internal rhyme. But it is easy to dismiss a simple poet; yet to do so in the case of McLachlan would be to miss qualities of value. McLachlan's best poems are a direct expression of his own strength of character, his sturdy self-dependence, his honesty, and his charity. A sincere love of nature and humanity and an angry hatred of hypocrisy and tyranny are the compulsions under which he writes, but his most intense feeling is

81

usually controlled by common sense and humor. The radical sentiment of his earlier poetry will be found in the spirited "Old England
Is Eaten by Knaves," and it persists, in spite of a good deal of conventional piety and patriotism, from early verses like "We Live in
a Rickety House" to the scattered satirical pieces in his later volumes. McLachlan's radicalism is independent, personal, and non-
doctrinaire. It derives from Burns and the poet's own experience,
and its sturdy gruffness reminds one of Cobbett.

The Emigrant, his most ambitious poem, was a projected pioneer
epic that was to present the history of a backwoods settlement. Only
the first part was written. Its seven chapters are entitled: "Leaving
Home," "The Journey," "The Arrival," "Cutting the First Tree,"
"The Log Cabin," "The Indian Battle," and "Donald Ban."
It is written in short, heavily accented rhyming couplets that rather
quickly become monotonous, though it is relieved here and there
by some pleasant, lyrical interludes.

As a nature poet McLachlan belongs to the old school of Cowper
and Thomson, but when he went into the woods he kept his eyes
open and his wits about him. As a result he sometimes saw the familiar with the eye of the imagination, as when, to give but a single
instance, he notices that

> The humming bird above the flower
> Is like a halo bending.

At night, we learn from one of his poems, he found time to read. His
books were Homer, Shakespeare, Burns, and Sir Walter Scott. These
authors and the wilderness itself gave him his education. Throughout the bulk of his verse, the good and the mediocre alike, we discern
the figure of a man who hated cant and believed in the brotherhood
of man and the Fatherhood of God.

YOUNG CANADA, OR JACK'S AS
GOOD AS HIS MASTER

> I love this land of forest grand!
>   The land where labour's free;
> Let others roam away from home,
>   Be this the land for me!
> Where no one moils, and strains and toils,
>   That snobs may thrive the faster;
> And all are free, as men should be,
>   And Jack's as good's his master!

Where none are slaves, that lordly knaves
   May idle all the year;
For rank and caste are of the past,—
   They'll never flourish here!
And Jew or Turk if he'll but work,
   Need never fear disaster;
He reaps the crop he sowed in hope,
   For Jack's as good's his master!

Our aristocracy of toil
   Have made us what you see—
The nobles of the forge and soil,
   With ne'er a pedigree!
It makes one feel himself a man,
   His very blood leaps faster,
Where wit or worth's preferred to birth,
   And Jack's as good's his master!

Here's to the land of forests grand!
   The land where labour's free;
Let others roam away from home,
   Be this the land for me!
For here 'tis plain, the heart and brain,
   The very soul grows vaster!
Where men are free, as they should be,
   And Jack's as good's his master!

OLD CANADA; OR, GEE BUCK GEE

The country's goin' fast to ruin!
This edication's our undoin',
We're comin' to a pretty pass,
Our boys who scarce have been to grass,
Have all gone off, bound to the teachers,
Or city clerks, or peddlin' preachers;
Our darters too, are quite Sultanas,
All strummin' on them cuss'd pianos,
And try to trip us up with rules
They've learn'd away at Grammar Schools,
And look upon the likes o' me—
Who nurs'd them criters on my knee—
As far beneath them,—Gee Buck Gee!

And then they're all Book Farmers too!
And they would teach me what to do;

Manurin', ploughin', drainin', seedin',
All farmin's to be done by readin'!
O Lord! O Lord! it makes me mad,
When every striplin' o' a lad,
And every edicated ass,
Who scarce knows growin' wheat from grass,
Must teach the like o' me to farm,
Wi' Latin names as long's my arm;
Them criters teach the like o' me?
Who farm'd ere they could reach my knee,
Ain't it presumption?—Gee Buck Gee!

I tell ye what! them and their books,
Are getting to be perfect pukes;
And sure enough this edication
Will be the ruin o' the nation;
We'll not ha' men, it's my opinion,
Fit to defend our New Dominion;
Not one o' them can swing an axe,
But they will bore you with the facts;
I'd send the criters off to work,
But that, by any means they'll shirk!
Grandad to some o' them I be,
O, that's what riles and vexes me!
Ain't it a caution?—Gee Buck Gee!

WE LIVE IN A RICKETY HOUSE

We live in a rickety house,
    In a dirty dismal street,
Where the naked hide from day,
    And thieves and drunkards meet.

And pious folks with their tracts,
    When our dens they enter in,
They point to our shirtless backs,
    As the fruits of beer and gin.

And they quote us texts to prove
    That our hearts are hard as stone,
And they feed us with the fact
    That the fault is all our own.

It will be long ere the poor
    Will learn their grog to shun

While it's raiment, food and fire,
  And religion all in one.

I wonder some pious folks
  Can look us straight in the face,
For our ignorance and crime
  Are the Church's shame and disgrace.

We live in a rickety house,
  In a dirty dismal street,
Where the naked hide from day,
  And thieves and drunkards meet.

From *THE EMIGRANT*

[SONG]

Old England is eaten by knaves,
  Yet her heart is all right at the core,
May she ne'er be the mother of slaves,
  Nor a foreign foe land on her shore.

I love my own country and race,
  Nor lightly I fled from them both,
Yet who would remain in a place
  Where there's too many spoons for the broth.

The squire's preserving his game.
  He says that God gave it to him,
And he'll banish the poor without shame,
  For touching a feather or limb.

The Justice he feels very big,
  And boasts what the law can secure,
But has two different laws in his wig,
  Which he keeps for the rich and the poor.

The Bishop he preaches and prays,
  And talks of a heavenly birth,
Bur somehow, for all that he says,
  He grabs a good share of the earth.

Old England is eaten by knaves,
  Yet her heart is all right at the core,
May she ne'er be the mother of slaves,
  Nor a foreign foe land on her shore.

[IN THE FOREST]

Soon we entered in the woods,
On the trackless solitudes,
Where the spruce and cedar made
An interminable shade;
And the pine and hemlock stood,
Monarchs of the solitude,
And we picked our way along,
Sometimes right and sometimes wrong;
For a long and weary day,
Thus we journeyed on our way,
Picked a path through swale and swamp,
And at evening fixed our camp;
Where a lovely little spring
Murmured like a living thing . . . .

There we laid us down to rest,
With the cold earth for our bed,
And the green boughs overhead;
And again at break of day,
Started on our weary way;
Through morasses, over bogs,
Wading rivers, crossing logs,
Scrambling over fallen trees,
Wading pond holes to the knees;
Sometimes wandering from the track;
And to find it turning back;
Scorning ills that would betide us,
Stout hearts and the sun to guide us.

Then there came a change of scene,
Groves of beech and maple green,
Streams that murmured through the glade,
Little flowers that loved the shade,
Lovely birds of gorgeous dye,
Flitted 'mong the branches high,
Coloured like the setting sun,
But were songless every one;
No one like the linnet gray,
In our home so far away;
No one singing like the thrush,
To his mate within the bush;

No one like the gentle lark,
Singing between light and dark;
Soaring from the dewy sod,
Like a herald up to God.
Some had lovely amber wings,
Round their necks were golden rings;
Some were purple, others blue,
All were lovely, strange and new;
But although surpassing fair,
Still the song was wanting there;
Then we heard the rush of pigeons,
Flocking to those lonely regions;
And anon when all was still,
Paused to hear the whip-poor-will;
And we thought of the cuckoo,
But this stranger no one knew.

CHARLES SANGSTER (1822-93)

CHARLES SANGSTER was born at the Navy Yard, Kingston, Ontario, July 16, 1822. At an early age he was left fatherless, the youngest of a large family, and at fifteen he found work in the ordnance department at Fort Henry making cartridges. There he remained for ten years in very humble employment. In 1849 he became editor of the *Amherstburg Courier* but shortly returned to Kingston, where he engaged in journalism. He died in Ottawa in 1893, where he had been a clerk in the civil service department.

Sangster was given high praise in the first Canadian anthology, Rev. Edward Hartley Dewart's *Selections from Canadian Poets* (1864). Wrote Dr. Dewart:

His genius is more truly Canadian than that of any other poet of distinction in this Province. . . . . Mr. S., while cherishing a loyal attachment to the mother land, gives Canada the chief place in his heart. Her mighty lakes and rivers—her forests and hills—her history, religion, and laws—her homes and liberties—her brave sons and fair daughters—are all objects of his most ardent affection, graven alike upon the pages of his poetry, and upon the tablets of his heart. The most prominent characteristics of his genius are, a wonderful fertility of thought, which inables him to pour forth images, and forms of expression with lavish prodigality;—an intense sympathy with Nature, in all her varied moods and forms;—and that peculiar freshness and originality of language that is the sure distinction of those, to whom belong "the vision and the faculty divine."

The modern reader can hardly praise Sangster's poems in terms like these, for many of them are imitative, some are awkward and imperfect, and others are strained and sentimental. The best of them, however, are the product of a fervid and tender spirit and of an excited imagination brought under the control of a considerable technical skill. Sangster's two volumes are *The St. Lawrence and the Saguenay and Other Poems* (1856) and *Hesperus, and Other Poems and Lyrics* (1860). In later years he published nothing.

The chief poem in the first volume is a kind of sentimental journey, or Childe Harold's pilgrimage, in which the poet and some fair but imaginary companion sail down the great river and respond with appropriate emotions to the beauty and variety of the scenery or the sacredness of historical associations. The poem consists of a hundred and ten Spenserian stanzas with some lyrical interludes. The mingling of various literary influences—Byron and Scott particularly, and even (in one couplet at least) Pope's *Pastorals*—with Sangster's direct observations make these skilfully handled Spenserian stanzas interesting to the student of literature as well as to the lover of pure poetry or to the sentimental traveler. The poem is episodic and not without some dull and inflated passages, but the description of the Thousand Islands is a beautiful and successful piece of writing. The volume as a whole is uneven and imperfect, but it contains, along with many crude and sentimental effusions, some poems of more than ordinary interest. Among these are "Morning in Summer," with its vision of the civilizing influence of the railway, and "Bertram and Lorenzo: A Dramatic Fragment," an ambitious poem in excellent Wordsworthian blank verse that tells a somewhat Alastor-like story of a poet's love and death in a romantic setting of soul-enkindling mountains.

Sangster's second volume was less bulky than the first, and it contained fewer weak and imperfect pieces and most of the best of Sangster's lyrics. It included three or four poems of some magnitude. The title poem is a masque—"A Legend of the Stars"—written in blank verse interspersed with a number of odelike lyrics. Its theme is the divine spirit of light and creation. Another important poem is "The Happy Harvesters: A Cantata." In this a group of country villagers gather to celebrate with music and song the completion of the harvest. In addition to "An Autumn Change," it contains two rollicking lyrics of country life, "A Song for the Flail" and "The Soldiers of the Plough," and some very pretty heroic couplets.

> Autumn, like an old poet in a haze
> Of golden visions, dreams away his days,
> So Hafiz-like that one may almost hear
> The singer's thoughts imbue the atmosphere;
> Sweet as the dreamings of the nightingales
> Ere yet their songs have waked the eastern vales,
> Or stirred the airy echoes of the wood. . . . .

Such lines have an old-fashioned artificial charm to which Sangster's fervid sensibility gives a warmth of feeling that is quite delightful. It is regrettable that this quality does not seem to come at the poet's command but to arise spontaneously and spasmodically. The few lines which introduce the lyric, "An Autumn Change," are another happy instance of it:

> Fair was the maid, and lovely as the morn
> From starry Night and rosy Twilight born. . . . .
> The health and beauty of her youthful face
> Made it the Harem of each maiden grace;
> And such perfection blended with her air,
> She seemed some stately Goddess moving there:
> Beholding her, you thought she might have been
> The long-lost, flower-loving Proserpine.

Sangster's patriotic poems are significant in intention, perhaps, but their robust martial ardor hardly finds a technically satisfying expression. One of his occasional pieces, however, is something of an exception. This is the poem, "Brock." It was written for the dedication on October 13, 1859, of a new monument to the hero of Queenston Heights, the original one having been defaced by rebel sympathizers during the rebellion of 1837. The poem is interesting as an early statement of the patriotic sentiments which were crystallizing round the idea of Confederation. A more polished expression of the same feelings is found in the later "Canada" of Charles G. D. Roberts. The last two stanzas of Sangster's poem, however, have a tortuous grandeur that redeems what otherwise would be merely conventional.

LOST AND FOUND

> In the mildest, greenest grove
>   Blest by sprite or fairy,
> Where the melting echoes rove,
>   Voices sweet and airy;
>   Where the streams
>   Drink the beams
>   Of the Sun,
>   As they run
>   Riverward
>   Through the sward,
>   A shepherd went astray—
>   E'en gods have lost their way.
>
> Every bird had sought its nest,
>   And each flower-spirit
> Dreamed of that delicious rest
>   Mortals ne'er inherit;

Through the trees
Swept the breeze,
Bringing airs
Unawares
Through the grove,
Until love
Came down upon his heart,
Refusing to depart.

Hungrily he quaffed the strain,
  Sweeter still, and clearer,
Drenched with music's mellow rain,
  Nearer—nearer—dearer!
    Chains of sound
    Gently bound
    The lost Youth,
    Till, in sooth,
    He stood there
    A prisoner,
  Raised between earth and heaven
  By love's divinest leaven.

Was there ever such a face?
  Was it not a vision?
Had he climbed the starry space,
  To the fields Elysian?
    Through the glade
    The milk-maid
    With her pail,
    To the vale
    Passed along,
    Breathing song
  Through all his ravished sense,
  To gladden his suspense.

"Love is swift as hawk or hind,
  Chamois-like in fleetness,
None are lost that love can find,"
  Sang the maid, with sweetness.
    "True, in sooth,"
    Thought the Youth,
    "Strong, as swift,
    Love can lift
    Mountain weights
    To the gates

Of the celestial skies,
Where all else fades and dies."

Lightly flew the sunny days,
  Joy and gladness sending;
Life becomes a song of praise
  When true hearts are blending.
    Guileless truth
    Won the Youth,
    Kept him there,
    A prisoner;
    While dear Love
    From above
Poured down enduring dreams,
In calm supernal gleams.

BROCK

October 13th, 1859

One voice, one people, one in heart
  And soul, and feeling, and desire!
  Re-light the smouldering martial fire,
  Sound the mute trumpet, strike the lyre,
  The hero deed can not expire,
    The dead still play their part.

Raise high the monumental stone!
  A nation's fealty is theirs,
  And we are the rejoicing heirs,
  The honored sons of sires whose cares
  We take upon us unawares,
    As freely as our own.

We boast not of the victory,
  But render homage, deep and just,
  To his—to their—immortal dust,
  Who proved so worthy of their trust
  No lofty pile nor sculptured bust
    Can herald their degree.

No tongue need blazon forth their fame—
  The cheers that stir the sacred hill
  Are but mere promptings of the will
  That conquered then, that conquers still;
  And generations yet shall thrill
    At Brock's remembered name.

Some souls are the Hesperides
  Heaven sends to guard the golden age,
  Illuming the historic page
  With records of their pilgrimage;
  True Martyr, Hero, Poet, Sage:
    And he was one of these.

Each in his lofty sphere sublime
  Sits crowned above the common throng,
  Wrestling with some Pythonic wrong,
  In prayer, in thunder, thought, or song;
  Briareus-limbed, they sweep along,
    The Typhons of the time.

From THE ST. LAWRENCE AND THE SAGUENAY
[THE THOUSAND ISLANDS]

The bark leaps love-fraught from the land; the sea
Lies calm before us. Many an isle is there,
Clad with soft verdure; many a stately tree
Uplifts its leafy branches through the air;
The amorous current bathes the islets fair,
As we skip, youth-like, o'er the limpid waves;
White cloudlets speck the golden atmosphere,
Through which the passionate sun looks down, and graves
His image on the pearls that boil from the deep caves,

And bathe the vessel's prow. Isle after isle
Is passed, as we glide tortuously through
The opening vistas, that uprise and smile
Upon us from the ever-changing view.
Here nature, lavish of her wealth, did strew
Her flocks of panting islets on the breast
Of the admiring River, where they grew,
Like shapes of Beauty, formed to give a zest
To the charmed mind, like waking Visions of the Blest.

The silver-sinewed arms of the proud Lake,
Love-wild, embrace each islet tenderly,
The zephyrs kiss the flowers when they wake
At morn, flushed with a rare simplicity;
See how they bloom around yon birchen tree,
And smile along the bank, by the sandy shore,
In lovely groups—a fair community!
The embossed rocks glitter like golden ore,
And here, the o'erarching trees form a fantastic bower.

Red walls of granite rise on either hand,
Rugged and smooth; a proud young eagle soars
Above the stately evergreens, that stand
Like watchful sentinels on these God-built towers;
And near yon beds of many-colored flowers
Browse two majestic deer, and at their side
A spotted fawn all innocently cowers;
In the rank brushwood it attempts to hide,
While the strong-antlered stag steps forth with lordly stride,

And slakes his thirst, undaunted, at the stream.
Isles of o'erwhelming beauty! surely here
The wild enthusiast might live, and dream
His life away. No Nymphic trains appear,
To charm the pale Ideal Worshipper
Of Beauty; nor Neriads from the deeps below;
Nor hideous Gnomes, to fill the breast with fear:
But crystal streams through endless landscapes flow,
And o'er the clustering Isles the softest breezes blow.
.   .   .   .

And now 'tis Night. A myriad stars have come
To cheer the earth, and sentinel the skies.
The full-orbed moon irradiates the gloom,
And fills the air with light. Each Islet lies
Immersed in shadow, soft as thy dark eyes;
Swift through the sinuous path our vessel glides,
Now hidden by the massive promontories,
Anon the bubbling silver from its sides
Spurning, like a wild bird, whose home is on the tides.

Here Nature holds her Carnival of Isles.
Steeped in warm sunlight all the merry day,
Each nodding tree and floating greenwood smiles,
And moss-crowned monsters move in grim array;
All night the Fisher spears his finny prey;
The piney flambeaux reddening the deep,
Past the dim shores, or up some mimic bay:
Like grotesque banditti they boldly sweep
Upon the startled prey, and stab them while they sleep.

Many a tale of legendary lore
Is told of these romantic Isles. The feet
Of the Red Man have pressed each wave-zoned shore,
And many an eye of beauty oft did greet

The painted warriors and their birchen fleet,
As they returned with trophies of the slain.
That race has passed away; their fair retreat
In its primeval loneness smiles again,
Save where some vessel snaps the isle-enwoven chain:

Save where the echo of the huntsman's gun
Startles the wild duck from some shallow nook,
Or the swift hounds' deep baying, as they run,
Rouses the lounging student from his book;
Or where, assembled by some sedgy brook,
A pic-nic party, resting in the shade,
Spring pleasedly to their feet, to catch a look
At the strong steamer, through the watery glade
Ploughing, like a huge serpent from its ambuscade.

From "MARILINE"

I

At the wheel plied Mariline,
Beauteous and self-serene,
Never dreaming of that mien
Fit for lady or for queen.

Never sang she, but her words,
Music-laden, swept the chords

Of the heart, that eagerly
Stored the subtle melody,
Like the honey in the bee;
Never spake, but showed that she

Held the golden master-key
That unlocked all sympathy

Pent in souls where Feeling glows,
Like the perfume in the rose,
Like her own innate repose,
Like the whiteness in the snows.

Richly thoughted Mariline!
Nature's heiress!—nature's queen!

II

By her side, with liberal look,
Paused a student o'er a book,

Wielder of a shepherd's crook,
Reveller by grove and brook:

. . . .

With exalted eye serene
Gazed he on fair Mariline.

Swifter whirled the busy wheel,
Piled the thread upon the reel—
Saw she not his spirit kneel,
Praying for her after-weal?

Like the wife of Collatine,
Busily spun Mariline.

. . . .

V

Brightly broke the summer morn,
Like a lark from out the corn,—
Broke like joy just newly born
From the depths of woe forlorn,—

Broke with grateful songs of birds,
Lowings of well-pastured herds;

Hailed by childhood's happy looks,
Cheered by anthems of the brooks—
Chants beyond the lore of books—
Cawing crows, instead of rooks.

Glowed the heavens—rose the sun,
Mariline was up, for one.

VI

Like a chatterer tongue-tied,
Lo, the wheel is placed aside!—
Not from indolence or pride—
Mariline must be a Bride!

Fairest maid of maids terrene!
Bride of Brides, dear Mariline!

. . . .

X

Up the air, across the moor,
As they left the cottage door,

Chiméd the merry village-bells,
Music-wrapt the neighbouring fells,
Stirréd the heart's awakened cells,
Like fine strains from fairy dells.

Past the orchard, down the lane,
By fresh wavy fields of grain,

By the brook, that told its love
To the pasture, glen, and grove—
Sacred haunts, that well could prove
Vows enregistered above.

By the restless mill, where stood,
Bowing in his amplest mood,

The old miller, hat in hand,
Rich in goodness, rich in land,
On whose features, grave and bland,
Glowed a blessing for the band.

Through the village, where, behind
Many a half-uplifted blind,

Eyes, that might have lit the skies
Of Mahomet's Paradise,
Flashed behind the curtains' dyes,
With a cheerful, half-surprise.

Through the village, underneath
Many a blooming flower-wreath

Garlanding the arches green
Reared in honour of the queen
Of this day of days serene,
Day of days to Mariline.

To the church, whose cheering bells
Told the tale in music-swells—

Told it to the country wide,
With an earnest kind of pride—
Something not to be denied—
"Mariline must be a Bride!"

.   .   .   .

XIII

Ye whose souls are strong and firm,
In whom love's electric germ

Has been fanned into a flame
At the mention of a name;
Ye whose souls are still the same
As when first the Victor came,

Stinging every nerve to life,
In the beatific strife,

Till the man's divinest part
Ruled triumphant in the heart,
And, with shrinking, sudden start,
The bleak old world stood apart,

Periling the wild Ideal
By the presence of the Real:

Ye, and ye alone, can know
How these twain souls burn and glow,
Can interpret every throe
Of the full heart's overflow,

That imparts that light serene
To the brow of Mariline.

From "THE HAPPY HARVESTERS"

AN AUTUMN CHANGE

"Oh, dreamy autumn days!
I seek your faded ways,
As one who calmly strays
    Through visions of the past;
I walk the golden hours,
And where I gathered flowers
The stricken leaves in showers
    Are hurled upon the blast."

Thus mused the lonely maid,
As through the autumn glade,
With pensive heart, she strayed,
    Regretting Love's delay;
In vain the traitor flies!
To pleading lips and eyes,
Sweet looks, and tender sighs,
    He falls an easy prey.

"Oh, dreamy autumn days!
I tread your bridal ways,
As one who homeward strays,
    Through realms divinely fair;
I walk Love's radiant hours,
Fragrant with passion flowers,
And blessings fall like dowers
    Down the elysian air."

Thus mused the maiden now,
With sunny heart and brow,
For Love had turned his prow
    Towards the Golden Isles,
Where from Pierean springs
The soul of Music sings
Its sweet imaginings,
    Through all the Land of Smiles.

THE SOLDIERS OF THE PLOUGH

No maiden dream, nor fancy theme,
    Brown Labour's muse would sing;
Her stately mien and russet sheen
    Demand a stronger wing.
Long ages since, the sage, the prince,
    The man of lordly brow,
All honour gave that army brave,
    The Soldiers of the Plough.
            Kind heaven speed the Plough!
            And bless the hands that guide it;
                God gives the seed—
                The bread we need,
            Man's labour must provide it.

In every land, the toiling hand
    Is blest as it deserves;
Not so the race who, in disgrace,
    From honest labour swerves.
From fairest bowers bring rarest flowers,
    To deck the swarthy brow
Of those whose toil improves the soil,
    The Soldiers of the Plough.
            Kind heaven speed the Plough!
            And bless the hands that guide it;

God gives the seed—
The bread we need,
Man's labour must provide it.

Blest is his lot, in hall or cot,
    Who lives as nature wills,
Who pours his corn from Ceres' horn,
    And quaffs his native rills!
No breeze that sweeps trade's stormy deeps,
    Can touch his golden prow;
Their foes are few, their lives are true,
    The Soldiers of the Plough.
        Kind heaven speed the Plough!
        And bless the hands that guide it;
        God gives the seed—
        The bread we need,
Man's labour must provide it.

THOMAS D'ARCY McGEE (1825–68)

THOMAS D'ARCY McGEE was born in Ireland in 1825. He received his education in Wexford and came to the United States when he was seventeen. He went to work on the *Boston Pilot* and two years later became chief editor. At the request of Daniel O'Connell he returned to Ireland in 1845 to join the staff of the *Dublin Freeman's Journal*. He became a leading spirit in the revolutionary party known as "Young Ireland" and was compelled to escape arrest by fleeing to America. Here in 1848 he again took up journalism. He ceased to advocate Irish rebellion and sought instead to promote the welfare of his countrymen through legislation, cultural development, and philanthropy. He came to Canada in 1857 and settled in Montreal, where he edited the *New Era*. He quickly became an important figure in the political life of the country and was one of the most ardent champions of Confederation. Within a year of his arrival he was elected to the parliament of Lower Canada as a member for Montreal. He served at different times as president of the Executive Council and as minister of agriculture. His popularity was very great, but his outspoken opposition to the Fenian movement made him many bitter enemies among the more radical of his countrymen. It was by some of these that he was assassinated at Ottawa on the night of April 6, 1868.

McGee was an effective orator and the author of much political writing. He was also a prolific poet, whose *Complete Poems*, edited with a memoir by Mrs. Sadlier in 1870, is as bulky a volume as any Canadian can show. *Canadian Ballads and Occasional Verses* was published in 1858.

THE ARCTIC INDIAN'S FAITH

We worship the Spirit that walks unseen
Through our land of ice and snow;
We know not His face, we know not His place,
But His presence and power we know.

101

Does the Buffalo need the Pale-face word
    To find his pathway far?
What guide has he to the hidden ford,
    Or where the green pastures are?
Who teacheth the Moose that the hunter's gun
    Is peering out of the shade?
Who teacheth the doe and the fawn to run
    In the track the Moose has made?

Him do we follow, Him do we fear,
    The Spirit of earth and sky;
Who hears with the *Wapiti's* eager ear
    His poor red children's cry;
Whose whisper we note in every breeze
    That stirs the birch canoe;
Who hangs the reindeer-moss on the trees
    For the food of the Caribou.

The Spirit we worship, who walks unseen
    Through our land of ice and snow;
We know not His face, we know not His place,
    But His presence and power we know.

THOMAS MOORE AT ST. ANNE'S

I

On these swift waters borne along,
    A poet from the farther shore,
Framed as he went his solemn song,
    And set it by the boatman's oar.

II

It was his being's law to sing
    From morning dawn to evening light;
Like nature's choristers, his wing
    And voice were only still'd at night.

III

Nor did all nights bring him repose;
    For by the moon's auspicious ray,
Like Philomela on her rose,
    His song eclipsed the songs of day.

IV

He came a stranger summer-bird,
  And quickly pass'd; but as he flew
Our river's glorious song, he heard,
  His tongue was loosed—he warbled too!

V

And, mark the moral, ye who dream
  To be the poets of the land:
He nowhere found a nobler theme
  Than you, ye favor'd, have at hand.

VI

Not in the storied Summer Isles,
  Not 'mid the classic Cyclades,
Not where the Persian sun-god smiles,
  Found he more fitting theme than these.

VII

So, while the boat glides swift along,
  Behold above there looketh forth
The star that lights the path of song—
  The constant star that loves the north.

PAMELIA VINING YULE (1825–97)

PAMELIA S. VINING was born in Clarendon, New York, in 1825 and was educated at Albion College, Michigan, where, after graduation, she taught for a time. She moved with her family to Canada and became a teacher of English and art at the newly opened Canadian Literary Institute at Woodstock in Upper Canada. In 1866 she married James C. Yule, a divinity student at the college, and thereafter devoted the greater part of her life to evangelical religion and good works. She died at Ingersoll, Ontario, in 1897.

The fugitive verses of many years were collected in *Poems of the Heart and Home* (1881). As early as 1864 a number of Miss Vining's poems had been included in Dewart's *Selections from Canadian Poets*, and the poet was highly praised by this first Canadian anthologist.

In the eighties every poet seemed anxious to claim that his work was an expression of a peculiar national spirit. Although her book is made up for the most part of pious and sentimental "heart songs," edifying narratives, and conventional descriptive pieces, Mrs. Yule wrote in her Preface: "These poems are essentially Canadian. They have nearly all been written on Canadian soil; and they are mainly the outgrowth of many and varied experiences in Canadian life. To the author, there is hardly one that . . . . does not awaken reminiscences of . . . . some morning or evening walk amidst Canadian scenery, or some pleasant sail over Canadian waters."

Mrs. Yule was a prolific, competent, sentimental versifier, but in one or two poems a greater intensity of feeling indicates that she could be something more. The best of these is "Littlewit and Loftus." This spirited piece is a more remarkable achievement than the reader with modern prejudices may realize. Particularly effective is the sharp-witted and sharp-tongued analysis of Squire Loftus' enlightened deism, but most remarkable of all is the heightened intensity of the ending, where the rhythms of light verse are used to increase the tension and bring what started out as satire to a triumphant conclusion on an intensely serious note of personal faith. The faint shrillness of tone is an indication of the bitterness of the sacrifice of worldly glory that evangelical Christianity demanded.

LITTLEWIT AND LOFTUS

John Littlewit, friends, was a *credulous* man,
    In the good time long ago,
Ere men had gone wild o'er the latter-day dream
Of turning the world upside down with steam,
Or of chaining the lightning down to a wire,
And making it talk with its tongue of fire.

He was perfectly sure that the world stood still,
    And the sun and moon went round;—
He believed in fairies, and goblins ill,
And witches that rode over vale and hill
On wicked broom-sticks, studying still
    Mischief and craft profound.

"What a fool was John Littlewit!" somebody cries;—
    Nay, friend, not so fast, if you please!
    A humble man was John Littlewit—
    A gentle, loving man;
He clothed the needy, the hungry fed,
Pitied the erring, the faltering led,
Joyed with the joyous, wept with the sad,
Made the heart of the widow and orphan glad,
And never left for the lowliest one
An act of kindness and love undone;—
    And when he died, we may well believe
    God's blessed angels bore
John Littlewit's peaceful soul away
To the beautiful Heaven for which we pray,
Where the tree of knowledge blooms for aye,
    And ignorance plagues no more.

Squire Loftus, friends, was a *cultured* man,
    You knew him—so did I:
He had studied the "Sciences" through and through,
Had forgotten far more than the ancients knew,
    Yet still retained enough
To demonstrate clearly that all the old,
Good, practical Bible-truths we hold
    Are delusions, nonsense, stuff!

He could show that the earth had begun to grow
Millions and millions of ages ago;

That men had developed up and out
From something Moses knew nothing about;—
Held with Pope that all are but parts of a whole
Whose body is Nature, and God its Soul;—
And, since *he* was a part of that same great whole,
Then the soul of all Nature was also his soul;—
Or, more plainly—to be not obscure or dim—
That God had *developed Himself* in him:—
That what is called *Sin* in mankind, is not so,
But is just *misdirection*, all owing, you know,
To defectiveness either of body or brain,
Or both, which the soul is not thought to retain;—
In the body it acts as it *must*, but that dead
All stain from the innocent soul will have fled!

"How wise was Squire Loftus!" there's somebody cries;—
        Nay, friend, not so fast, if you please;
His wisdom was that of the self-deceived fool
Who quits the clear fount for the foul, stagnant pool,
Who puts out his eyes lest the light he descry,
Then shouts 'mid the gloom "how clear-sighted am I!"
Who turns from the glorious fountain of Day,
To follow the wild *ignis fatuus'* ray
Through quagmire and swamp, ever farther astray,
        With every step that he takes.

But he died as he lived; and the desolate night
He had courted and loved better far than the light,
Grew more and more dark, till he passed from our sight,
        And what shall I say of him more?—
Give me rather John Littlewit's questionless faith,
To illume my lone path through the valley of death—
The arm that he leaned on, the mansion of light
That burst through the gloom on his kindling sight,
        And I'll leave the poor sceptic his lore!—
Let me know only this—*I was lost and undone,*
But am saved by the blood of the Crucified One,
        And I'm *wise* although knowing no more!

WILLIAM WYE SMITH (1827–1917)

THE Reverend William Wye Smith was born in Jedburgh, Scotland, and came to Canada at an early age, where he lived for nearly eighty years. He was a journalist and a Congregational minister and for a time edited the *Canadian Independent*. He published two volumes of verse, *Alazon, and Other Poems* (1850) and *Poems* (1888), and a translation, *The New Testament in Broad Scotch* (1896).

W. D. Lighthall, in his *Songs of the Great Dominion*, wrote: " 'The Second Concession of Deer' strikes a Canadian as familiarly as roast beef would a Briton abroad. 'Concession' is a term for a range of farms. The 'first concession' is usually the row facing on a river; the 'second concession' would mean the row just behind them, and so on. The term comes from the 'conceding' of lands by the early French *seigneurs* to their vassal tenants."

THE SECOND CONCESSION OF DEER

John Tompkins lived in a house of logs,
  On the second concession of Deer;
The front was logs, all straight and sound—
The gable was logs, all tight and round—
The roof was logs, so firmly bound—
And the floor was logs, all down to the ground—
  The warmest house in Deer.

And John, to my mind, was a log himself,
  On the second concession of Deer;—
None of your birch, with bark of buff—
Nor basswood, weak and watery stuff—
But he was hickory, true and tough,
And only his outside bark was rough;—
  The grandest old man in Deer!

But John had lived too long, it seemed,
  On the second concession of Deer!

107

For his daughters took up the governing rein,
With a fine brick house on the old domain,
All papered, and painted with satinwood stain,
Carpeted stairs, and best ingrain—
     The finest house in Deer!

Poor John, it was sad to see him now,
     On the second concession of Deer!
When he came in from his weary work,
To strip off his shoes like a heathen Turk,—
Or out of the *company's* way to lurk,
And ply in the *shanty* his knife and fork—
     The times were turned in Deer!

But John was hickory to the last,
     On the second concession of Deer!
And out on the river-end of his lot
He laid up the logs in a cosy spot,
And self and wife took up with a cot,
And the great brick house might swim or not—
     He was done with the pride of Deer!

But the great house could not go at all,
     On the second concession of Deer;
'Twas *mother* no more, to wash or bake,
Nor *father* the gallants' steeds to take—
From the kitchen no more came pie nor cake—
And even their butter they'd first to make!—
     There were lessons to learn in Deer!

And the lesson they learned a year or more,
     On the second concession of Deer!
Then the girls got back the brave old pair—
And gave the mother her easy chair—
She told them how, and they did their share—
And John the honours once more did wear
     Of his own domain in Deer.

JOHN HUNTER DUVAR (1830-99)

JOHN HUNTER DUVAR, the "Bard of Hernewood," was born in Scotland in 1830. He came to Canada early in life and took up the army as a career. He became a lieutenant colonel of a brigade of the Halifax Garrison Artillery and later commanded a Prince Edward Island battalion of the active militia. For ten years he was Dominion Inspector of Fisheries for Prince Edward Island. He then went into comparative retirement on his estate at Hernewood, Fortune Cove, P.E.I., where he lived like a Canadian Sir Walter Scott—half feudal lord and half man of letters. Besides a mass of scattered pamphlets, he wrote *The Enamorado: A Drama* (1879) and *De Roberval: A Drama* (1888). With the latter was published two narrative poems in mock-heroic vein, *The Emigration of the Fairies* and *The Triumph of Constancy: A Romaunt*. He published privately some lyrics under the title of *John a'Var: His Lais*. *Annals of the Court of Oberon* appeared in 1895. He died at Hernewood in 1899.

Duvar, perhaps because of the aristocratic superiority of his point of view, has not received his proper due from the historians of Canadian literature. There is only a perfunctory line or two about his work in Logan and French's comprehensive *Highways of Canadian Literature*, and no mention of him at all in Rhodenizer's *Handbook of Canadian Literature*. Critics who praise Mair's *Tecumseh* ought to look into *De Roberval*. There they would find a genuine Canadian theme treated with intelligence and wit and presented in a blank verse that has the variety needed for drama and that can be rhetorical when rhetoric is called for and easy, colloquial, and terse when those qualities are wanted. Here are a few lines that might have come out of one of the dramas by a modern poet like Gordon Bottomley or Lascelles Abercrombie. It is a common soldier speaking:

> I saw a savage once from Africa;
> Black as a lump of charcoal, kettle black,
> But fat as any high Church dignitary,
> And greasy as a friar mendicant;
> Bohemians bought her for a kind of show,
> As a descendant of the Queen of Sheba.

109

And here is De Roberval's apostrophe to the Indian maid, the hero-
ine of the drama:

> Ha! are there wood-ghosts in this solitude,
> Such as we read of in roman de rou?
> No, it is Dian, or Diana's maid,
> And fully armed with arrow, belt and bow,
> Though tricked out in a somewhat antic guise.
> By heathen Venus, what a shape it has!
> If nymph it be, and not an airy form
> Evoked from out the rainbows of the place: *
> Small head well set, arched neck, svelt frame and limbs,
> Lissome as steel, as active as a deer,
> And skin no duskier than I oft have seen
> Among the peasant maids of warm Provence,
> At time of grapes, when browned by vintage sun;
> It lives, it moves, it answers to my gaze,
> Yet I have heard these dryades are dumb;
> If this should be a woman, now, and she
> An average sample of the belle sauvage,
> 'Twould be no task to populate the land.

This is a presentation of the Noble Savage in the light of an earlier
tradition than that of eighteenth-century sentimentalism, the neo-
classic tradition of Dryden's heroic plays, more intelligent because
more conscious in its artificiality and in wit and realism closer to the
facts of human nature.

There is no need to describe the special, if limited, excellence of
The Emigration of the Fairies. The tone is obviously derived from the
Byron of *Don Juan*, and the whole invention is happy in its lightness
and precision. A few lines from the earliest section will illustrate the
gracefulness of Duvar's fancy in delicate miniature work:

> The upper plates of fragile sea-brought shells,
> Like tiny tazzas filled with dips of lymph,
> Flecked the gay sands, minute oasis wells,
> Each one a tub-bath for a tinier nymph,
> While small white molluscs, like Carrara domes,
> Of hermit crabs and mite fays were the homes.
>
> The hugest marine monsters of that shore
> Were launces lithe and lean, with silvery scales,
> Four inches long (which in the silex bore,
> Or, swimming snake-like, undulate their tails),
> And so ferocious seemed, so glib and gleaming,
> They made the shore fays scuttle off a screaming.
>
> The largest game were sandpipers, whose feet,
> In dancing step, stamped deltas on the sand. . . . .

* The romantic scene was close by the cataract of Niagara.

The poem is divided into three sections: "Their Emigration"; "At Sea"; and "Their New Home." The three parts consist of twenty-five, fifty-three, and thirty-nine stanzas, respectively.

The Triumph of Constancy is also charming and successful. It is as though one of the milder of Chaucer's tales had been retold by a slightly irreverent Tennyson, and the result, while not very important, is pleasanter reading than some of the *Idylls of the King*.

There is a brief essay on Duvar in Lawrence J. Burpee's *A Little Book of Canadian Essays* (1909).

From *THE EMIGRATION OF THE FAIRIES*

(*The fairies in their floating island have been wafted from the shores of England by a severe storm, which has driven them for many days across the Atlantic.*)

A few days more they drifted, ever west,
Where seabirds now would fly around and swim,
And the air freshened more, from which they guessed
Land near—indeed they saw its outlines dim
Lie low like smoke, till one elf at the prow
Sung out, "A stretch of land on the lee bow!"

A long low line of beach, with crest of trees,
With openings of rich verdure, emerald hued,
And as the string o' the tide and landward breeze
Wafted them nearer, in a thankful mood
They blessed the land and beach of ruddy brown,
And off the shore lay bobbing up and down.

Now this fair land was Epaygooyat* called,
An isle of golden grain and healthful clime,
With vast fish-teeming waters, ocean-walled,
The smallest province of the Maritime.
Up on the beach the Fairies' Raft was cast,
And on Canadian land stuck hard and fast.

. . . .

Here many things were new and passing strange
To eyes familiarized to English scenes;
The skies were bluer, larger was the range
Of color, ruddier reds and brighter greens,
The skyline farther, longer was the trail,
And everything upon a larger scale.

* Prince Edward Island.

The trees grew thicker, rougher, taller stemmed,
Set in a thicker copse of underwood,
The roads were narrower and with bushes hemmed,
The horizon line more well-defined and shrewd,
The land less under tilth, enclosures fewer,
And the whole aspect inchoate and newer.

First halt. They heard within a sugar patch
The rhyming tic-a-tac of axes chopping,
So scouts were sent ahead to try to catch
A glimpse of whom or what 'twas caused the lopping,
And bring back a description of the natives—
If they were cannibals, or friends, or caitiffs.

The scouts returned, and said where they had stole
They'd seen a score or so of stalwart creatures
In flannel shirts, not smock-frocks; on the whole
They rather liked their friendly bearded features,
And that the first glance of these live Canadians
Impressed them favorably—(they were Acadians).

. . . .

They reached a scaffold frame beside a weir,
With criss-cross beams and rafters gaunt and slewed,
And in it agonizing screams could hear,
And saw a whirling fiend devouring wood—
It was a sawmill—and, too feared for speech,
They skirred away beyond the monster's reach.

. . . .

At length they reached a log hut in a clearing,
The habitation of a pioneer,
And broke off when they were the house a-nearing,
That through the settler's window they might peer
To see the inside of the habitation,
And learn some traits and habits of the nation.

They saw a strong-built mother boiling porridge,
All in a chamber somewhat bare but neat
(The goodman with his gun had gone to forage,
While the goodwife kept home alive and feat),
And, helping her, six barefoot little spartans,
All clad in homespun grey instead of tartans.

Then one of our most grizzled, shrewd, and wise
Of elfmen said: "Lads! look you here, and find out
The worth of health, strength, will, and enterprise,

For in such life as this you will see lined out
The elements of a strong, healthy State—
This is a nation destined to be great."

When through the farmer's window they were poking
They noticed something that amused them much;
It was that in no grate no coals were smoking,
Nor porcelain stove, as used among the Dutch,
But fire of wood, such as the hearthstone ruddies
With faces in the fire and back-log studies.

The water-well was not with moss o'ergrown,
Nor oaken bucket floated in its deep,
But 'stead of wheel there was a chunk of stone
Appended to a young fir as a sweep,
On principle of Archimedes' lever;
Yet the device was clumsier than clever.

Another thing they noticed between whiles
Failed not their curiosity to catch,
The which was houses roofed with wooden tiles
Instead of comfortable wheaten thatch,
And much they marvelled if the fireside ingles
Could be kept warm beneath these roofs of shingles.

They, above all things, missed the hawthorn hedges,
And cottages with ivy-trellised gables,
And rows of beehives resting on the ledges,
And neat gates leading to the fields and stables—
And grieved the unaesthetical pretenses
That farmers plead for building zigzag fences.

.   .   .   .

Between two brooks, both running diamond-bright,
A mile apart, there rose a flat-topped mound,
So low the acclivity was very slight
And suitable to form a camping ground;
Fair grass fields, too, and interspersed with these
Were groves and scattered clumps of standing trees.

Behind the fields, with outline brave and bold,
Besprent with many a tint of greenerie,
There stood a great belt of the forest old,
Whose topmost sprays aye rippled like a sea
To every breath of wind that that way strayed,
And a soft susurrus of whisper made.

.   .   .   .

It was, in truth, a quiet shady place,
A nook apart from traffic's toil and moil;
Nor fair nor market, but unbroken face
Of lush green pastures on a fertile soil,
Well clothed with wealth of woods, by nature's bounty,
And known as HERNEWOOD all throughout the county;

For the blue herons there would build their nests
High up on the tall tops of withered pines,
And sit there with their bills upon their breasts,
Or on one leg erect would stand in lines,
Fishing along the inlet's marish sedges,
Like sculptured ibises on old Nile's edges.

The fairies much approved the meads so green,
But yet they missed the daisies and primroses,
Though thyme and violets and herbs unseen
Sent a most grateful perfume to their noses,
And all the ground was dotted with white stars
Of bird-berry blooms and yellow butter-jars.

In short, 'twas just the spot for fairy raids,
With shifting points of view and ample space,
With cloistered avenues and sheltered shades,
Not yet infested by the human race,
But lying in the bosom of the woods
And full alike of fields and solitudes.

Which, when our pilgrims saw, with wild delight
They cried "Eureka! we have found it now!
Here are new meads, new woods, new brooks of light,
A Home as fair as our old haunts, we trow,
And" (as in Indian tongue it is expressed),
"Here, ala-ba-ma, we set up our rest."
. . . .

It happened luckily the place was not
Reserved by Government, nor was it fit
To sell as building lots, but was a spot
Belonged to one who loved (and lived on) it,
A man who, with a harmless eccentricity,
In a rude country life sought his felicity.

So that, so far from sending for a bailiff,
Or for a clergyman to exorcise them,
He (like Haroun al Raschid, the good caliph),

Sat down to ponder how he could devise them
In shape of a small permanent annuity,
The lands they'd squatted on, in perpetuity.

Therefore he framed some rules for his dependents,
A sort of autocratic moral law,
Binding upon himself and his descendants
That, under pain of dog-whip, hoof nor claw
Nor boy should trespass on the fairies' spot,
And all men who disturbed them should be shot.

Under this guiding and paternal care
The Fairy Folk have grown and multiplied,
And in their New Home, wilder, not less fair
Than their old English haunt, they now abide,
And have resumed their frolicsome old habits—
As lithe as squirrels and as smug as rabbits.

CHARLES MAIR (1838–1927)

CHARLES MAIR was one of the first writers to realize the poetic possibilities in purely Canadian themes, particularly in the opening-up of the West, though the load of traditional diction he carried over from Keats, Wordsworth, Longfellow, Bryant, and other popular poets prevented him from achieving a full measure of success. There is a good deal of accurate observation and precise description in poems like "The Fireflies," "August," and "The Last Bison," but the diction too often falls into artificiality and the sentiment into bookishness. Mair's most ambitious work was the chronicle drama *Tecumseh* (1886). Professor E. K. Broadus wrote: "The materials of the play—Tecumseh's efforts to federate the Indian tribes against the encroachments of the Americans, the assistance which he tendered General Brock in defeating the Americans at Detroit, and his last fight at Amherstburg—do not 'compose' into a drama. Neither the personality of the central figure nor the interwoven love-plot avails to fuse the different elements of the story. Even as a dramatic poem—an heroic pageant—it is marred by the stiffness, the grandiloquence and the mechanical uniformity of the style." The work has been praised as an ambitious if not entirely successful effort to portray a significant and heroic episode of Canadian history.

Mair himself took an active part in the development of the West. He was born in 1838, of English and Scottish ancestry, in Lanark, Upper Canada. He was educated at Perth Grammar School and at Queen's University. In 1868 he entered government service at Ottawa, and as one of the five members of the "Canada First" group he was associated with the movement to acquire for the nation the northwest territories of the Hudson Bay Company. He was a member of a road-building expedition into the Lake-of-the-Woods region northwest of Winnipeg. When the first Riel rebellion broke out in 1869, he and his young bride were made prisoners by the rebels. He was sentenced to death but managed to escape. Later he engaged in fur-trading and served as quartermaster in the Governor-General's Body Guard during the second Riel rebellion. He served on govern-

ment expeditions into British Columbia and subsequently entered
the service of the Immigration Department. He retired in 1921 and
died in 1927 in Victoria, British Columbia.

The following are Mair's works: *Dreamland and Other Poems* (1868);
Tecumseh: A Drama (1886); *The American Bison* (*Transactions of the
Royal Society of Canada* [1890]); *Tecumseh: A Drama, and Canadian
Poems* (1901); and *Through the Mackenzie Basin* (1908). A collected
edition of his works in verse and prose was published by the Radisson
Society in 1926. The book contained, in addition to the works listed
above, some previously unpublished autobiographical material and
an enthusiastic Introduction by Robert Norwood.

AUGUST

Dull August! Maiden of the sultry days,
And Summer's latest born! When all the woods
Grow dim with smoke, and smirch their lively green
With haze of long-continued drought begot;
When every field grows yellow, and a plague
Of thirst dries up its herbage to the root,
So that the cattle grow quite ribby-lean
On woody stalks whose juices all are spent;
When every fronded fern in mid-wood hid
Grows sick and yellow with the jaundice heat,
Whilst those on hill-sides glare with patchy red;
When streamlets die upon the lichened rocks,
And leave the bleaching pebbles shining bare,
And every mussel shell agape and parched,
And small snail-craft quite emptied of their crews;
When not one angel-cloud is to be seen
To image coolness and the coming rain,
But all the air with stour and dust is filled,
Through which the sun stares with a pallid face
On which one long may look, and turn, and read
Some prophecy of old with eyes undimmed;
When every morn is fiery as the noon,
And every eve is fiery as the morn,
And every night a prison hot and dark,
Where one doth sleep and dream of pleasant snow,
And winter's icicles and blessed cold,
But soon awakes, with limbs uneasy cramped,

And garments drenched, and stifled, panting breath;
When life itself grows weary of its use,
And mind is tarnished with the hue of things,
And thoughts are sickened with o'erdarkened food;
When man uneasy strolls, a listless mome
In museless misery, a wretch indeed—
Say, fiery maiden, with the scorching eyes,
What has thou left to chain us to the earth?

Ah, there are busy forms which, all unsought,
Find yet a relish in thy scanty store.
And, for that blooms are scarce, therefore the bee
Wades knee-deep in the purple thistle tops,
And shares their sweetness with the hungry wasp.
Therefore the butterfly comes sailing down,
And, heedless, lighting on a hummer's back,
Soon tacks aloft in sudden strange alarm,
Whilst bee and wasp quick scurry out of sight,
And leave their treasures to the plodding ant.
The beetle in the tree-top sits and sings
His brassy tune with increase to the end,
And one may peep and peer amongst the leaves,
Yet see him not though still he sits aloft,
And winds his reedy horn into the noon.
Now many a sob is heard in thickets dim,
Where little birds sit, pensive, on the spray,
And muse mayhap on the delights of Spring;
And many a chitmunk whistles out its fear,
And jerks and darts along the panneled rails,
Then stops, and watches with unwinking eyes
Where you do stand, as motionless as death;
But should you wag a finger through the air,
Or move a-tiptoe o'er the crispy sod,
'Twill snudge away beneath the balsam brush,
Quick lost and safe among the reddened spray.
Now one may sit within a little vale,
Close to the umbrage of some wood whose gums
Give heavy odours to the heavy air,
And watch the dusty crackers snap their wings,
Whilst gangs of blue-flies fetch a buzzing teaze
Of mad, uneasy whirlings overhead.
Now one may mark the spider trim his web
From bough to bough, and sorrow at the fate

Of many a sapless fly quite picked and bare,
Still hanging lifeless in the silken mesh,
Or muse upon the maze of insect brede
Which finds a home and feeds upon the leaves
Till naught but fibre-skeletons are hung
From branch to branch up to the highest twig.
And many a curious pleasance may be seen
And strange disport. Of such the wondrous glee
The joinéd gnats have in their headlong flight;
The wild'ring quest of horse-flies humming past
In twos and threes, and the small cloud of wings
Which mix and throng together in the sun.
A num'rous kin dart shining o'er some pool
Spared from the general wreck of water store,
And from the lofty woods crow-blackbird trains
Chuck o'er the barren leas with long-drawn flight.
Far o'er the hills the grouse's feath'ry drum
Beats quick and loud within a beechen copse,
And, sometimes, when the heavy woods are still,
A single tap upon a hemlock spire
Dwells with the lonely glades in echoes deep.

Then with the eve come sounds of varied note.
The boys troop clam'ring to the woods, and curs
Yelp sharply where the groundhog's lair is found.
The horn has called the reapers from the fields,
And, now, from cots half-hid by fruited trees,
The homely strains of fiddle or of fife,
Which distance sweetens with a needed art,
Come dropping on the ear. And sometimes, too,
If sparks are deemed sincere, and rustic love
Run smooth, the merry milkmaids sing
A fallow's length with pails at elbow slung,
Or, while they thrust the draw-well dangler down,
'Gainst which the swains oppose their yielding strength,
Laugh loud and long, or scold with mimicked heat.
These find a pleasure in the waste of days,
And strive against the mis'ry of the time
With am'rous snares and artifice of love.
Not less those faithful ones who look upon
This weather-sorrow with sufficing joy—
The old, who still would linger with their seed,
And snatch a little comfort from the earth.

Still would they gaze upon the simmering sun,
And take the warmth into their agéd bones,
Nor cavil with the hindrances which stay
The lethal hour when death shall come and bend
Their reverend heads into the restful grave.

Hail August! Maiden of the sultry days,
To thee I bring the measured meed of praise.
For, though thou hast besmirched the day and night,
And hid a wealth of glory from our sight,
Thou still dost build in musing, pensive mood,
Thy blissful idyls in the underwood.
Thou still dost yield new beauties, fair and young,
With many a form of grace as yet unsung,
Which ripens o'er thy pathway and repays
The toil and languor of the sultry days.

From "THE FIREFLIES"

How dreamy-dark it is!
Men yawn for weariness, and hoard their gains,
While careful housewives drown the kitchen fires. . . . .
The plodding oxen, dragging creaky wains
O'er bosky roads, their ancient horns entwine,
Lick their huge joles, and think of bedded stalls,
And munching of sweet corn. The lick'rous swine
Huddled in routed turf, neglect the calls
And pinches of their young, and hide their dugs,
Swoll'n with a lazy milk, whilst timid sheep,
Far from their winter-folds of knotty fir,
Dream of lean wolves and bleatings in their sleep.

Yet there are those that oft the silence mock,
For life wings through the darkness everywhere,
And night's dull, ugly brood is all astir.
The flapping bat and hungry-snapping hawk
Now glut themselves with innocent, droning flies,
Whisked from the dingy commonwealth of air.
The loathsome toad, which foul infection breeds
And lep'rous sores, hops o'er the dusty walk,
And, in the hollows where the river lies,
The hoarse frogs sprawl among the bedded reeds,
And croak harsh ditties to their uncouth mates. . . . .

> This is the hour
When fire-flies flit about each lofty crag,
And down the valleys sail on lucid wing. . . . .
I see them glimmer where the waters lag
By winding bays, and to the willows sing;
And, far away, where stands the forest dim,
Huge-built of old, their tremulous lights are seen.
High overhead they gleam like trailing stars,
Then sink adown, until their emerald sheen
Dies in the darkness like an evening hymn—
Anon to float again in glorious bars
Of streaming rapture, such as man may hear
When the soul casts its slough of mortal fear.
And now they make rich spangles in the grass,
Gilding the night-dew on the tender blade;
Then hover o'er the meadow-pools to gaze
At their bright forms shrined in the dreamy glass
Which earth, and air, and bounteous rain have made.
One moment, and the thicket is ablaze
With twinkling lamps which swing from bough to bough:
Another, and like sylphids they descend
To cheer the brook-side where the bell-flow'rs grow.
Near and more near they softly come, until
Their little life is busy at my feet;
They glow around me, and my fancies blend
Capriciously with their delight, and fill
My wakeful bosom with unwonted heat.
One lights upon my hand, and there I clutch
With an alarming finger its quick wing:
Erstwhile so free, it pants, the tender thing!
And dreads its captor and his handsel touch.

From *TECUMSEH*

I

There was a time on this fair continent
When all things throve in spacious peacefulness.
The prosperous forests unmolested stood,
For where the stalwart oak grew there it lived
Long ages, and then died among its kind.
The hoary pines—those ancients of the earth—
Brimful of legends of the early world,

Stood thick on their own mountains unsubdued.
And all things else illumined by the sun,
Inland or by the lifted wave, had rest.
The passionate or calm pageants of the skies
No artist drew; but in the auburn west
Innumerable faces of fair cloud
Vanished in silent darkness with the day.
The prairie realm—vast ocean's paraphrase—
Rich in wild grasses numberless, and flowers
Unnamed save in mute Nature's inventory,
No civilized barbarian trenched for gain.
And all that flowed was sweet and uncorrupt.
The rivers and their tributary streams,
Undammed, wound on forever, and gave up
Their lonely torrents to weird gulfs of sea,
And ocean wastes unshadowed by a sail.
And all the wild life of this western world
Knew not the fear of man; yet in those woods,
And by those plenteous streams and mighty lakes,
And on stupendous steppes of peerless plain,
And in the rocky gloom of canyons deep,
Screened by the stony ribs of mountains hoar
Which steeped their snowy peaks in purging cloud,
And down the continent where tropic suns
Warmed to her very heart the mother earth,
And in the congeal'd north where silence self
Ached with intensity of stubborn frost,
There lived a soul more wild than barbarous;
A tameless soul—the sunburnt savage free—
Free, and untainted by the greed of gain:
Great Nature's man content with Nature's food.

II

Tecumseh. Once all this mighty continent was ours,
And the Great Spirit made it for our use.
He knew no boundaries, so had we peace
In the vast shelter of His handiwork,
And, happy here, we cared not whence we came.
We brought no evils thence—no treasured hate,
No greed of gold, no quarrels over God;
And so our broils, to narrow issues joined,
Were soon composed, and touched the ground of peace.

Our very ailments, rising from the earth,
And not from any foul abuse in us,
Drew back, and let age ripen to death's hand.
Thus flowed our lives until your people came,
Till from the East our matchless misery came!
Since then our tale is crowded with your crimes,
With broken faith, with plunder of reserves—
The sacred remnants of our wide domain—
With tamp'rings, and delirious feasts of fire,
The fruit of your thrice-curséd stills of death
Which make our good men bad, our bad men worse,
Ay! blind them till they grope in open day
And stumble into miserable graves.
Oh, it is piteous, for none will hear!
There is no hand to help, no heart to feel,
No tongue to plead for us in all your land.
But every hand aims death, and every heart,
Ulcered with hate, resents our presence here;
And every tongue cries for our children's land
To expiate their crime of being born.
Oh, we have ever yielded in the past,
But we shall yield no more! Those plains are ours!
Those forests are our birth-right and our home!
Let not the Long-Knife build one cabin there—
Or fire from it will spread to every roof,
To compass you, and light your souls to death!

III

Lefroy. We left
The silent forest, and, day after day,
Great prairies swept beyond our aching sight
Into the measureless West; uncharted realms,
Voiceless and calm, save when tempestuous wind
Rolled the rank herbage into billows vast,
And rushing tides which never found a shore.
And tender clouds, and veils of morning mist,
Cast flying shadows, chased by flying light,
Into interminable wildernesses,
Flushed with fresh blooms, deep perfumed by the rose,
And murmurous with flower-fed bird and bee.
The deep-grooved bison-paths like furrows lay,
Turned by the cloven hoofs of thundering herds

Primeval, and still travelled as of yore.
And gloomy valleys opened at our feet—
Shagged with dusk cypresses and hoary pine;
And sunless gorges, rummaged by the wolf,
Which through long reaches of the prairie wound,
Then melted slowly into upland vales,
Lingering, far-stretched amongst the spreading hills.

Brock. What charming solitudes! And life was there!

Lefroy. Yes, life was there! inexplicable life,
Still wasted by inexorable death.
There had the stately stag his battle-field—
Dying for mastery among his hinds.
There vainly sprung the affrighted antelope,
Beset by glittering eyes and hurrying feet.
The dancing grouse, at their insensate sport,
Heard not the stealthy footstep of the fox;
The gopher on his little earthwork stood,
With folded arms, unconscious of the fate
That wheeled in narrowing circles overhead;
And the poor mouse, on heedless nibbling bent,
Marked not the silent coiling of the snake.
At length we heard a deep and solemn sound—
Erupted moanings of the troubled earth
Trembling beneath innumerable feet.
A growing uproar blending in our ears,
With noise tumultuous as ocean's surge,
Of bellowings, fierce breath and battle shock,
And ardour of unconquerable herds.
A multitude whose trampling shook the plains,
With discord of harsh sound and rumblings deep
As if the swift revolving earth had struck,
And from some adamantine peak recoiled,
Jarring. At length we topped a high-browed hill—
The last and loftiest of a file of such—
And, lo! before us lay the tameless stock,
Slow wending to the northward like a cloud!
A multitude in motion, dark and dense—
Far as the eye could reach, and farther still,
In countless myriads stretched for many a league.

GEORGE T. LANIGAN (1846–86)

GEORGE THOMAS LANIGAN, the author of one immortal piece of newspaper ribaldry, was born at Three Rivers, Lower Canada, in 1846. As a young man he founded the newspaper that is now the *Montreal Star*, and in the seventies he worked on the *New York World*, for which he wrote a series of brilliant brief prose fables published in 1878 under the title, *Fables Out of the World*. They are said to have been much admired by Mark Twain. "The Ahkoond of Swat" was written one night in the office of the *World* as an expression of Lanigan's reaction to the cryptic message that came in over the wires, "The Ahkoond of Swat is dead." Edward Lear has also written a poem on the subject. Lear had read Lanigan, we may suppose, in a little book of American humorous verse in Walter Scott's *Canterbury Poets*, which had been published in the eighties. Lear's poem is a much more sophisticated piece of work.

Lanigan translated a few of the old French-Canadian chansons and published when he was nineteen a little volume entitled *National Ballads of Canada, Imitated and Translated from the Originals*, by "Allid" (Montreal, 1865).

A THRENODY

"The Ahkoond of Swat is dead."—Press dispatch

What, what, what,
What's the news from Swat?
    Sad news,
    Bad news,
Comes by the cable led
Through the Indian Ocean's bed,
Through the Persian Gulf, the Red
Sea and the Med-
Iterranean—he's dead;
The Ahkoond is dead!

For the Ahkoond I mourn.
    Who wouldn't?
He strove to disregard the message stern,
    But he Ahkoondn't.

Dead, dead, dead;
    Sorrow, Swats!
Swats wha' hae wi' Ahkoond bled,
Swats whom he had often led
Onward to a gory bed,
    Or to victory,
    As the case might be.
    Sorrow, Swats!
Tears shed,
    Shed tears like water,
Your great Ahkoond is dead!
    That Swat's the matter!

Mourn, city of Swat!
Your great Ahkoond is not,
But lain 'mid worms to rot:
His mortal part alone, his soul was caught
(Because he was a good Ahkoond)
Up to the bosom of Mahound.
Though earthly walls his frame surround
(For ever hallowed be the ground!)
And sceptics mock the lowly mound
And say, "He's now of no Ahkound!"
(His soul is in the skies!)

The azure skies that bend above his loved
    Metropolis of Swat
He sees with larger, other eyes,
Athwart all earthly mysteries—
    He knows what's Swat.

Let Swat bury the great Ahkoond
    With a noise of mourning and of lamentation!
Let Swat bury the great Ahkoond
    With the noise of the mourning of the Swattish nation!
    Fallen is at length
    Its tower of strength,
Its sun had dimmed ere it had nooned:
Dead lies the great Ahkoond.
    The great Ahkoond of Swat
    Is not.

PART III
THE NEW NATIONALISM
"THE GOLDEN AGE"

ISABELLA VALANCY CRAWFORD
(1850–87)

BORN in 1850 in Dublin into a cultivated Irish family of Highland Scottish descent, Isabella Valancy Crawford was brought to the backwoods of Ontario at the age of eight. Her father struggled to make a living as a country doctor and to educate a family of twelve children. Suffering from an inherited heart disease, all but three of the children succumbed to the hard life of the woodland settlement (Paisley, on the Saugeen River). Eight years after coming to Canada the family moved to the village of Lakefield, the scene of some of the events described by the pioneer writers, Susanna Moodie and Catherine Parr Trail, and later to Peterborough. But even a larger practice in town did not enable Dr. Crawford to free his family from poverty, and Isabella began to make a serious effort to help. She contributed short stories and poems to Toronto newspapers and the magazines. When her father died in 1875, she became the sole support of her mother and one remaining invalid sister, and upon the death of her sister she went with her mother to Toronto, where the two women took lodgings over a grocery store on King Street. Here, living in proud retirement, Miss Crawford wrote tirelessly, contributing a long and varied series of poems to the periodicals and the press.

In 1884 she published at her own expense a cheaply bound volume of verse under the forbidding title, *Old Spookses' Pass, Malcolm's Katie, and Other Poems*. Although the book was praised in the *Week* and in some of the best English literary journals, only about fifty of the thousand copies were sold. Its failure was a keen disappointment to the poet, but she continued her work with undiminished energy. She wrote a novel, *The Little Bacchante*, which came out as a serial in the *Toronto Evening Globe* in 1886. Miss Crawford died suddenly February 12, 1887, without knowing the high place that her poetry was to occupy in Canadian literature. It was not until 1905, when a collected edition of her poems was edited by J. W. Garvin, with an Introduction by Ethelwyn Wetherald, that her importance was recognized. This volume contained eighty-six poems, of which fifty-two were newly collected.

Energy is the outstanding quality of Miss Crawford's best poems, and among these, as well as the Canadian pieces, "Malcolm's Katie" and "The Canoe," must be numbered some poems of classical inspiration, such as "Curtius" and the fine ballad, "The Helot." With these for vigor and intensity must be named her striking saga of the Norse gods, "Gisli, the Chieftain," and her imaginative evocation of the West, "Old Spookses' Pass." The last contains a vivid description of the stampede of a herd of wild cattle, as powerful as anything in Masefield, which triumphs over the handicap of the dialect, though the poem as a whole, perhaps, makes too heavy a demand on the ear.

THE CANOE

My masters twain made me a bed
Of pine-boughs resinous, and cedar;
Of moss, a soft and gentle breeder
Of dreams of rest; and me they spread
With furry skins, and laughing said,
"Now she shall lay her polish'd sides,
As queens do rest, or dainty brides,
Our slender lady of the tides!"

My masters twain their camp-soul lit,
Streamed incense from the hissing cones,
Large, crimson flashes grew and whirl'd,
Thin, golden nerves of sly light curl'd
Round the dun camp, and rose faint zones,
Half way about each grim bole knit,
Like a shy child that would bedeck
With its soft clasp a Brave's red neck;
Yet sees the rough shield on his breast,
The awful plumes shake on his crest,
And fearful drops his timid face,
Nor dares complete the sweet embrace.

Into the hollow hearts of brakes,
Yet warm from sides of does and stags,
Pass'd to the crisp dark river flags;
Sinuous, red as copper snakes,
Sharp-headed serpents, made of light,
Glided and hid themselves in night.

My masters twain the slaughter'd deer
Hung on fork'd boughs—with thongs of leather.
Bound were his stiff, slim feet together—
His eyes like dead stars cold and drear;
The wand'ring firelight drew near
And laid its wide palm, red and anxious,
On the sharp splendor of his branches;
On the white foam grown hard and sere
    On flank and shoulder.
Death—hard as breast of granite boulder,
    And under his lashes
Peer'd thro' his eyes at his life's grey ashes.

My masters twain sang songs that wove
(As they burnish'd hunting blade and rifle)
A golden thread with a cobweb trifle—
Loud of the chase, and low of love.

"O Love, art thou a silver fish?
Shy of the line and shy of gaffing,
Which we do follow, fierce, yet laughing,
Casting at thee the light-wing'd wish,
And at the last shall we bring thee up
From the crystal darkness under the cup
    Of lily folden,
    On broad leaves golden?

"O Love! art thou a silver deer,
Swift thy starr'd feet as wing of swallow,
While we with rushing arrows follow;
And at the last shall we draw near,
And over thy velvet neck cast thongs—
Woven of roses, of stars, of songs?
    New chains all moulden
    Of rare gems olden!"

They hung the slaughter'd fish like swords
On saplings slender—like scimitars
Bright, and ruddied from new-dead wars,
Blaz'd in the light—the scaly hordes.

They pil'd up boughs beneath the trees,
Of cedar-web and green fir tassel;
Low did the pointed pine tops rustle,
The camp fire blush'd to the tender breeze.

The hounds laid dew-laps on the ground,
With needles of pine sweet, soft and rusty—
Dream'd of the dead stag stout and lusty;
A bat by the red flames wove its round.

The darkness built its wigwam walls
Close round the camp, and at its curtain
Press'd shapes, thin woven and uncertain,
As white locks of tall waterfalls.

From "MALCOLM'S KATIE"

I

The South Wind laid his moccasins aside,
Broke his gay calumet of flow'rs, and cast
His useless wampum, beaded with cool dews,
Far from him, northward; his long, ruddy spear
Flung sunward, whence it came, and his soft locks
Of warm, fine haze grew silver as the birch.
His wigwam of green leaves began to shake;
The crackling rice-beds scolded harsh like squaws;
The small ponds pouted up their silver lips;
The great lakes ey'd the mountains, whisper'd "Ugh!
"Are ye so tall, O chiefs? Not taller than
"Our plumes can reach." And rose a little way,
As panthers stretch to try their velvet limbs,
And then retreat to purr and bide their time.
At morn the sharp breath of the night arose
From the wide prairies, in deep-struggling seas,
In rolling breakers, bursting to the sky;
In tumbling surfs, all yellow'd faintly thro'
With the low sun—in mad, conflicting crests,
Voic'd with low thunder from the hairy throats
Of the mist-buried herds; and for a man
To stand amid the cloudy roll and moil,
The phantom waters breaking overhead,
Shades of vex'd billows bursting on his breast,
Torn caves of mist wall'd with a sudden gold,
Reseal'd as swift as seen—broad, shaggy fronts,
Fire-ey'd and tossing on impatient horns
The wave impalpable—was but to think
A dream of phantoms held him as he stood.

The late, last thunders of the summer crash'd,
Where shrieked great eagles, lords of naked cliffs.
The pulseless forest, lock'd and interlock'd
So closely, bough with bough, and leaf with leaf,
So serf'd by its own wealth, that while from high
The moons of summer kiss'd its green-gloss'd locks;
And round its knees the merry West Wind danc'd;
And round its ring, compacted emerald;
The south wind crept on moccasins of flame;
And the red fingers of th' impatient sun
Pluck'd at its outmost fringes—its dim veins
Beat with no life—its deep and dusky heart,
In a deep trance of shadow, felt no throb
To such soft wooing answer: thro' its dream
Brown rivers of deep waters sunless stole;
Small creeks sprang from its mosses, and amaz'd,
Like children in a wigwam curtain'd close
Above the great, dead heart of some red chief,
Slipp'd on soft feet, swift stealing through the gloom,
Eager for light and for the frolic winds.
In this shrill moon the scouts of winter ran
From the ice-belted north, and whistling shafts
Struck maple and struck sumach—and a blaze
Ran swift from leaf to leaf, from bough to bough;
Till round the forest flash'd a belt of flame
And inward lick'd its tongues of red and gold
To the deep, tranced inmost heart of all.
Rous'd the still heart—but all too late, too late.
Too late, the branches welded fast with leaves,
Toss'd, loosen'd, to the winds—too late the sun
Pour'd his last vigor to the deep, dark cells
Of the dim wood. The keen, two-bladed Moon
Of Falling Leaves roll'd up on crested mists
And where the lush, rank boughs had foiled the sun
In his red prime, her pale, sharp fingers crept
After the wind and felt about the moss,
And seem'd to pluck from shrinking twig and stem
The burning leaves—while groan'd the shudd'ring wood.
Who journey'd where the prairies made a pause,
Saw burnish'd ramparts flaming in the sun,
With beacon fires, tall on their rustling walls.
And when the vast, horn'd herds at sunset drew

Their sullen masses into one black cloud,
Rolling thund'rous o'er the quick pulsating plain,
They seem'd to sweep between two fierce red suns
Which, hunter-wise, shot at their glaring balls
Keen shafts, with scarlet feathers and gold barbs,
By round, small lakes with thinner forests fring'd,
More jocund woods that sung about the feet
And crept along the shoulders of great cliffs;
The warrior stags, with does and tripping fawns,
Like shadows black upon the throbbing mist
Of Evening's rose, flash'd thro' the singing woods—
Nor tim'rous, sniff'd the spicy, cone-breath'd air;
For never had the patriarch of the herd
Seen limn'd against the farthest rim of light
Of the low-dipping sky, the plume or bow
Of the red hunter; nor when stoop'd to drink,
Had from the rustling rice-beds heard the shaft
Of the still hunter hidden in its spears;
His bark canoe close-knotted in its bronze,
His form as stirless as the brooding air,
His dusky eyes, too, fix'd unwinking, fires;
His bow-string tighten'd till it subtly sang
To the long throbs, and leaping pulse that roll'd
And beat within his knotted, naked breast.

II

The mighty morn strode laughing up the land,
And Max, the labourer and the lover, stood
Within the forest's edge, beside a tree;
The mossy king of all the woody tribes,
Whose clatt'ring branches rattl'd, shuddering,
As the bright axe cleav'd moon-like thro' the air,
Waking strange thunders, rousing echoes link'd
From the full, lion-throated roar, to sighs
Stealing on dove-wings thro' the distant aisles.
Swift fell the axe, swift follow'd roar on roar,
Till the bare woodland bellow'd in its rage,
As the first-slain slow toppl'd to his fall.
"O King of Desolation, art thou dead?"
Thought Max, and laughing, heart and lips, leap'd on
The vast, prone trunk. "And have I slain a King?
"Above his ashes will I build my house—
"No slave beneath its pillars, but—a King!"

III

O, Love builds on the azure sea,
  And Love builds on the golden sand;
And Love builds on the rose-wing'd cloud,
  And sometimes Love builds on the land.

O, if Love build on sparkling sea—
  And if Love build on golden strand—
And if Love build on rosy cloud—
  To Love these are the solid land.

O, Love will build his lily walls,
  And Love his pearly roof will rear,—
On cloud or land, or mist or sea—
  Love's solid land is everywhere!

IV

It was not all his own, the axe-stirr'd waste.
In these new days men spread about the earth,
With wings at heel—and now the settler hears,
While yet his axe rings on the primal woods,
The shrieks of engines rushing o'er the wastes;
Nor parts his kind to hew his fortunes out.
And as one drop glides down the unknown rock
And the bright-threaded stream leaps after it,
With welded billions, so the settler finds
His solitary footsteps beaten out,
With the quick rush of panting, human waves
Upheav'd by throbs of angry poverty,
And driven by keen blasts of hunger, from
Their native strands—so stern, so dark, so dear!
O, then, to see the troubl'd, groaning waves,
Throb down to peace in kindly, valley beds;
Their turbid bosoms clearing in the calm
Of sun-ey'd Plenty—till the stars and moon,
The blessed sun himself, has leave to shine
And laugh in their dark hearts! So shanties grew
Other than his amid the blacken'd stumps;
And children ran with little twigs and leaves
And flung them, shouting, on the forest pyres,
Where burn'd the forest kings—and in the glow
Paus'd men and women when the day was done.
There the lean weaver ground anew his axe,

Nor backward look'd upon the vanish'd loom,
But forward to the plowing of his fields;
And to the rose of Plenty in the cheeks
Of wife and children—nor heeded much the pangs
Of the rous'd muscles tuning to new work.
The pallid clerk look'd on his blister'd palms
And sigh'd and smil'd, but girded up his loins
And found new vigour as he felt new hope.
The lab'rer with train'd muscles, grim and grave,
Look'd at the ground and wonder'd in his soul,
What joyous anguish stirr'd his darken'd heart,
At the mere look of the familiar soil,
And found his answer in the words—*"Mine own!"*
Then came smooth-coated men, with eager eyes,
And talk'd of steamers on the cliff-bound lakes;
And iron tracks across the prairie lands;
And mills to crush the quartz of wealthy hills;
And mills to saw the great, wide-arm'd trees;
And mills to grind the singing stream of grain;
And with such busy clamour mingled still
The throbbing music of the bold, bright Axe—
The steel tongue of the Present, and the wail
Of falling forests—voices of the Past.

V

"Bite deep and wide, O Axe, the tree,
  What doth thy bold voice promise me?"

"I promise thee all joyous things,
  That furnish forth the lives of kings!

"For ev'ry silver ringing blow,
  Cities and palaces shall grow!"

"Bite deep and wide, O Axe, the tree,
  Tell wider prophecies to me."

"When rust hath gnaw'd me deep and red,
  A nation strong shall lift his head!

"His crown the very Heav'ns shall smite,
  Æons shall build him in his might!"

"Bite deep and wide, O Axe, the tree;
  Bright Seer, help on thy prophecy!"

Max smote the snow-weigh'd tree and lightly laugh'd.
"See, friend," he cried to one that look'd and smil'd,
"My axe and I—we do immortal tasks—
"We build up nations—this my axe and I!"
"O," said the other with a cold, short smile,
"Nations are not immortal! is there now
"One nation thron'd upon the sphere of earth,
"That walk'd with the first Gods, and saw
"The budding world unfold its slow-leav'd flow'r?
"Nay; it is hardly theirs to leave behind
"Ruins so eloquent, that the hoary sage
"Can lay his hand upon their stones, and say:
" 'These once were thrones!' The lean, lank lion peals
"His midnight thunders over lone, red plains,
"Long-ridg'd and crested on their dusty waves,
"With fires from moons red-hearted as the sun;
"And deep re-thunders all the earth to him.
"For, far beneath the flame-fleck'd, shifting sands,
"Below the roots of palms, and under stones
"Of younger ruins, thrones, tow'rs and cities
"Honeycomb the earth. The high, solemn walls
"Of hoary ruins—their foundings all unknown
"(But to the round-ey'd worlds that walk
"In the blank paths of Space and blanker Chance).
"At whose stones young mountains wonder, and the seas'
"New-silv'ring, deep-set valleys pause and gaze;
"Are rear'd upon old shrines, whose very Gods
"Were dreams to the shrine-builders, of a time
"They caught in far-off flashes—as the child
"Half thinks he can remember how one came
"And took him in her hand and shew'd him that
"He thinks, she call'd the sun. Proud ships rear high
"On ancient billows that have torn the roots
"Of cliffs, and bitten at the golden lips
"Of firm, sleek beaches, till they conquer'd all,
"And sow'd the reeling earth with salted waves.
"Wrecks plunge, prow foremost, down still, solemn slopes,
"And bring their dead crews to as dead a quay;
"Some city built before that ocean grew,
"By silver drops from many a floating cloud,
"By icebergs bellowing in their throes of death,
"By lesser seas toss'd from their rocking cups,

"And leaping each to each; by dew-drops flung
"From painted sprays, whose weird leaves and flow'rs
"Are moulded for new dwellers on the earth,
"Printed in hearts of mountains and of mines.
"Nations immortal? where the well-trimm'd lamps
"Of long-past ages, when Time seem'd to pause
"On smooth, dust-blotted graves that, like the tombs
"Of monarchs, held dead bones and sparkling gems?
"She saw no glimmer on the hideous ring
"Of the black clouds; no stream of sharp, clear light
"From those great torches, pass'd into the black
"Of deep oblivion. She seem'd to watch, but she
"Forgot her long-dead nations. When she stirr'd
"Her vast limbs in the dawn that forc'd its fire
"Up the black East, and saw the imperious red
"Burst over virgin dews and budding flow'rs,
"She still forgot her molder'd thrones and kings,
"Her sages and their torches, and their Gods,
"And said, 'This is my birth—my primal day!'
"She dream'd new Gods, and rear'd them other shrines,
"Planted young nations, smote a feeble flame
"From sunless flint, re-lit the torch of mind;
"Again she hung her cities on the hills,
"Built her rich towers, crown'd her kings again,
"And with the sunlight on her awful wings
"Swept round the flow'ry cestus of the earth,
"And said, 'I build for Immortality!'
"Her vast hand rear'd her tow'rs, her shrines, her thrones;
"The ceaseless sweep of her tremendous wings
"Still beat them down and swept their dust abroad;
"Her iron finger wrote on mountain sides
"Her deeds and prowess—and her own soft plume
"Wore down the hills! Again drew darkly on
"A night of deep forgetfulness; once more
"Time seem'd to pause upon forgotten graves—
"Once more a young dawn stole into her eyes—
"Again her broad wings stirr'd, and fresh clear airs,
"Blew the great clouds apart;—again Time said,
" 'This is my birth—my deeds and handiwork
" 'Shall be immortal.' Thus and so dream on
"Fool'd nations, and thus dream their dullard sons.
"Naught is immortal save immortal—Death!"

Max paus'd and smil'd: "O, preach such gospel, friend,
"To all but lovers who most truly love;
"For *them*, their gold-wrought scripture glibly reads,
"All else is mortal but immortal—Love!"

From "GISLI, THE CHIEFTAIN"

THE SONG OF THE ARROW

What know I,
As I bite the blue veins of the throbbing sky;
To the quarry's breast,
Hot from the sides of the sleek smooth nest?

What know I
Of the will of the tense bow from which I fly!
What the need or jest,
That feathers my flight to its bloody rest.

What know I
Of the will of the bow that speeds me on high?
What doth the shrill bow
Of the hand on its singing soul-string know?

Flame-swift speed I—
And the dove and the eagle shriek out and die;
Whence comes my sharp zest
For the heart of the quarry? the Gods know best.

Deep pierc'd the red gaze of the eagle—
The breast of a cygnet below him;
Beneath his dun wing from the eastward
Shrill-chaunted the long shaft of Gisli!

Beneath his dun wing from the westward
Shook a shaft that laugh'd in its biting—
Met in the fierce breast of the eagle
The arrows of Gisli and Brynhild!

[EPILOGUE]

Said the voice of Evil to the ear of Good,
    "Clasp thou my strong, right hand,
Nor shall our clasp be known or understood
    By any in the land.

"I, the dark giant, rule strongly on the earth,
      Yet thou, bright one, and I
  Sprang from the one great mystery—at one birth
      We looked upon the sky!

"I labour at my bleak, my stern toil accurs'd
      Of all mankind—nor stay
  To rest, to murmur 'I hunger!' or 'I thirst!'
      Nor for my joy delay.

"My strength pleads strongly with thee; doth any
          beat
      With hammer and with stone
  Past tools to use them to his deep defeat—
      To turn them on his throne?

"Then I of God the mystery—toil thou with me
      Brother; but in the sight
  Of men who know not, I, the stern son shall be
      Of Darkness—Thou of Light!"

JOHN E. LOGAN (1852-1915)

JOHN EDWARD LOGAN was born in Hamilton, Ontario, and, after some years of his youth spent in the West, he settled permanently in Montreal, where he played a prominent part in the business, social, and athletic life of the city. After his death in 1915 his poems were collected by the Pen and Pencil Club of Montreal and published under the title, *Verses*. A few poems on Indian themes and some vivid dialect ballads of the old West are the most interesting of these. Logan wrote a good deal of fugitive verse under the pseudonym "Barry Dane."

"THE INJUN"

(*An Incident in the Minnesota Massacre of 1862*)

Ye say the Injuns all alike,
    A bad an' sneakin' lot;
An' a'int no use for nuthin',
    So the cusses should be shot?

Well, p'raps they is, an' p'raps they a'int,
    A lazy, wuthless crowd;
Yet durn my skin ef I kin see
    Why white men chin so loud.

Ef some o' them poor devils kicks
    'Cause things a'int run quite squar',
An' jumps an Indian agent's ranch,
    An' yanks his bloomin' har,

Thar' a'int no thought uv causes,
    An' no one cares a cuss,
It's jes' call out the Blue Coats
    An' give 'em somethin' wuss.

Thar's good an' bad in Injun,
    An' thar's good an' bad in White;
But, somehow, they is always wrong,
    An' we is allus right.

But I'm an old, old timer,
    I've jes' bin here so long,
That I kin mostly allus tell
    The ones that's right an' wrong.

An' ye can bet yer sainted life,
    When things get steamin' hot,
That some white fool or knave has lit
    The fire that biles the pot.

Ye think the Injun isn't squar'?
    That's jes' whar' ye mistake;
Fer bein' true to them that's true
    The Injun scoops the cake.

Fer I kin tell ye what occurr'd
    Way back in 'sixty-two,
When things in Minnesota State
    Wuz lookin' kinder blue.

The Sioux wuz up an' on the shoot
    A-slingin' round their lead,
An' scalpin' every mother's son
    That wuzn't bald or dead.

Thar' warn't a livin' Yankee—
    An' lots wuz brave an' bold—
That would have crossed them plains alone
    For a waggon load uv gold.

'Cause why? We know'd the Guv'ment
    Wuzn't treatin' Injuns fair;
That's why they riz an' painted things,
    An' raised the settlers' hair.

That summer a fur-trader
    Came up from Montreal,
An' on his way to Garry
    He landed at Saint Paul.

An' all the guides an' hunters said
   He couldn't cross the plains,
Fer them thar' painted devils
   Wuz layin' low fer trains.

He only laffed, and said, he know'd
   The Injuns all his life,
An' he was goin' to mosey through
   An' take along his wife.

An' she, you bet, wuz plucky,
   An' said she'd go along,
Fer Injuns only went fer them
   As allus done 'em wrong.

Now I should smile, 'twuz riskey—
   An' all the fellers sed
The chances of their gettin' through
   Warn't wuth an ounce uv lead.

But sure's yer born they started,
   Right out the northern trail,
Aboard a praree schooner,
   With a Texan steer fer sail.

An' right a-top that creekin' cart,
   Upon the highest rack,
That trader nailed a bloomin' rag—
   An English Union Jack.

So thar' he'd gone an' done it,
   Es stubborn as a mule;
An' knowin' fellers said we'd seen
   The last of that damn fool.

They wuzn't long upon the trail
   Before a band of Reds
Got on their tracks, an' foller'd up,
   A-goin' to shave their heads.

But when they seen that little flag
   A-stickin' on that cart,
They jes' said, "Hudson Bay. Go on.
   Good trader with good heart!"

An' when they struck the river,
   An' took to their canoe,

'Twuz that thar' bit uv culler
   That seen 'em safely through.

Fer thar' that cussed little rag
   Went floatin' through the State—
A-flappin' in the face uv death,
   An' smilin' right at fate.

That wuz the way them 'tarnal fools
   Crossed them thar' blazin' plains,
An' floated down the windin' Red
   Through waves with bloody stains.

What give that flag its virtoo?
   What's thar' in red an' blue,
To make a man an' woman dar'
   What others dassn't do?

Jes' this—an' Injuns know'd it—
   That whar' them cullers flew,
The men that lived beneath them
   Wuz mostly straight an' true.

That when they made a bargain,
   'Twuz jes' as strong an' tight
As if 't were drawn on sheep-skin
   An' signed in black an' white.

That's how them Hudson traders done
   Fer mor'n two hundred year;
That's why that trader feller crossed
   Them plains without a fear.

An' jes' so long es white men
   Don't try some little game,
To euchre out the red man,
   So long he'll act the same.

But when the men beneath that flag
   Tries any monkey ways,
Then, good-bye, old time friendship,
   For the Injuns goin' ter raise.

But jes' believe me, onst for all,
   To them that treats him fair,
The Injun mostly allus wuz,
   And is, and will be, square.

GEORGE FREDERICK CAMERON
(1854–85)

THREE of Canada's greatest poets were cut off just when their work had reached maturity—Isabella Valancy Crawford died at the age of thirty-seven, Archibald Lampman at thirty-eight, and George Frederick Cameron at thirty-one. It is useless to speculate what added riches Canadian literature would possess had they lived as long as C. G. D. Roberts or Duncan Campbell Scott.

Cameron published no volume during his lifetime, but a selection of his poems was made by his brother, Charles J. Cameron, of Queen's University, and published in 1887 at Kingston and Boston. Its accurate title was *Lyrics on Freedom, Love and Death*. The editor prefaced the book with some biographical and critical material, which, as the book is extremely rare, it will be useful to quote:

George Frederick Cameron, the author of the following poems, the eldest son of James Grant Cameron and Jessie Sutherland, was born in New Glasgow, Nova Scotia, September 24th, 1854. He received his preliminary education at the High School of his native town, and had read the greater part of Virgil and Cicero in the original before his fourteenth year. Even at this age he employed most of his spare time in poetry. Removing with his family to Boston in the spring of 1869, he entered the Boston University of Law in 1872. After graduation, he entered the law office of Dean, Butler and Abbot in the same city. From this period until 1882 his attention was mainly devoted to literature and he was a frequent contributor to the *Commercial Bulletin, Traveller, Courier* and *Transcript* of the new Athens of America. In 1882 he entered Queen's University and was the prize poet in 1883.

In March of the same year he became Editor of the Kingston *News*, which position he held until a few weeks before his death. The latter event took place during a visit to the country, where, on the 17th of September [1885], he expired of heart disease after a few hours sickness. . . . .

In addition to this factual information, the Preface included some criticism and appreciation:

It was impossible, being what he was, that his poetry should be free from occasional pessimism. This was the natural product of the circumstances of his life. It was necessary from the character of the age in which he wrote: It was inevitable from the quality of his own mind. . . . .

That the author did not bubble over in his verse with loyalty to the throne and all it represents was perhaps his infirmity. I tried to persuade him of the advantages such a course would offer to a poor poet like himself, but, I regret to say, to no purpose. Whether the reason of failure lay in the weakness of the cause or in his want of faith in my sincerity is a moot question with me to this day.

The poet's brother was a man of wit and good sense, and it is fitting to insert here an epigram in the classical vein which George Frederick Cameron had written in his honor:

TO CHARLEY

Hast thou the poet-gift? Thou hast,
    O golden-tongued and hearted Greek!
    To find thy prototype, I seek
Far down along the shadowy Past,
    Where half-gods and whole poets speak:

Wit, song, and eloquence divine—
    Where are they in the list of names?
    I halt at his of many fames,
And boldly call thee, brother mine,
    A Sheridan—without his shames!

The reader should have little difficulty in setting Cameron's poetry apart from the dominant tradition of Canadian verse in the eighties and nineties. There is nothing in it of the conscious effort to be "Canadian" which played an important part in the work of the younger group that was to follow Roberts. There is, instead, an awareness of classical culture—the culture of Anacreon or Catullus—that is approached in something of the spirit of a Jonson or a Landor and that sets Cameron apart from Roberts and Lampman, whose approach to the classics is mainly through Keats, and from Carman, whose subjectivity and undisciplined emotionalism make something new and personal out of his classical attempts.

~~~~~~

THE WAY OF THE WORLD

We sneer and we laugh with the lip—the most of us do it,
    Whenever a brother goes down like a weed with the tide;
We point with the finger and say—Oh, we knew it! we knew it!
    But, see! we are better than he was, and we will abide.

He walked in the way of his will—the way of desire,
  In the Appian way of his will without ever a bend;
He walked in it long, but it led him at last to the mire,—
  But we who are stronger will stand and endure to the end.

His thoughts were all visions—all fabulous visions of flowers,
  Of bird and of song and of soul which is only a song;
His eyes looked all at the stars in the firmament, ours
  Were fixed on the earth at our feet, so we stand and are strong.

He hated the sight and the sound and the sob of the city;
  He sought for his peace in the wood and the musical wave;
He fell, and we pity him never, and why should we pity—
  Yea, why should we mourn for him—we who still stand, who are
    brave?

Thus speak we and think not, we censure unheeding, unknowing,—
  Unkindly and blindly we utter the words of the brain;
We see not the goal of our brother, we see but his going,
  And sneer at his fall if he fall, and laugh at his pain.

Ah, me! the sight of the sod on the coffin lid,
  And the sound, and the sob, and the sigh of it as it falls!
Ah, me! the beautiful face forever hid
  By four wild walls!

You hold it a matter of self-gratulation and praise
  To have thrust to the dust, to have trod on a heart that was true,—
To have ruined it there in the beauty and bloom of its days?
  Very well! There is somewhere a Nemesis waiting for you.

'TIS STRANGE, YOU THINK

'Tis strange, you think, that I remember yet
  The word, the kiss, the parting place, the date,
  When Love fell dead before the feet of Fate?
  Strange? It were strange indeed, did I forget.

The moon was westward, and her upper rim
  Was barely visible o'er the mountain head;
  Hand locked in hand we stood, and then you said—
  Even as she set and all the land grew dim:—

"I wonder will this love of ours set so,
  And all our lives grow dark, and cold, and drear,
  With but a star-beam floating there and here?"
  And then you shuddered, and I answered—"No."

And yet I know not how it came to be—
    Half fault perhaps of yours, half fault of mine,
We parted there amid the laurestine;
    And with you anger went, regret with me.

You cherished anger—I espoused regret:
    And as the moon now sets behind the hills,
Through every vein the ancient memory thrills.
    That was the time—ah, how could I forget!

YSOLTE

Well, I am young and the world is wide,
    And I have gold enough and to spare,
And I could buy, if I would, a bride
    To give me, perchance, a son and heir;
But single my heart is, and I will abide
As single, and float on my own gulf-tide
    Of desire, now here, now there,
Wherever my silver shallop may ride
    And my sails of silver bear,—
Until I drift on the unknown shore,
And beach my boat to roam no more.

How easily men are caught with chaff!
An ankle, an eye, or a light-lipt laugh,
    And down they go on their knees.
Was I caught myself? Oh, not by half!
    No, thank you, if you please.
I will be caught? No, thank you, again!
    I sound myself on all these things,
And find I am not like the most of men
    To be led in leading strings.
No painted, or pretty, or perilous girl
    Shall put my soul in pain;
No ruby lips o'er teeth of pearl,
Gazelle-like eye, or wind-kist curl
    Shall break my heart in twain.

Oh, I do laugh to see men cringe
    Before some delicate, dainty doll,—
Some mass of foolishness, fuss, and fringe,
    Some delicate—nothing at all.

To see men fawn and flatter and lie—
　　At the feet of these dolls, I mean,—and swear
That they for sake of them would die;
　　They might die did they dare:
For men in love are fools—or nigh,
　　Though cap nor bells they wear.
To see them, knowing so well man's mind,
　　And knowing so well that woman's power
　　Is that of beauty, but of an hour;
And knowing well of womankind,—
　　To see them and hear—oh, I do laugh!
　　Why are they crows to be caught with chaff.

Oh, I do weep to see men creep
　　Through mire, and dirt, and deadly shame,
To drag the gold from its æon-sleep
　　Or to snatch a kiss from Fame.
Can place or power avail to keep
　　Star-clear a tarnished name?
Well, what of this? But this, no more:
　　For dunces we need not rake the schools;
For the most of men—'twas said before—
　　Are arrant fools—are arrant fools.

And now that my say is said of men,
　　I leave them alone, and nothing loth;
Let them sink to themselves, if they will, again,—
　　To their love and life—I leave them to both.
For I am young and the world is wide,
　　And I have gold enough and to spare,
And I could buy, if I would, a bride
　　To give me, perchance, a son and heir;
But single my heart is, and I will abide
As single, and float on my own gulf-tide
　　Of desire, now here, now there,—
Wherever my shallop of silver may ride
　　And my sails of silver bear,—
Until I drift on the unknown shore
And beach my bark to launch no more!

.　.　.　.　.　.　.　.　.　.　.　.　.

It seems as if a change
　　Had come across the earth,—

A something sweet and strange:
  Gone is the gloom and gone the dearth
  Of sunshine and soft air and mirth,—
I feel as if again a boy;
  Departed is my old annoy,
And all is life and peace and joy
  Befitting second birth.
I have been born again;
  And in my new-found mood
I say that beasts and birds and men,
  All things that are or that have been,
Are good—are very good.

But will it, can it last—
  This life that is so sweet?—
Where all the past is past
  And buried 'neath my feet?
Can it be as a shadow cast—
  Not real, but a cheat?
I think not. It is said,
  When one is born anew
That all the former life is fled
  And that then present true.

Is't substance, or a sham?
  I know the stars shine brighter
    Than they before had shone:
The air is warm and calm:
  I know my heart is lighter,—
    Its heaviness is gone:
I do not lean on broken reed,—
This is a newer life indeed.

  .   .   .   .

There is a stranger in the place,
  A stranger who no doubt looks down,
Scorn on his lip and ashy face,
  Upon the God-made country clown.
  And he is stopping there in town:
And he has seen the one I love:
  And he will love her—that I know,
  A voice within me tells me so.

But, sooth, I swear by the stars above,
  By the tides at my feet that ebb and flow,
  Whatever may come, whatever may go,
He shall not harm my harmless dove.

I swear he shall not harm her! still,
Her lord shall be her own sweet will.
And if her own sweet will shall put
  My love aside, I shall but say—
This trampling true love 'neath her foot
  For false, is only woman's way.

His face is lined and worn, although
  'Tis fashioned fairly and might pass—
A female mirror flatters so—
  At muster in a lady's glass:
But his hand is as a lady's fair,
  His foot is as his hand is—small;
  So should you take them all in all
They would be quite a pretty pair.

The prowling fox has found his prey,—
  An easy prey, an easy prize:
So easy that some people say
  It was a willing sacrifice.
But I say neither yea nor nay,
  Not having other people's eyes.

He angled and she took the bait.
  Perchance he used a noble line
And golden hook,—at any rate
  He has no reason to repine:
If I have reason, "Such is fate!"
  I say, or—"Such is fate of mine!"

.   .   .   .

They are together much of late,
  They passed me by to-day:
I was standing there at my gate:
  He nodded a cloudy brow—not ill,
She shot me a smile as they rode away
  To the house beyond the hill:
I would hate him could I hate,—
  If I learn to hate, I will.

.   .   .   .

Oh, that we had not met to part
  As we are parted now,—
The stain of anger on each heart,
  Of anger on each brow!

Would that the love which shone so bright
  Had killed me with its blaze;
Ere I had seen it robed in night,
  And robb'd of all its rays!

Would that the hours so fleet and fair
  Had never come to me!—
Ere I had known that once they were,
  That they no more can be.

Would I had slept the dreamless sleep,
  Ere I had come to know
That Love may sow in joy, yet reap
  A harvest wild with woe!

Would love had faded ere my birth
  Or blossomed on my tomb:
Nor ever mocked my youth with mirth,
  To curse my age with gloom!

And oh, that we had never met
  And dreamed a dream of bliss,
To wake again to cold regret,
  To wake again to—this!

*   *   *

Where often I have found relief,
  I went to seek for peace to-day,—
A temporal balm for temporal grief:
    Amid fair Nature's solitudes,
    Within the ivy-fretted woods,
  I found it in a novel way.

Upon the moss beside a spring
Whose limpid waves go spattering
    Adown the ancient rocks and gray,
    As often I had lain I lay
When to my hand came wandering—
    The wind had tossed it there in play—
A vagrant scroll bound by a ring,
  A golden circlet old and thin.

I seized it, and half jestingly
  Spake to it, opening, "Let me see
What omen may be here for me!
  And this is what I read therein:—

What though, my brother, to-day be drear
  And dark and sad?
To-morrow, to-morrow will soon be here—
  Perchance to make thee glad.

Sorrow and heaviness—these are things
  That come to men:
They come to the commons, they come to kings,
  They come to go again.

Why should a season of bitterness bear
  Thee down to dust?
To-day may be foul yet to-morrow be fair;
  Trust in to-morrow—trust!

And if to-morrow be darker yet
  With pain and ill,
Though the heart be dry and the eyelids wet,
  Trust in to-morrow still!

It was enough,—a hopeful song!
  Had some good genius sent it here,
Borne on the kindly winds along
    Inscribed with promise of good cheer
    For some dear future day or year?
I may be right, or may be wrong;
    But thus I will interpret what
    The day and accident have brought:
Perhaps there is a generous Fate,
    A generous Fate! but time will tell
    If all be ill or all be well,—
And, for the present—I can wait.

Though she be false as coquette's kiss,
    From this sweet mood I must not stir
    In which Love, as interpreter,
Reads all the auguries for bliss;
But bring myself to chime with this,—
    'Tis well, if all be well with her.

.   .   .   .

Now hear the end of all the play!—
    I hold her fair and firm and true
    To eyesight and to soul-sight, too:
She is the sweetest piece of clay
    God ever sculptured into form!
And who on earth shall say me nay,
    If to the wide, wild world I say,
Until life's storms forever stay,
    I shall defend her from all storm!

I hear along the air a wedding bell;
Say, heart of mine! how is it?
                                        It is well!

DEATH*

Dear friend, I know this world is kin,
    And all of hate is but a breath:
We all are friends, made perfect in
    Our near relationship by death.

And so, although it was not mine
    To meet thee in thy walk below,
Or know of thee till feet of thine
    Were on the hills no man can know;

For friendship's sake I fain would bring
    A flower, or two, to thee to prove
That memory lives, that death's sharp sting
    Hath still an antidote in love.

                    *   *   *

Devoured by his desire of her
    The king, who ever loved her best,
    Hath stilled the billowing of her breast,
Hath kissed her so no pulse doth stir,
    But all of her doth lie at rest.

Then, knowing she may never now
    Wish any else, he takes his leave,
    And little recks how they may grieve
Who see the splendor of her brow
    Gleam ghastly through the gathering eve;

* In memoriam Maggie Meagher.

Who see her lying pale, supine,
    With wild red roses twined with fair
    About her throat, and in her hair,
And on her bosom,—all divine
    If but a little life were there.

Nor heeds he aught the sunless glooms
    And fair forms folded from the light
    In close graves crowded far from sight
In lone lands dedicate to tombs
    And scarce to starbeams known at night;

But goes his way; and as he goes
    Leaves that we hold as sorrow here,—
    The pain of parting and the tear,
The broken lily and the rose
    Down fallen with the fallen year.

Cold king, most lone and absolute!
    What maid would be desired of thee?
    From thy embrace who would not flee?
What though a monarch, being mute
    In love of thine what love could be?

Can any good be silent so?
    Be dumb, and do its work and pass
    Swift as an image in a glass?
Ah, all of good that we can know
    Thus comes to us, and leaves, alas!

While we, who have no key to ope
    Death's cabinet of mysteries,
    Can only vainly strain our eyes,
And hold to heaven and that high hope
    That death is good in any guise!

                    *   *   *

And if but slight to thee appear
    The tribute brought, now that thine eyes
May view through all the eternal year
    The fairer flowers of Paradise,—

If dim and all unworthy look
    The offering, yet remember well
We do not sleep by Eden's brook,
    Or dream on beds of Asphodel:

So only bring the flowers that bloom
　　Beside us, fresh enough and fair;
Enough to wither on thy tomb:
　　And with our hearts—behold them there!

MY POLITICAL FAITH

I am not of those fierce, wild wills,
　　Albeit from loins of warlike line,
　　To wreck laws human and divine
Alike, that on a million ills
　　I might erect one sacred shrine

To Freedom: nor again am I
　　Of *these* who could be sold and bought
　　To fall before a Juggernaut:
I hold all "royal right" a lie—
　　Save that a royal soul hath wrought!

It is in the extreme begins
　　And ends all danger: if the Few
　　Would feel, or if the Many knew
This fact, the mass of fewer sins
　　Would shrive them in their passing through:

O'er all God's footstool not a slave
　　Should under his great glory stand,
　　For men would rise, swift sword in hand,
And give each tyrant to his grave
　　And freedom to each lovely land.

IN AFTER DAYS

I will accomplish that and this,
　　And make myself a thorn to Things—
　　Lords, councillors and tyrant kings—
Who sit upon their thrones and kiss

The rod of Fortune; and are crowned
　　The sovereign masters of the earth
　　To scatter blight and death and dearth
Wherever mortal man is found.

I will do this and that, and break
　　The backbone of their large conceit,
　　And loose the sandals from their feet,
And show 'tis holy ground they shake.

So sang I in my earlier days,
    Ere I had learned to look abroad
    And see that more than monarchs trod
Upon the form I fain would raise.

Ere I, in looking toward the land
    That broke a triple diadem,
    That grasped at Freedom's garment hem,
Had seen her, sword and torch in hand,

A freedom-fool: ere I had grown
    To know that Love is freedom's strength—
    France taught the world that truth at length!—
And Peace her chief foundation stone.

Since then, I temper so my song
    That it may never speak for blood;
    May never say that ill is good;
Or say that right may spring from wrong:

Yet am what I have ever been—
    A friend of Freedom, staunch and true,
    Who hate a tyrant, be he—you—
A people,—sultan, czar, or queen!

And then the Freedom-haters came
    And questioned of my former song,
    If *now* I held it right, or wrong:
And still my answer was the same:—

The good still moveth towards the good:
    The ill still moveth towards the ill:
    But who affirmeth that we will
Not form a nobler brotherhood

When communists, fanatics, those
    Who howl their *"vives"* to Freedom's name
    And yet betray her unto shame,
Are dead and coffined with her foes.

THE FUTURE

O poet of the future! I,
    Of the dead present, bid thee hail!
Come forth and speak,—our speech shall die:
    Come forth and sing,—our song shall fail:
Our speech, our song fall barren,—we go by!

Our heart is weak. In vain it swells
    And beats to bursting at the wrong:
There never sets a sun but tells
    Of weak ones trampled down by strong,
Of Truth and Justice both immured in cells.

We would aspire, but round us lies
    A maze of high desires and aims;
Would seek a prize, but, ah! our eyes
    Fail as we face the fallen fames
Of the great world's Olympian games.

Seeing the victors vanquished, we
    Grow heartsick at the sight, and choose
To hold in fee what things there be
    Rather than in the hazard use,—
Than stake the all we have—to lose!

We all are feeble. Still we tread
    An ever-upward sloping way;
Deep chasms and dark are round us spread
    And bale-fires beckon us astray:
But thou shalt stand upon the mountain head.

But thou wilt look with gladdened eyes
    And see the mist of error flee,
And see the happy sons arise
    Of happier days that are to be,—
On greener, gladder earth, and clearer skies.

We, of the Morning, but behold
    The dawn afar: thine eyes shall see
The full and perfect day unfold,—
    The full and perfect day to be,
When Justice shall return as lovely as of old.

Thou, with unloosened tongue, shalt speak
    In words of subtle, silver sound,—
In words not futile now, nor weak,
    To all the nations listening round
Until they seek the light,—nor vainly seek!

We only ask it as our share,
    That, when your day-star rises clear,—
A perfect splendor in the air,—
    A glory ever, far and near,—
Ye write such words—*as these of those who were!*

September, 1885

STANDING ON TIPTOE

Standing on tiptoe ever since my youth
  Striving to grasp the future just above,
I hold at length the only future—Truth,
  And Truth is Love.

I feel as one who being awhile confined
  Sees drop to dust about him all his bars:—
The clay grows less, and, leaving it, the mind
  Dwells with the stars.

September, 1885

WILLIAM HENRY DRUMMOND
(1854–1907)

ONE of the best loved and in some respects the most original of all Canadian poets was born in the village of Mohill, County Leitrim, Ireland, on the thirteenth of April, 1854. While he was still a small boy, the family immigrated to Canada, where after only a few months the father died, leaving his widow with limited means to rear four boys between the ages of five and eleven. William, the eldest, studied telegraphy and at the age of fifteen was stationed at the little French village of Bord-à-Plouffe on the Rivière des Prairies, behind Montreal. He saved enough money to finish at the Montreal High School and to go on to McGill University and Bishop's College, Lennoxville, from which he was graduated as Doctor of Medicine in 1884. After several years as a country doctor, in the Notre Dame Mountains and at Knowlton, in Brome County, he took up practice in Montreal. He was extremely popular and won for himself a prominent place in the social and athletic life of the community. He was a brilliant after-dinner speaker and an enthusiastic devotee of fishing, snowshoeing, and tobogganing. The poems of habitant life that he had written to please himself and amuse his friends were submitted after some hesitation to a publisher, but when in 1897 *The Habitant and Other French Canadian Poems* was published in New York and London their success was immediate. The book was introduced by a courteous and sympathetic tribute from Louis Fréchette, the most distinguished of French-Canadian poets, and was illustrated by the artist F. S. Coburn. This was followed by *Phil-o-Rum's Canoe and Madeleine Vercheres* (two poems) (1898), *Johnnie Courteau and Other Poems* (1901), and *The Voyageur and Other Poems* (1905). Drummond's brothers had acquired important mining interests in the Cobalt district, and it was there that the poet died unexpectedly of cerebral hemorrhage after a strenuous visit he had paid to the mining camps to combat an outbreak of smallpox among the miners. For several years he had been professor of medical jurisprudence at Bishop's College and in 1902 had been honored with the degree of LL.D. by the University of Toronto. His unpublished poems were edited with a memoir by his wife, May Harvey Drummond, and issued in a volume entitled *The Great Fight* (1908). A handsome collected edition appeared in 1912 with the Introduction by Louis Fréchette and an appreciation by the Scottish writer Neil Munro. A brief volume of selections, with excellent critical and bibliographical material, was edited for the "Makers of Canadian Literature Series" by J. F. Macdonald.

Although he wrote a few poems in common English and one or two in Irish dialect, it is the vast majority written in the patois of the French-Canadian that show the original and genuinely attractive qualities of Drummond's best poetry. The English pieces are for the most part occasional, and even the best of them are somewhat stilted and conventional. The broken English of the habitant poems and the objectivity of the characterization seemed to set the poet free to express without shyness or restraint his deeper or tenderer feelings. The dialect, of course, was never intended to be mainly humorous. Drummond's humor gains something from the quaintness (to English ears) of the language, but its genuine source is in character and situation. The dialect is realistic. It is a brilliant representation of the idiom and inflection with which the habitant speaks when he expresses himself in English.

Humor and pathos are the essential characteristics of Drummond's poems. As an interpreter of the French-Canadian, he is undoubtedly limited. He shows the pleasanter side of life and the more lovable traits of character. But it is real as far as it goes. The humor is never puerile, and the pathos never becomes mawkish. The ease and success with which Drummond accomplished his purpose perhaps deceives us as to the difficulty of his task. Louis Fréchette has expressed, as only a Frenchman can appreciate it, the true nature of Drummond's originality: "N'est-elle pas, en effet, d'une originalité peu commune, l'idée de prendre un pauvre illettré, de le présenter comme un type national à part, de lui mettre aux lèvres une langue qui n'est pas la sienne et qu'il ne connaît qu'à demi; d'en faire en même temps un personnage bon, doux, aimable, honnête, intelligent et droit, l'esprit en éveil, le cœur plein d'une poésie native stimulant son patriotisme, jetant un rayon lumineux dans son modeste intérieur, berçant ses heures rêveuses de souvenirs lointains et mélancoliques?"

THE WRECK OF THE "JULIE PLANTE"

A LEGEND OF LAC ST. PIERRE

On wan dark night on Lac St. Pierre,
    De win' she blow, blow, blow,
An' de crew of de wood scow "Julie Plante"
    Got scar't an' run below—
For de win' she blow lak hurricane,
    Bimeby she blow some more,
An' de scow bus' up on Lac St. Pierre
    Wan arpent from de shore.

De captinne walk on de fronte deck,
    An' walk de hin' deck too—
He call de crew from up de hole,
    He call de cook also.
De cook she's name was Rosie,
    She come from Montreal,
Was chambre maid on lumber barge,
    On de Grande Lachine Canal.

De win' she blow from nor'-eas'-wes',—
    De sout' win' she blow too,
W'en Rosie cry, "Mon cher captinne,
    Mon cher, w'at I shall do?"
Den de captinne t'row de beeg ankerre,
    But still de scow she dreef,
De crew he can't pass on de shore,
    Becos' he los' hees skeef.

De night was dark lak wan black cat,
    De wave run high an' fas',
W'en de captinne tak' de Rosie girl
    An' tie her to de mas'.
Den he also tak' de life preserve,
    An' jomp off on de lak',
An' say, "Good-bye, ma Rosie dear,
    I go drown for your sak'."

Nex' morning very early
    'Bout ha'f-pas' two—t'ree—four—
De captinne—scow—an' de poor Rosie
    Was corpses on de shore,

For de win' she blow lak hurricane,
  Bimeby she blow some more,
An' de scow bus' up on Lac St. Pierre,
  Wan arpent from de shore.

MORAL

Now all good wood scow sailor man
  Tak' warning by dat storm
An' go an' marry some nice French girl
  An' leev on wan beeg farm.
De win' can blow lak hurricane
  An' s'pose she blow some more,
You can't get drown on Lac St. Pierre
  So long you stay on shore.

LE VIEUX TEMPS

Venez ici, mon cher ami, an' sit down by me—so
An' I will tole you story of old tam long ago—
W'en ev'ryt'ing is happy—w'en all de bird is sing
An' me!—I'm young an' strong lak moose an' not afraid no t'ing.

I close my eye jus' so, an' see de place w'ere I am born—
I close my ear an' lissen to musique of de horn,
Dat's horn ma dear ole moder blow—an only t'ing she play
Is "viens donc vite Napoléon—'peche toi pour votre souper."—

An' w'en he's hear dat nice musique—ma leetle dog "Carleau"
Is place hees tail upon hees back—an' den he's let heem go—
He's jomp on fence—he's swimmin' crik—he's ronne two forty gait,
He say "dat's somet'ing good for eat—Carleau mus' not be late."

O dem was pleasure day for sure, dem day of long ago
W'en I was play wit' all de boy, an' all de girl also;
An' many tam w'en I'm alone an' t'ink of day gone by
An' pull latire an' spark de girl, I cry upon my eye.

Ma fader an' ma moder too, got nice, nice familee,
Dat's ten garçon an' t'orteen girl, was mak' it twenty t'ree,
But fonny t'ing de Gouvernement don't geev de firs' prize den
Lak w'at dey say dey geev it now, for only wan douzaine.

De English peep dat only got wan familee small size
Mus' be feel glad dat tam dere is no honder acre prize
For fader of twelve chil'ren—dey know dat mus' be so,
De Canayens would boss Kebeck—mebbe Ontario.

But dat is not de story dat I was gone tole you
About de fun we use to have w'en we leev a chez nous
We're never lonesome on dat house, for many cavalier
Come at our place mos' every night—especially Sun-day.

But tam I 'member bes' is w'en I'm twenty wan year—me—
An' so for mak' some pleasurement—we geev wan large soirée.
De whole paroisse she be invite—de Curé he's come too—
Wit plaintee peep from 'noder place—dat 's more I can tole you.

De night she's cole an' freeze also, chemin she's fill wit snow
An' on de chimley lak phantome, de win' is mak' it blow—
But boy an' girl come all de sam an' pass on grande parloir
For warm itself on beeg box stove, was mak' on Trois Rivières—

An' w'en Bonhomme Latour commence for tune up hees fidelle
It mak' us all feel very glad—l'enfant! he play so well,
Musique suppose to be firs' class, I offen hear, for sure
But mos' bes' man, beat all de res', is ole Bateese Latour—

An' w'en Bateese play Irish jeeg, he's learn on Mattawa
Dat tam he's head boss cook Shaintee—den leetle Joe Leblanc
Tak' hole de beeg Marie Juneau an' dance upon de floor
Till Marie say "Excuse to me, I cannot dance no more."—

An' den de Curé 's mak' de speech—ole Curé Ladouceur!
He say de girl was spark de boy too much on some cornerre—
An' so he's tole Bateese play up ole fashion reel a quatre
An' every body she mus' dance, dey can't get off on dat.

Away she go—hooraw! hooraw! plus fort Bateese, mon vieux!
Camille Bisson, please watch your girl—dat's bes' t'ing you can do.
Pass on de right an' tak' your place Mamzelle Des Trois Maisons
You're s'pose for dance on Paul Laberge, not Telesphore Gagnon.

Mon oncle Al-fred, he spik lak' dat—'cos he is boss de floor,
An' so we do our possibill an' den commence encore.
Dem crowd of boy an' girl I'm sure keep up until nex' day
If ole Bateese don't stop heseff, he come so fatigué.

An' affer dat, we eat some t'ing, tak' leetle drink also
An' de Curé, he 's tole story of many year ago—
W'en Iroquois sauvage she's keel de Canayens an' steal deir hair,
An' say dat 's only for Bon Dieu, we don't be here—he don't be
  dere.

But dat was mak' de girl feel scare—so all de cavalier
Was ax hees girl go home right off, an' place her on de sleigh,
An' w'en dey start, de Curé say, "Bonsoir et bon voyage
Menagez-vous—tak' care for you—prenez-garde pour les sau-
  vages."

An' den I go meseff also, an' tak' ma belle Elmire—
She's nicer girl on whole Comté, an' jus' got eighteen year—
Black hair—black eye, an' chick rosée dat 's lak wan fameuse on
  de fall
But don't spik much—not of dat kin', I can't say she love me at all.

Ma girl—she's fader beeg farmeur—leev 'noder side St. Flore
Got five-six honder acre—mebbe a leetle more—
Nice sugar bush—une belle maison—de bes' I never see—
So w'en I go for spark Elmire, I don't be mak' de foolish me—

Elmire!—she's pass t'ree year on school—Ste. Anne de la Perade
An' w'en she's tak' de firs' class prize, dat's mak' de ole man glad;
He say "Ba gosh—ma girl can wash—can keep de kitchen clean,
Den change her dress—mak' politesse before God save de Queen."

Dey 's many way for spark de girl, an' you know dat of course,
Some way dey might be better way, an' some dey might be worse,
But I lak' sit some cole night wit' my girl on ole burleau
Wit' lot of hay keep our foot warm—an' plaintee buffalo—

Dat 's geev good chances get acquaint—an' if burleau upset
An' t'row you out upon de snow—dat's better chances yet—
An' if you help de girl go home, if horse he ronne away
De girl she 's not much use at all—don't geev you nice baiser!

Dat 's very well for fun ma frien', but w'en you spark for keep
She's not sam t'ing an' mak' you feel so scare lak' leetle sheep
Some tam you get de fever—some tam you're lak snowball
An' all de tam you ack lak' fou—can't spik no t'ing at all.

Wall! dat 's de way I feel meseff, wit Elmire on burleau,
Jus' lak' small dog try ketch hees tail—roun' roun' ma head she go,
But bimeby I come more brave—an' tak' Elmire she's han'
"Laisse-moi tranquille" Elmire she say "You mus' be crazy man."

"Yass—yass" I say "mebbe you t'ink I'm wan beeg loup garou,
Dat 's forty t'ousand 'noder girl, I lef' dem all for you,
I s'pose you know Polique Gauthier your frien' on St. Cesaire
I ax her marry me nex' wick—she tak' me—I don't care."

Ba gosh; Elmire she don't lak dat—it mak' her feel so mad—
She commence cry, say " 'Poleon you treat me very bad—
I don't lak see you t'row you'seff upon Polique Gauthier,
So if you say you love me sure—we mak' de mariée."—

Oh it was fine tam affer dat—Castor I t'ink he know,
We 're not too busy for get home—he go so nice an' slow,
He 's only upset t'ree—four tam—an' jus' about daylight
We pass upon de ole man's place—an' every t'ing's all right.

Wall! we leev happy on de farm for nearly fifty year,
Till wan day on de summer tam—she die—ma belle Elmire.
I feel so lonesome lef' behin'—I tink 't was bes' mebbe—
Dat w'en le Bon Dieu tak' ma femme—he should not forget me.

But dat is hees biz-nesse ma frien'—I know dat's all right dere;
I'll wait till he call " 'Poleon" den I will be prepare—
An' w'en he fin' me ready, for mak' de longue voyage
He guide me t'roo de wood hesef upon ma las' portage.

JOHNNIE COURTEAU

Johnnie Courteau of de mountain,
Johnnie Courteau of de hill—
Dat was de boy can shoot de gun,
Dat was de boy can jomp an' run,
An' it's not very offen you ketch heem still—
　　Johnnie Courteau!

Ax dem along de reever,
Ax dem along de shore,
Who was de mos' bes' fightin' man
From Managance to Shaw-in-i-gan,
De place w'ere de great beeg rapide roar?
　　Johnnie Courteau!

Sam' t'ing on ev'ry shaintee
Up on de Mekinac,
Who was de man can walk de log,
W'en w'ole of de reever she's black wit' fog,
An' carry de beeges' load on hees back?
　　Johnnie Courteau!

On de rapide you want to see heem
If de raf' she's swingin' roun',
An' he's yellin', "Hooraw, Bateese! good man!"
W'y de oar come double on hees han'
W'en he's makin' dat raf' go flyin' down,
     Johnnie Courteau!

An' Tête de Boule chief can tole you
De feller w'at save hees life,
W'en big moose ketch heem up a tree,
Who's shootin' dat moose on de head, sapree!
An' den run off wit' hees Injun wife?
     Johnnie Courteau!

An' he only have pike pole wit' heem
On Lac à la Tortue
W'en he meet de bear comin' down de hill,
But de bear very soon is get hees fill!
An' he sole dat skin for ten dollar too,
     Johnnie Courteau!

Oh, he never was scare for no'ting
Lak de ole coureurs de bois,
But w'en he's gettin' hees winter pay
De bes' t'ing sure is kip out de way,
For he's goin' right off on de Hip Hooraw!
     Johnnie Courteau!

Den pullin' hees sash aroun' heem
He dance on hees botte sauvage
An' shout, "All aboar' if you want to fight!"
Wall! you never can see de finer sight
W'en he go lak dat on de w'ole village!
     Johnnie Courteau!

But Johnnie Courteau get marry
On Philomene Beaurepaire,
She's nice leetle girl was run de school
On w'at you call parish of Sainte Ursule
An' he see her off on de pique-nique dere,
     Johnnie Courteau!

Den somet'ing come over Johnnie
W'en he marry on Philomene,
For he stay on de farm de w'ole year roun',

He chop de wood an' he plough de groun'
An' he's quieter feller was never seen,
            Johnnie Courteau!

An' ev'ry wan feel astonish,
From La Tuque to Shaw-in-i-gan,
W'en dey hear de news was goin' aroun',
Along on de reever up an' down,
How wan leetle woman boss dat beeg man,
            Johnnie Courteau!

He never come out on de evening
No matter de hard we try,
'Cos he stay on de kitchen an' sing hees song:

        "A la claire fontaine,
          M'en allant promener,
          J'ai trouvé l'eau si belle
          Que je m'y suis baigner!
          Lui y'a longtemps que je t'aime,
          Jamais je ne t'oublierai."

Rockin' de cradle de w'ole night long
Till baby's asleep on de sweet bimeby,
            Johnnie Courteau!

An' de house, wall! I wish you see it,
De place she's so nice an' clean,
Mus' wipe your foot on de outside door,
You're dead man sure if you spit on de floor,
An' he never say not'ing on Philomene,
            Johnnie Courteau!

An' Philomene watch de monee
An' put it all safe away
On very good place; I dunno w'ere,
But anyhow nobody see it dere,
So she's buyin' new farm de noder day,
            Madame Courteau!

S. FRANCES HARRISON
(1859-1935)

SUSAN FRANCES RILEY was born in Toronto in 1859 of Irish-Canadian stock. She was educated in private schools in Toronto and Montreal and early made a reputation as a professional pianist and singer. In her twenty-first year she married J. W. F. Harrison, a prominent church organist of Montreal, who later held a position in Ottawa and finally in Toronto.

Under the nom de plume of "Seranus," Mrs. Harrison began to contribute sketches and poems to the leading journals and for a time was literary editor of the *Week*. In 1886 she published *Crowded Out and Other Sketches*—"the first attempt to put . . . . the feeling and landscape of Lower Canada before our people in an artistic way." This was followed the next year by *The Canadian Birthday Book*, a small anthology of Canadian poetry, significant as being the first collection of its kind since Dewart's pioneer work of 1864. In 1891 appeared *Pine, Rose, and Fleur de Lis*. An easy, colloquial, sympathetic, and often witty series of impressions of French-Canadian life cast easily into the strict mold of the villanelle forms the most interesting part of the book and gives Mrs. Harrison a place only inferior to that of Drummond. The unpretentiousness of the work must be included among its virtues; for, though penetrating, it is not profound: its goodness is the goodness of excellent light verse. In marked contrast is a moving "Monody: To the Memory of Isabella Valancy Crawford." Mrs. Harrison has also written two novels. *In Northern Skies and Other Poems* appeared in 1912, and *Later Poems and New Villanelles* in 1928. She died in 1935.

AT STE. THÉRÈSE

I

The quaint stiff metres of olden France!
Strange, to hear them in St. Thérèse,
Metres that speak of duel and dance,

169

Of gay parterre and of trim pleasance,
    Of swords that flash and fringe that frays—
The quaint stiff metres of olden France!

In his sash and *tuque* with his keen gay glance,
    Hark to Maxime as he lustily brays
Metres that speak of duel and dance,

Measures that ring with old-world romance,
    Ballads, rondels, and virelays,
The quaint stiff metres of olden France.

A troubadour with a whip for his lance,
    In his rude calash his song betrays
Metres that speak of duel and dance.

Strange, is it not, by a happy chance
    I should hear in the streets of Ste. Thérèse,
The quaint stiff metres of olden France,
Metres that speak of duel and dance?

II

The tall twin towers of the grim *église*
    Loom up over the wharf and street,
Over the Lombardy poplar trees.

Whichever way one goes one sees
    The *séminaire*, and is sure to meet
The tall twin towers of the grim *église*,

And but for the keen Canadian breeze
    Blowing the sharp Canadian sleet
Over the Lombardy popular trees.

To me and Pierre, who says it will freeze
    By night, I feel as if I must greet
The tall twin towers of the grim *église*

For an Old World church with Old World fees,
    The Old World *carillon* sounding sweet
Over the Lombardy poplar trees.

Vite donc, my Pierre! For the time it flees;
    Once more would I see from my snug low seat
The tall twin towers of the grim *église*
Over the Lombardy poplar trees.

PETITE STE. ROSALIE

Father Couture loves a fricassee,
  Serv'd with a sip of home-made wine,
He is the Curé, so jolly and free,

And lives in Petite Ste. Rosalie.
  On Easter Sunday when one must dine,
Father Couture loves a fricassee.

No stern ascetic, no stoic is he,
  Preaching a rigid right divine.
He is the Curé, so jolly and free,

That while he maintains his dignity,
  When Lent is past and the weather is fine,
Father Couture loves a fricassee.

He kills his chicken himself—*on dit*,
  And who is there dare the deed malign?
He is the Curé, so jolly and free.

Open and courteous, fond of a fee,
  The village deity, bland and benign,
Father Couture loves a fricassee,
He's a sensible Curé, so jolly and free!

HELENA COLEMAN (1860———)

MISS COLEMAN was born at Newcastle, Ontario, in 1860. She was the daughter of a Methodist clergyman and, through her mother, was descended from John Quincy Adams. For some years she was a teacher at the Ontario Ladies' College, Whitby. In 1906 her *Songs and Sonnets* was published by the Tennyson Club of Toronto, although her verses had been appearing under a nom de plume for many years in such magazines as the *Atlantic Monthly* and *Scribner's*. *Marching Men* was published in 1917, and more recently a selection entitled *Songs* appeared in the series of "Ryerson Chapbooks." Precision, clarity, simplicity, and nobility of sentiment are the characteristics of Miss Coleman's best verses and are well illustrated by this beautiful sonnet.

AS DAY BEGINS TO WANE

Encompassed by a thousand nameless fears,
I see life's little day begin to wane,
And hear the well-loved voices call in vain
Across the narrowing margin of my years;
And as the Valley of the Shadow nears,
Such yearning tides of tenderness and pain
Sweep over me that I can scarce restrain
The gathering flood of ineffectual tears.

Yet there are moments when the shadows bring
No sense of parting or approaching night,
But, rather, all my soul seems broadening
Before the dawn of unimagined light—
As if within the heart a folded wing
Were making ready for a wider flight.

CHARLES G. D. ROBERTS
(1 8 6 0———)

CHARLES G. D. ROBERTS was born near Fredericton, New Brunswick, January 10, 1860. His father was a classical scholar and a clergyman, and his mother came of a distinguished United Empire Loyalist family that traced its lineage back to Concord and to the great-grandfather of Emerson. Her sister was the mother of Bliss Carman. At Fredericton Collegiate School, Charles G. D. Roberts came under the influence of the headmaster, George R. Parkin, later Sir George Parkin, whose methods and ideals resembled those of Arnold of Rugby. Here and at the University of New Brunswick he received a classical education, winning honors in Greek and Latin. He graduated in 1879, having specialized in his later years in philosophy and political economy.

Schoolmastering, postgraduate study at his alma mater, marriage, and some free-lance journalism filled the years until 1885, when Roberts became professor of English and French literature and political economy at King's College, Windsor, Nova Scotia. He had published in 1880 his first volume of poems, *Orion, and Other Poems*, and for a few months in 1883 he had edited, in Toronto, Goldwin Smith's periodical, the *Week*. His ardent imperialist-nationalism had made it impossible for him to remain long with a journal whose proprietor believed that Canada's best future lay in annexation by the United States. Nevertheless, he attracted to the *Week* the best poetic talent in the Dominion. Lampman, Campbell, Isabella Valancy Crawford, Pauline Johnson, Mair, and D. C. Scott became regular contributors. In addition to teaching, Roberts was writing assiduously—poetry, adventure stories for boys, and a colorful, enthusiastic *History of Canada*. His second book of poems, *In Divers Tones*, appeared in 1886, and a sonnet sequence, *Songs of the Common Day*, in 1893. With this was published "Ave," an elegy in honor of Shelley.

Roberts gave up teaching in 1896 and went to make his living as a writer in New York. With remarkable industry he turned out poems, adventure tales, romances, and a series of stories of animals and wild life. He remained in New York until 1907, when he went abroad to live. In 1914 he enlisted as a private but was soon given a commission.

He rose to the rank of major, and in the final years of the war he assisted Lord Beaverbrook in the preparation of the official history of Canada's part in the war. Roberts remained in England until 1925, when he returned to live in Toronto. He took a prominent part in the activities of the Canadian Authors' Association and gradually has come to be considered the dean of Canadian men of letters. Besides those already named, Roberts published the following volumes of poetry: *The Book of the Native* (1896); *New York Nocturnes* (1898); *Poems* (a collection of all he wished to preserve of his earlier volumes) (1901); *The Book of the Rose* (1903); *New Poems* (1919); *The Vagrant of Time* (1927); *The Iceberg and Other Poems* (1934); *Selected Poems* (1936); *Twilight over Shaugamauk* (1937); and *Canada Speaks of Britain* (1941).

In his best work Roberts is a national poet—both directly and indirectly. His "Canada" gives classic expression to the feelings which actuated those who labored for Confederation. Sangster, in the opening stanzas of "Brock," had already made poetry out of this enthusiasm; and Mair, an original member of the little group known as "Canada First," had in an elegy on its founder, William A. Foster, attempted, though without great success, to do the same. But no Canadian poet, before or since, has succeeded in writing so polished and perfect a statement of the ideals that inspired the Fathers of Confederation as Roberts did in "Canada" and "An Ode for the Canadian Confederacy." Yet the deepest and most enduring expression of nationalism is to be found in Roberts' poems of nature and the Acadian countryside, where its expression is implicit and indirect, as it is in the best of his sonnets of country life, in the delicate little idyl, "The Solitary Woodsman," and in his masterpiece of recollected emotion, "Tantramar Revisited."

James Cappon's *Roberts and the Influences of His Time* (1905) remains the most valuable critical study of the poet.

~~~~~~

CANADA

O Child of Nations, giant-limbed,
    Who stand'st among the nations now
Unheeded, unadored, unhymned,
    With unanointed brow,—

How long the ignoble sloth, how long
    The trust in greatness not thine own?
Surely the lion's brood is strong
    To front the world alone!

How long the indolence, ere thou dare
    Achieve thy destiny, seize thy fame,—
Ere our proud eyes behold thee bear
    A nation's franchise, nation's name?

The Saxon force, the Celtic fire,
    These are thy manhood's heritage!
Why rest with babes and slaves? Seek higher
    The place of race and age.

I see to every wind unfurled
    The flag that bears the Maple Wreath;
Thy swift keels furrow round the world
    Its blood-red folds beneath;

Thy swift keels cleave the furthest seas;
    Thy white sails swell with alien gales;
To stream on each remotest breeze
    The black smoke of thy pipes exhales.

O Falterer, let thy past convince
    Thy future,—all the growth, the gain,
The fame since Cartier knew thee, since
    Thy shores beheld Champlain!

Montcalm and Wolfe! Wolfe and Montcalm!
    Quebec, thy storied citadel
Attest in burning song and psalm
    How here thy heroes fell!

O Thou that bor'st the battle's brunt
    At Queenston and at Lundy's Lane,—
On whose scant ranks but iron front
    The battle broke in vain!—

Whose was the danger, whose the day,
    From whose triumphant throats the cheers,
At Chrysler's Farm, at Chateauguay,
    Storming like clarion-bursts our ears?

On soft Pacific slopes,—beside
    Strange floods that northward rave and fall,—
Where chafes Acadia's chainless tide—
    Thy sons await thy call.

They wait; but some in exile, some
  With strangers housed, in stranger lands,—
And some Canadian lips are dumb
  Beneath Egyptian sands.

O mystic Nile! Thy secret yields
  Before us; thy most ancient dreams
Are mixed with far Canadian fields
  And murmur of Canadian streams.

But thou, my country, dream not thou!
  Wake, and behold how night is done,—
How on thy breast, and o'er thy brow,
  Bursts the uprising sun!

THE SOLITARY WOODSMAN

When the grey lake-water rushes
Past the dripping alder-bushes,
  And the bodeful autumn wind
In the fir-tree weeps and hushes,—

When the air is sharply damp
Round the solitary camp,
  And the moose-bush in the thicket
Glimmers like a scarlet lamp,—

When the birches twinkle yellow,
And the cornel bunches mellow,
  And the owl across the twilight
Trumpets to his downy fellow,—

When the nut-fed chipmunks romp
Through the maples' crimson pomp,
  And the slim viburnum flushes
In the darkness of the swamp,—

When the blueberries are dead,
When the rowan clusters red,
  And the shy bear, summer-sleekened,
In the bracken makes his bed,—

On a day there comes once more
To the latched and lonely door,
  Down the wood-road striding silent,
One who has been here before.

Green spruce branches for his head,
Here he makes his simple bed,
　　Couching with the sun, and rising
When the dawn is frosty red.

All day long he wanders wide
With the grey moss for his guide,
　　And his lonely axe-stroke startles
The expectant forest-side.

Toward the quiet close of day
Back to camp he takes his way,
　　And about his sober footsteps
Unafraid the squirrels play.

On his roof the red leaf falls,
At his door the bluejay calls,
　　And he hears the wood-mice hurry
Up and down his rough log walls;

Hears the laughter of the loon
Thrill the dying afternoon;
　　Hears the calling of the moose
Echo to the early moon.

And he hears the partridge drumming,
The belated hornet humming,—
　　All the faint, prophetic sounds
That foretell the winter's coming.

And the wind about his eaves
Through the chilly night-wet grieves,
　　And the earth's dumb patience fills him,
Fellow to the falling leaves.

THE MOWING

This is the voice of high midsummer's heat.
　　The rasping vibrant clamour soars and shrills
　　O'er all the meadowy range of shadeless hills,
As if a host of giant cicadae beat
The cymbals of their wings with tireless feet,
　　Or brazen grasshoppers with triumphing note
　　From the long swath proclaimed the fate that smote
The clover and timothy-tops and meadowsweet.

The crying knives glide on; the green swath lies.
　　And all noon long the sun, with chemic ray,
　　Seals up each cordial essence in its cell,
That in the dusky stalls, some winter's day,
　　The spirit of June, here prisoned by his spell,
　　May cheer the herds with pasture memories.

IN AN OLD BARN

Tons upon tons the brown-green fragrant hay
　　O'erbrims the mows beyond the time-warped eaves,
　　Up to the rafters where the spider weaves,
Though few flies wander his secluded way.
Through a high chink one lonely golden ray,
　　Wherein the dust is dancing, slants unstirred.
　　In the dry hush some rustlings light are heard,
Of winter-hidden mice at furtive play.

Far down, the cattle in their shadowed stalls,
　　Nose-deep in clover fodder's meadowy scent,
　　Forget the snows that whelm their pasture streams,
The frost that bites the world beyond their walls.
　　Warm housed, they dream of summer, well content
　　In day-long contemplation of their dreams.

IN THE BARN-YARD'S SOUTHERLY CORNER

When the frost is white on the fodder-stack,
The haws in the thorn-bush withered and black,
When the near fields flash in a diamond mail
And the far hills glimmer opaline pale,
Oh, merrily shines the morning sun
　　In the barn-yard's southerly corner.

When the ruts in the cart-road ring like steel
And the birds to the kitchen door come for their meal,
And the snow at the gate is lightly drifted
And over the wood-pile thinly sifted,
Oh, merrily shines the morning sun
　　In the barn-yard's southerly corner.

When the brimming bucket steams at the well,
And the axe on the beech-knot sings like a bell,
When the pond is loud with the skaters' calls,

And the horses stamp in the littered stalls,
Oh, merrily shines the morning sun
   In the barn-yard's southerly corner.

When the hay lies loose on the wide barn-floor,
And a sharp smell puffs from the stable door,
When the pitchfork handle stings in the hand
And the stanchioned cows for the milking stand,
Oh, merrily shines the morning sun
   In the barn-yard's southerly corner.

And the steers, let out for a drink and a run
Seek the warm corner one by one,
And the huddling sheep, in their dusty white,
Nose at the straw in the pleasant light,
When merrily shines the morning sun
   In the barn-yard's southerly corner.

TANTRAMAR REVISITED

Summers and summers have come, and gone with the flight of the
   swallow;
Sunshine and thunder have been, storm, and winter, and frost;
Many and many a sorrow has all but died from remembrance,
Many a dream of joy fall'n in the shadow of pain.
Hands of chance and change have marred, or moulded, or broken,
Busy with spirit or flesh, all I most have adored;
Even the bosom of Earth is strewn with heavier shadows,—
Only in these green hills, aslant to the sea, no change!
Here where the road that has climbed from the inland valleys and
   woodlands,
Dips from the hill-tops down, straight to the base of the hills,—
Here, from my vantage-ground, I can see the scattering houses,
Stained with time, set warm in orchards, meadows, and wheat,
Dotting the broad bright slopes outspread to southward and east-
   ward,
Wind-swept all day long, blown by the south-east wind.

Skirting the sunbright uplands stretches a riband of meadow,
Shorn of the labouring grass, bulwarked well from the sea,
Fenced on its seaward border with long clay dikes from the turbid
Surge and flow of the tides vexing the Westmoreland shores.
Yonder, toward the left, lie broad the Westmoreland marshes,—
Miles on miles they extend, level, and grassy, and dim,

Clear from the long red sweep of flats to the sky in the distance,
Save for the outlying heights, green-rampired Cumberland Point;
Miles on miles outrolled, and the river-channels divide them,—
Miles on miles of green, barred by the hurtling gusts.

Miles on miles beyond the tawny bay is Minudie.
There are the low blue hills; villages gleam at their feet.
Nearer a white sail shines across the water, and nearer
Still are the slim, grey masts of fishing boats dry on the flats.
Ah, how well I remember those wide red flats, above tide-mark,
Pale with scurf of the salt, seamed and baked in the sun!
Well I remember the piles of blocks and ropes, and the net-reels
Wound with the beaded nets, dripping and dark from the sea!
Now at this season the nets are unwound; they hang from the rafters
Over the fresh-stowed hay in upland barns, and the wind
Blows all day through the chinks, with the streaks of sunlight, and
    sways them
Softly at will; or they lie heaped in the gloom of a loft.

Now at this season the reels are empty and idle; I see them
Over the lines of the dikes, over the gossiping grass.
Now at this season they swing in the long strong wind, thro' the lone-
    some
Golden afternoon, shunned by the foraging gulls.
Near about sunset the crane will journey homeward above them;
Round them, under the moon, all the calm night long,
Winnowing soft grey wings of marsh-owls wander and wander,
Now to the broad, lit marsh, now to the dusk of the dike.
Soon, thro' their dew-wet frames, in the live keen freshness of morn-
    ing,
Out of the teeth of the dawn blows back the awakening wind.
Then, as the blue day mounts, and the low-shot shafts of the sunlight
Glance from the tide to the shore, gossamers jewelled with dew
Sparkle and wave, where late sea-spoiling fathoms of drift-net,
Myriad-meshed, uploomed sombrely over the land.

Well I remember it all. The salt, raw scent of the margin;
While, with men at the windlass, groaned each reel, and the net,
Surging in ponderous lengths, uprose and coiled in its station;
Then each man to his home,—well I remember it all!

Yet, as I sit and watch, this present peace of the landscape,—
Stranded boats, these reels empty and idle, the hush,
One grey hawk slow-wheeling above yon cluster of haystacks,—
More than the old-time stir this stillness welcomes me home.

Ah, the old-time stir, how once it stung me with rapture,—
Old-time sweetness, the winds freighted with honey and salt!
Yet will I stay my steps and not go down to the marshland,—
Muse and recall far off, rather remember than see,—
Lest on too close sight I miss the darling illusion,
Spy at their task even here the hands of chance and change.

ICE

When Winter scourged the meadow and the hill
And in the withered leafage worked his will,
The water shrank, and shuddered, and stood still,—
Then built himself a magic house of glass,
Irised with memories of flowers and grass,
Wherein to sit and watch the fury pass.

ARCHIBALD LAMPMAN
(1 8 6 1 – 9 9)

ARCHIBALD LAMPMAN was born at Morpeth, Ontario, November 17, 1861, where his father was rector of Trinity Church. He was educated at Trinity College School, Port Hope, and at Trinity College, Toronto, where he received a classical training. After graduating in 1882, he made a brief, uncongenial attempt at schoolmastering and then secured a place in the civil service at Ottawa. He married in 1887 and had a daughter in 1892 and a son, who only lived a few months, in 1894. His chief recreation was camping trips into the woodland lake regions surrounding Ottawa, and on one of these he overstrained his heart and incurred the weakness that was responsible for his death on February 10, 1899, when his power as a poet was in its full maturity. Lampman published two books, *Among the Millet* (1888) and *Lyrics of Earth* (1893), and was correcting the proofs of a third, *Alcyone*, at the time of his death. A collected edition, *The Poems of Archibald Lampman*, was edited with a "Memoir" by his friend, Duncan Campbell Scott in 1900; and a volume of selections, with a critical Introduction by Dr. Scott, appeared in 1925 under the title, *Lyrics of Earth*. At the Long Sault and Other Poems, a selection of verses from Lampman's unpublished manuscripts, edited by Professor E. K. Brown and Duncan Campbell Scott, is to be published in 1943.

Lampman had been introduced to poetry and to some extent trained in the art by his father, a classical scholar and a disciple of Pope. In all his work one can detect the health-giving influence of a genuine classicism. He read the Greek tragic poets in Greek, and the English poets he admired most were Milton, Keats, Wordsworth, and Arnold. The influence of Keats is inescapable in his early poetry (as in that of C. G. D. Roberts), but except for occasional epithets and images drawn from Morris and the Pre-Raphaelites literary influences are thoroughly assimilated and strengthen, rather than weaken, his individuality. Though, like Wordsworth, he finds nature a refuge and a source of spiritual strength, his descriptive method is essentially different. It is that of impressionism. Sensation, rather than idea, is what Lampman derives from landscape.

182

He is a painter's poet. He sees "the maple full of little crimson knots" in spring, and in autumn, "low thickets gray and reddish . . . . stroked white with birch . . . . pale greenish stems half hid in dry gray leaves." In winter "a few bronzed cedars . . . . lean their blue shadows on the puckered snow." Details of shape and color, seen always in the light of a precise minute, and valued for their own sake alone, give a special significance to Lampman's portrayal of Canada.

Lampman is not a philosophical poet, yet he sometimes expresses feelings and ideas of genuine human significance. He discerned in the everlasting movement of the elements and reiteration of the seasons a correspondence with his own inner life.

In some of his poems a landscape is presented as a state of the soul. And the state of that soul, although in his last years especially he was sometimes given to melancholy, was essentially one of love and joy. What he himself wrote of Robert Bridges is the best summing-up of his own qualities: "The essence of his verse is that unexcited pleasure in life which is the more lasting because it is contemplation, and is based upon the eternal truths and upon nothing shifty or compromising. So we get back . . . . to the springs of poetry, and see the beauty at its source where the water is clear and flows limpidly with a small, pure stream."

The work of Lampman is another illustration of the fact that the truly Canadian poet need not reject the culture of the classical world and of England in order to paint the landscape of his native country.

HEAT

From plains that reel to southward, dim,
    The road runs by me white and bare;
Up the steep hill it seems to swim
    Beyond, and melt into the glare.
Upward half-way, or it may be
    Nearer the summit, slowly steals
A hay-cart, moving dustily
    With idly clacking wheels.

By his cart's side the wagoner
    Is slouching slowly at his ease,
Half-hidden in the windless blur
    Of white dust puffing to his knees.

This wagon on the height above,
    From sky to sky on either hand,
Is the sole thing that seems to move
    In all the heat-held land.

Beyond me in the fields the sun
    Soaks in the grass and hath his will;
I count the marguerites one by one;
    Even the buttercups are still.
On the brook yonder not a breath
    Disturbs the spider or the midge.
The water-bugs draw close beneath
    The cool gloom of the bridge.

Where the far elm-tree shadows flood
    Dark patches in the burning grass,
The cows, each with her peaceful cud,
    Lie waiting for the heat to pass.
From somewhere on the slope near by
    Into the pale depth of the noon
A wandering thrush slides leisurely
    His thin revolving tune.

In intervals of dreams I hear
    The cricket from the droughty ground;
The grasshoppers spin into mine ear
    A small innumerable sound.
I lift mine eyes sometimes to gaze:
    The burning sky-line blinds my sight:
The woods far off are blue with haze:
    The hills are drenched in light.

And yet to me not this or that
    Is always sharp or always sweet;
In the sloped shadow of my hat
    I lean at rest, and drain the heat;
Nay more, I think some blessèd power
    Hath brought me wandering idly here:
In the full furnace of this hour
    My thoughts grow keen and clear.

IN NOVEMBER

With loitering step and quiet eye,
Beneath the low November sky,
I wandered in the woods, and found
A clearing, where the broken ground
Was scattered with black stumps and briers,
And the old wreck of forest fires.
It was a bleak and sandy spot,
And, all about, the vacant plot,
Was peopled and inhabited
By scores of mulleins long since dead.
A silent and forsaken brood
In that mute opening of the wood,
So shrivelled and so thin they were,
So gray, so haggard, and austere,
Not plants at all they seemed to me,
But rather some spare company
Of hermit folk, who long ago,
Wandering in bodies to and fro,
Had chanced upon this lonely way,
And rested thus, till death one day
Surprised them at their compline prayer,
And left them standing lifeless there.
There was no sound about the wood
Save the wind's secret stir. I stood
Among the mullein-stalks as still
As if myself had grown to be
One of their sombre company,
A body without wish or will.
And as I stood, quite suddenly,
Down from a furrow in the sky
The sun shone out a little space
Across that silent sober place,
Over the sand heaps and brown sod,
The mulleins and dead goldenrod,
And passed beyond the thickets gray,
And lit the fallen leaves that lay,
Level and deep within the wood,
A rustling yellow multitude.

And all around me the thin light,
So sere, so melancholy bright,
Fell like the half-reflected gleam
Or shadow of some former dream;
A moment's golden reverie
Poured out on every plant and tree
A semblance of weird joy, or less,
A sort of spectral happiness;
And I, too, standing idly there,
With muffled hands in the chill air,
Felt the warm glow about my feet,
And shuddering betwixt cold and heat,
Drew my thoughts closer, like a cloak,
While something in my blood awoke,
A nameless and unnatural cheer,
A pleasure secret and austere.

MIDNIGHT

From where I sit, I see the stars,
    And down the chilly floor
The moon between the frozen bars
    Is glimmering dim and hoar.

Without in many a peakéd mound
    The glinting snowdrifts lie;
There is no voice or living sound;
    The embers slowly die.

Yet some wild thing is in mine ear;
    I hold my breath and hark;
Out of the depth I seem to hear
    A crying in the dark;

No sound of man or wife or child,
    No sound of beast that groans,
Or of the wind that whistles wild,
    Or of the tree that moans:

I know not what it is I hear;
    I bend my head and hark:
I cannot drive it from mine ear,
    That crying in the dark.

THE SONG SPARROW

Fair little scout, that when the iron year
Changes, and the first fleecy clouds deploy,
Comest with such a sudden burst of joy,
Lifting on winter's doomed and broken rear
That song of silvery triumph blithe and clear;
Not yet quite conscious of the happy glow,
We hungered for some surer touch, and lo!
One morning we awake and thou art here.
And thousands of frail-stemmed hepaticas,
With their crisp leaves and pure and perfect hues,
Light sleepers, ready for the golden news,
Spring at thy note beside the forest ways—
Next to thy song, the first to deck the hour—
The classic lyrist and the classic flower.

SOLITUDE

How still it is here in the woods. The trees
Stand motionless, as if they did not dare
To stir, lest it should break the spell. The air
Hangs quiet as spaces in a marble frieze.
Even this little brook, that runs at ease,
Whispering and gurgling in its knotted bed,
Seems but to deepen, with its curling thread
Of sound, the shadowy sun-pierced silences.
Sometimes a hawk screams or a woodpecker
Startles the stillness from its fixéd mood
With his loud careless tap. Sometimes I hear
The dreamy white-throat from some far off tree
Pipe slowly on the listening solitude,
His five pure notes succeeding pensively.

A SUNSET AT LES EBOULEMENTS

Broad shadows fall. On all the mountain side
The scythe-swept fields are silent. Slowly home
By the long beach the high-piled hay-carts come,
Splashing the pale salt shallows. Over wide
Fawn-coloured wastes of mud the slipping tide,
Round the dun rocks and wattled fisheries,

Creeps murmuring in. And now by twos and threes,
O'er the slow spreading pools with clamorous chide,
Belated crows from strip to strip take flight.
Soon will the first star shine; yet ere the night
Reach onward to the pale-green distances,
The sun's last shaft beyond the gray sea-floor
Still dreams upon the Kamouraska shore,
And the long line of golden villages.

WINTER EVENING

To-night the very horses springing by
Toss gold from whitened nostrils. In a dream
The streets that narrow to the westward gleam
Like rows of golden palaces; and high
From all the crowded chimneys tower and die
A thousand aureoles. Down in the west
The brimming plains beneath the sunset rest,
One burning sea of gold. Soon, soon shall fly
The glorious vision, and the hours shall feel
A mightier master; soon from height to height,
With silence and the sharp unpitying stars,
Stern creeping frosts, and winds that touch like steel,
Out of the depth beyond the eastern bars,
Glittering and still shall come the awful night.

THE CITY OF THE END OF THINGS

Beside the pounding cataracts
Of midnight streams unknown to us
'Tis builded in the leafless tracts
And valleys huge of Tartarus.
Lurid and lofty and vast it seems;
It hath no rounded name that rings,
But I have heard it called in dreams
The City of the End of Things.

Its roofs and iron towers have grown
None knoweth how high within the night,
But in its murky streets far down
A flaming terrible and bright
Shakes all the stalking shadows there,
Across the walls, across the floors,

And shifts upon the upper air
From out a thousand furnace doors;
And all the while an awful sound
Keeps roaring on continually,
And crashes in the ceaseless round
Of a gigantic harmony.
Through its grim depths re-echoing
And all its weary height of walls,
With measured roar and iron ring,
The inhuman music lifts and falls.
Where no thing rests and no man is,
And only fire and night hold sway;
The beat, the thunder and the hiss
Cease not, and change not, night nor day.
And moving at unheard commands,
The abysses and vast fires between,
Flit figures that with clanking hands
Obey a hideous routine;
They are not flesh, they are not bone,
They see not with the human eye,
And from their iron lips is blown
A dreadful and monotonous cry;
And whoso of our mortal race
Should find that city unaware,
Lean Death would smite him face to face,
And blanch him with its venomed air:
Or caught by the terrific spell,
Each thread of memory snapt and cut,
His soul would shrivel and its shell
Go rattling like an empty nut.

It was not always so, but once,
In days that no man thinks upon,
Fair voices echoed from its stones,
The light above it leaped and shone:
Once there were multitudes of men,
That built that city in their pride,
Until its might was made, and then
They withered age by age and died.
But now of that prodigious race,
Three only in an iron tower,
Set like carved idols face to face,
Remain the masters of its power;

And at the city gate a fourth,
Gigantic and with dreadful eyes,
Sits looking toward the lightless north,
Beyond the reach of memories;
Fast rooted to the lurid floor,
A bulk that never moves a jot,
In his pale body dwells no more,
Or mind or soul,—an idiot!
But sometime in the end those three
Shall perish and their hands be still,
And with the master's touch shall flee
Their incommunicable skill.
A stillness absolute as death
Along the slacking wheels shall lie,
And, flagging at a single breath,
The fires shall moulder out and die.
The roar shall vanish at its height,
And over that tremendous town
The silence of eternal night
Shall gather close and settle down.
All its grim grandeur, tower and hall,
Shall be abandoned utterly,
And into rust and dust shall fall
From century to century;
Nor ever living thing shall grow,
Nor trunk of tree, nor blade of grass;
No drop shall fall, no wind shall blow,
Nor sound of any foot shall pass:
Alone of its accursèd state,
One thing the hand of Time shall spare,
For the grim Idiot at the gate
Is deathless and eternal there.

W. W. CAMPBELL (1861-1919)

WILLIAM WILFRED CAMPBELL was born at Berlin (Kitchener), Ontario, in 1861, and was educated at the University of Toronto and at Harvard. In 1885 he entered the ministry of the Episcopal church and served in several parishes in New England and New Brunswick. Six years later he resigned from the ministry to devote himself to literature—he claimed descent from the novelist Henry Fielding and the poet Thomas Campbell—and to work as a civil servant in the Dominion Archives Bureau at Ottawa, where he remained until his death in 1919. During the nineties he was associated with Archibald Lampman and Duncan Campbell Scott in writing criticism and literary journalism for the *Toronto Globe*.

Like all the members of the group of poets born in 1860 and 1861, Campbell was an ambitious poet and produced a large and varied body of work. His best poetry is found in the "Lake Lyrics"—descriptive nature poems and impressionistic sketches of the northern shores of Lake Huron—but he wrote also philosophical odes, dramatic narratives, and patriotic lyrics. Except for the lake poems, his work is for the most part bookish and derivative, though there is a curious and rather repulsive power in his vivid ballad, "The Mother." *The Collected Poems of Wilfred Campbell* was published in 1905, and three years later came his *Poetical Tragedies*, a series of Tennysonian closet dramas, among which were "Mordred," "Daulac," "Robespierre," and "Hildebrand." Campbell edited *The Oxford Book of Canadian Verse* and wrote two historical novels and other miscellaneous prose. In 1914 he published a selection of his verse under the title, *Sagas of Vaster Britain*. After his death *The Poetical Works of Wilfred Campbell* was published with a "Memoir" by W. J. Sykes. A recent Columbia doctoral dissertation, *Wilfred Campbell: A Study in Late Victorian Provincialism* (New York and Toronto, 1942), by C. F. Klinck, is a valuable interpretation of the poet's political and philosophical ideas. Neither his thought nor his personality is very attractive, but the effectiveness of his simpler nature lyrics remains undiminished.

HOW ONE WINTER CAME IN THE
LAKE REGION

For weeks and weeks the autumn world stood still,
   Clothed in the shadow of a smoky haze;
The fields were dead, the wind had lost its will,
And all the lands were hushed by wood and hill,
   In those grey, withered days.

Behind a mist the clear sun rose and set,
   At night the moon would nestle in a cloud;
The fisherman, a ghost, would cast his net;
The lake its shores forgot to chafe and fret,
   And hushed its caverns loud.

Far in the smoky woods the birds were mute,
   Save that from blackened tree a jay would scream,
Or far in swamps the lizard's lonesome lute
Would pipe in thirst, or by some gnarléd root
   The tree-toad trilled his dream.

From day to day still hushed the season's mood,
   The streams stayed in their runnels shrunk and dry;
Suns rose aghast by wave and shore and wood,
And all the world, with ominous silence, stood
   In weird expectancy:

When one strange night the sun like blood went down,
   Flooding the heavens in a ruddy hue;
Red grew the lake, the sere fields parched and brown,
Red grew the marshes where the creeks stole down,
   But never a wind-breath blew.

That night I felt the winter in my veins,
   A joyous tremor of the icy glow;
And woke to hear the north's wild vibrant strains,
While far and wide, by withered woods and plains,
   Fast fell the driving snow.

THE WINTER LAKES

Out in a world of death, far to the northward lying,
   Under the sun and the moon, under the dusk and the day;
Under the glimmer of stars and the purple of sunsets dying,
   Wan and waste and white, stretch the great lakes away.

Never a bud of spring, never a laugh of summer,
  Never a dream of love, never a song of bird;
But only the silence and white, the shores that grow chiller and
    dumber,
  Wherever the ice-winds sob, and the griefs of winter are heard.

Crags that are black and wet out of the gray lake looming,
  Under the sunset's flush, and the pallid, faint glimmer of dawn;
Shadowy, ghost-like shores, where midnight surfs are booming
  Thunders of wintry woe over the spaces wan.

Lands that loom like spectres, whited regions of winter,
  Wastes of desolate woods, deserts of water and shore;
A world of winter and death, within these regions who enter,
  Lost to summer and life, go to return no more.

Moons that glimmer above, waters that lie white under,
  Miles and miles of lake far out under the night;
Foaming crests of waves, surfs that shoreward thunder,
  Shadowy shapes that flee, haunting the spaces white.

Lonely hidden bays, moon-lit, ice-rimmed, winding,
  Fringed by forests and crags, haunted by shadowy shores;
Hushed from the outward strife, where the mighty surf is grinding
  Death and hate on the rocks, as sandward and landward it roars.

A LAKE MEMORY

The lake comes throbbing in with voice of pain
  Across these flats, athwart the sunset's glow.
I see her face, I know her voice again,
  Her lips, her breath, O God, as long ago.

To live the sweet past over I would fain,
  As lives the day in the red sunset's fire,
That all these wild, wan marshlands now would stain,
  With the dawn's memories, loves and flushed desire.

I call her back across the vanished years,
  Nor vain—a white-armed phantom fills her place;
Its eyes the wind-blown sunset fires, its tears
  This rain of spray that blows about my face.

LAZARUS

O Father Abram, I can never rest,
  Here in thy bosom in the whitest heaven,
  Where love blooms on through days without an even;
  For up through all the paradises seven,
There comes a cry from some fierce, anguished breast.

A cry that comes from out of hell's dark night,
  A piercing cry of one in agony,
  That reaches me here in heaven white and high;
  A call of anguish that doth never die;
Like dream-waked infant wailing for the light.

O Father Abram, heaven is love and peace,
  And God is good; eternity is rest.
  Sweet would it be to lie upon thy breast
  And know no thought but loving to be blest—
Save for that cry that never more will cease.

It comes to me above the angel-lyres,
  The chanting praises of the Cherubim;
  It comes between my upward gaze and Him,
  All-blessed Christ,—a voice from the vague dim,
"*O Lazarus, come and ease me of these fires.*

"*O Lazarus, I have called thee all these years,*
  It is so long for me to reach to thee,
  Across the ages of this mighty sea,
  That loometh dark, dense, like eternity;
Which I have bridged by anguished prayers and tears.

"*Which I have bridged by knowledge of God's love,*
  That even penetrates this anguished glare;
  A gleaming ray, a tremulous, star-built stair,
  A road by which love-hungered souls may fare
Past hate and doubt, to heaven and God above."

So calleth it ever upward unto me:
  It creepeth in through heaven's golden doors;
  It echoes all along the sapphire floors;
  Like smoke of sacrifice, it soars and soars;
It fills the vastness of eternity.

Until my sense of love is waned and dimmed,
  The music-rounded spheres do clash and jar:
  No more those spirit-calls from star to star,
  The harmonies that float and melt afar,
The belts of light by which all heaven is rimmed.

No more I hear the beat of heavenly wings,
  The seraph chanting in my rest-tuned ear;
  I only know a cry, a prayer, a tear,
  That rises from the depths up to me here;
A soul that to me suppliant leans and clings.

O, Father Abram, thou must bid me go
  Into the spaces of the deep abyss;
  Where far from us and our God-given bliss,
  Do dwell those souls that have done Christ amiss;
For through my rest I hear that upward woe.

I hear it crying through the heavenly night,
  When curvéd, hung in space, the million moons
  Lean planet-ward, and infinite space attunes
  Itself to silence, as from drear gray dunes
A cry is heard along the shuddering light,

Of wild dusk-bird, a sad, heart-curdling cry,
  So comes to me that call from out hell's coasts;
  I see an infinite shore with gaping ghosts;
  This is no heaven with all its shining hosts;
This is no heaven until that hell doth die.

So spake the soul of Lazarus, and from thence,
  Like new-fledged bird from its sun-jewelled nest,
  Drunk with the music of the young year's quest;
  He sank out into heaven's gloried breast,
Spaceward turned, toward darkness dim, immense.

Hellward he moved like radiant star shot out
  From heaven's blue with rain of gold at even,
  When Orion's train and that mysterious seven
  Move on in mystic range from heaven to heaven,
Hellward he sank, followed by radiant rout.

The liquid floor of heaven bore him up,
  With unseen arms, as in his feathery flight
  He floated down toward the infinite night;
  But each way downward, on the left and right,
He saw each moon of heaven like a cup

Of liquid, misty fire that shone afar
From sentinel towers of heaven's battlements;
But onward, winged by love's desire intense,
And sank, space-swallowed, into the immense,
While with him ever widened heaven's bar.

'Tis ages now long-gone since he went out,
Christ-urged, love-driven, across the jasper walls,
But hellward still he ever floats and falls,
And ever nearer come those anguished calls;
And far behind he hears a glorious shout.

BLISS CARMAN (1861–1929)

BLISS CARMAN was born in Fredericton, New Brunswick, in 1861. His father was a barrister, and his mother was a descendant of Rev. Daniel Bliss, a great-grandfather of Emerson. Carman was educated at Fredericton Collegiate, graduating in 1878 with a medal for proficiency in Greek and Latin. Like his cousin and schoolfellow, Charles G. D. Roberts, he came strongly under the influence of the headmaster, George R. Parkin. After graduating in 1881 from the University of New Brunswick, Carman spent two years at the University of Edinburgh. He returned to teach for a short time under Parkin, and then, after making an attempt to take up engineering and then law, he went to Harvard, where he studied history and philosophy. The teachings of Royce are said to have impressed him deeply. At Harvard he met Richard Hovey, the Dartmouth poet, and began a friendship that was fruitful for both and that was only terminated by Hovey's death in 1900.

In 1890 Carman went to New York and for two years was an assistant editor of the *Outlook*. After working on other magazines, including the *Atlantic Monthly*, he became editor of the *Chapbook* (Chicago) in 1894. His first volume of poetry, *Low Tide on Grand Pré*, had been published the previous year, and the first of the three series of *Songs from Vagabondia*, written in collaboration with Richard Hovey, appeared in 1894. The others were *More Songs from Vagabondia* (1896) and *Last Songs from Vagabondia* (1901). Carman wrote fluently and fast, and from this time on his books flowed from the presses like water. The best of them were: *Behind the Arras: A Book of the Unseen* (1895); *Ballads of Lost Haven* (1897); *The Pipes of Pan* (5 vols., 1902–5); and *Sappho: One Hundred Lyrics* (1904).

Between 1904 and 1908 Carman was mainly occupied with prose. He wrote a series of semiphilosophical, semi-inspirational essays, *The Kinship of Nature* (1904), *The Friendship of Art* (1904), *The Poetry of Life* (1905), and, in collaboration with Mary Perry King, *The Making of Personality* (1908). These add nothing to the poet's reputation. Indeed, with the publication of the *Sappho* lyrics and the last of the *Pipes of Pan* series Carman's finest work was done. His later poetry is an echo of his earlier, fainter and less compelling. The later volumes are: *Echoes from Vagabondia* (1912); *Daughters of Dawn* (1913); *Earth's Deities* (1914); *April Airs* (1916); *Later Poems* (1921); *Ballads and Lyrics* (1923); *Far Horizons* (1925); *Wild Garden* (1929); and *Sanctuary* (1929). Bliss Carman died in New Canaan, Connecticut, where he had spent the last years of his life.

The reader who wishes to have the best of Carman in small compass should get *Ballads and Lyrics* (1923), which is a selection of poems from six of Carman's early books. This should be supplemented by the definitive edition of *Pipes of Pan* and by *Sappho*.

LOW TIDE ON GRAND PRÉ

The sun goes down, and over all
  These barren reaches by the tide
Such unelusive glories fall,
  I almost dream they yet will bide
  Until the coming of the tide.

And yet I know that not for us,
  By any ecstasy of dream,
He lingers to keep luminous
  A little while the grievous stream,
  Which frets, uncomforted of dream—

A grievous stream, that to and fro
  Athrough the fields of Acadie
Goes wandering, as if to know
  Why one beloved face should be
  So long from home and Acadie.

Was it a year or lives ago
  We took the grasses in our hands,
And caught the summer flying low
  Over the waving meadow lands,
  And held it there between our hands?

The while the river at our feet—
  A drowsy inland meadow stream—
At set of sun the after-heat
  Made running gold, and in the gleam
  We freed our birch upon the stream.

There down along the elms at dusk
  We lifted dripping blade to drift,
Through twilight scented fine like musk,
  Where night and gloom awhile uplift,
  Nor sunder soul and soul adrift.

And that we took into our hands
  Spirit of life or subtler thing—
Breathed on us there, and loosed the bands
  Of death, and taught us, whispering,
  The secret of some wonder-thing.

Then all your face grew light, and seemed
  To hold the shadow of the sun;
The evening faltered, and I deemed
  That time was ripe, and years had done
  Their wheeling underneath the sun.

So all desire and all regret,
  And fear and memory, were naught;
One to remember or forget
  The keen delight our hands had caught;
  Morrow and yesterday were naught.

The night has fallen, and the tide . . . .
  Now and again comes drifting home,
Across these aching barrens wide,
  A sigh like driven wind or foam:
  In grief the flood is bursting home.

A NORTHERN VIGIL

Here by the gray north sea,
  In the wintry heart of the wild,
Comes the old dream of thee,
  Guendolen, mistress and child.

The heart of the forest grieves
  In the drift against my door;
A voice is under the eaves,
  A footfall on the floor.

Threshold, mirror and hall,
  Vacant and strangely aware,
Wait for their soul's recall
  With the dumb expectant air.

Here when the smouldering west
  Burns down into the sea,
I take no heed of rest
  And keep the watch for thee.

I sit by the fire and hear
  The restless wind go by,
On the long dirge and drear,
  Under the low bleak sky.

When day puts out to sea
  And night makes in for land,
There is no lock for thee,
  Each door awaits thy hand!

When night goes over the hill
  And dawn comes down the dale,
It's O for the wild sweet will
  That shall no more prevail!

When the zenith moon is round,
  And snow-wraiths gather and run,
And there is set no bound
  To love beneath the sun,

O wayward will, come near
  The old mad wilful way,
The soft mouth at my ear
  With words too sweet to say!

Come, for the night is cold,
  The ghostly moonlight fills
Hollow and rift and fold
  Of the eerie Ardise hills!

The windows of my room
  Are dark with bitter frost,
The stillness aches with doom
  Of something loved and lost.

Outside, the great blue star
  Burns in the ghostland pale,
Where giant Algebar
  Holds on the endless trail.

Come, for the years are long,
  And silence keeps the door,

Where shapes with the shadows throng
  The firelit chamber floor.

Come, for thy kiss was warm,
  With the red embers' glare
Across thy folding arm
  And dark tumultuous hair!

And though thy coming rouse
  The sleep-cry of no bird,
The keepers of the house
  Shall tremble at thy word.

Come, for the soul is free!
  In all the vast dreamland
There is no lock for thee,
  Each door awaits thy hand.

Ah, not in dreams at all,
  Fleering, perishing, dim,
But thy old self, supple and tall,
  Mistress and child of whim!

The proud imperious guise,
  Impetuous and serene,
The sad mysterious eyes,
  And dignity of mien!

Yea, wilt thou not return,
  When the late hill-winds veer,
And the bright hill-flowers burn
  With the reviving year?

When April comes, and the sea
  Sparkles as if it smiled,
Will they restore to me
  My dark Love, empress and child?

The curtains seem to part;
  A sound is on the stair,
As if at the last . . . . I start;
  Only the wind is there.

Lo, now far on the hills
  The crimson fumes uncurled,
Where the caldron mantles and spills
  Another dawn on the world!

DAPHNE

I know that face!
In some lone forest place,
When June brings back the laurel to the hills,
Where shade and sunlight lace,

Where all day long
The brown birds make their song—
A music that seems never to have known
Dismay nor haste nor wrong—

I once before
Have seen thee by the shore,
As if about to shed the flowery guise
And be thyself once more.

Dear, shy, soft face,
With just the elfin trace
That lends thy human beauty the last touch
Of wild, elusive grace!

Can it be true,
A god did once pursue
Thy gleaming beauty through the glimmering wood,
Drenched in the Dorian dew,

Too mad to stay
His hot and headstrong way,
Demented by the fragrance of thy flight,
Heedless of thy dismay?

But I to thee
More gently fond would be,
Nor less a lover woo thee with soft words
And woodland melody;

Take pipe and play
Each forest fear away;
Win thee to idle in the leafy shade
All the long summer day;

Tell thee old tales
Of love, that still avails
More than all mighty things in this great world,
Still wonder works nor fails;

Teach thee new lore,
How to love more and more,
And find the magical delirium
In joys unguessed before.

I would try over
And over to discover
Some wild, sweet, foolish, irresistible
New way to be thy lover—

New, wondrous ways
To fill thy golden days,
Thy lovely pagan body with delight,
Thy loving heart with praise.

For I would learn,
Deep in the brookside fern,
The magic of the syrinx whispering low
With bubbly fall and turn;

Mock every note
Of the green woodbird's throat,
Till some wild strain, impassioned yet serene,
Should form and float

Far through the hills,
Where mellow sunlight fills
The world with joy, and from the purple vines
The brew of life distils.

Ah, then indeed
Thy heart should have no need
To tremble at a footfall in the brake,
And bid thy bright limbs speed.

But night would come,
And I should make thy home
In the deep pines, lit by a yellow star
Hung in the dark blue dome—

A fragrant house
Of woven balsam boughs,
Where the great Cyprian mother should receive
Our warm unsullied vows.

IN THE HOUSE OF IDIEDAILY

Oh, but life went gayly, gayly,
In the house of Idiedaily!

There were always throats to sing
Down the river-banks with spring,

When the stir of heart's desire
Set the sapling's heart on fire.

Bobolincolns in the meadows,
Leisure in the purple shadows,

Till the poppies without number
Bowed their heads in crimson slumber

And the twilight came to cover
Every unreluctant lover.

Not a night but some brown maiden
Bettered all the dusk she strayed in,

While the roses in her hair
Bankrupted oblivion there.

Oh, but life went gayly, gayly,
In the house of Idiedaily!

But this hostelry, The Barrow,
With its chambers, bare and narrow,

Mean, ill-windowed, damp, and wormy,
Where the silence makes you squirmy,

And the guests are never seen to,
Is a vile place, a mere lean-to,

Not a traveller speaks well of,
Even worse than I heard tell of,

Mouldy, ramshackle, and foul.
What a dwelling for a soul!

Oh, but life went gayly, gayly,
In the house of Idiedaily!

There the hearth was always warm,
From the slander of the storm.

There your comrade was your neighbor,
Living on to-morrow's labor.

And the board was always steaming,
Though Sir Ringlets might be dreaming.

Not a plate but scoffed at porridge,
Not a cup but floated borage.

There were always jugs of sherry
Waiting for the makers merry,

And the dark Burgundian wine
That would make a fool divine.

Oh, but life went gayly, gayly,
In the house of Idiedaily!

LORD OF MY HEART'S ELATION

Lord of my heart's elation,
Spirit of things unseen,
Be thou my aspiration
Consuming and serene!

Bear up, bear out, bear onward
This mortal soul alone,
To selfhood or oblivion,
Incredibly thine own,—

As the foamheads are loosened
And blown along the sea,
Or sink and merge forever
In that which bids them be.

I, too, must climb in wonder,
Uplift at thy command,—
Be one with my frail fellows
Beneath the wind's strong hand,

A fleet and shadowy column
Of dust or mountain rain,
To walk the earth a moment
And be dissolved again.

Be thou my exaltation
Or fortitude of mien,
Lord of the world's elation,
Thou breath of things unseen!

FREDERICK GEORGE SCOTT
(1 8 6 1————)

FREDERICK GEORGE SCOTT was born in 1861 in Montreal of English parentage. His father for nearly forty years was professor of anatomy in McGill University. The poet was educated at the Montreal High School, at Bishop's College, Lennoxville, and later at King's College, London. He entered the church in 1884 and two years later was ordained a priest. For many years he was rector of Drummondville, in the Eastern Townships, Quebec, and then was moved to Quebec as rector of St. Matthew's Church, later becoming canon of Holy Trinity Cathedral. During World War I he was senior chaplain of the First Canadian Division, being awarded the D.S.O. for distinguished service in the front lines. As a fearless and sympathetic padre, he won the respect and love of all the Canadian soldiers. In 1922 he published *The Great War as I Saw It*, a volume of battle reminiscences.

The following are the most important of Archdeacon Scott's books of poetry: *The Soul's Quest, and Other Poems* (1888); *My Lattice, and Other Poems* (1894); *The Unnamed Lake, and Other Poems* (1897); *Poems, Old and New* (1900); *The Hymn of Empire, and Other Poems* (1906); *Poems* (1910) (a collected edition); *In the Battle Silences* (1916); and, more recently, a collection of patriotic verse inspired by World War II, *Lift Up Your Hearts* (1941).

THE UNNAMED LAKE

It sleeps among the thousand hills
　　Where no man ever trod,
And only nature's music fills
　　The silences of God.

Great mountains tower above its shore,
　　Green rushes fringe its brim,
And o'er its breast for evermore
　　The wanton breezes skim.

Dark clouds that intercept the sun
  Go there in Spring to weep,
And there, when Autumn days are done,
  White mists lie down to sleep.

Sunrise and sunset crown with gold
  The peaks of ageless stone,
Where winds have thundered from of old
  And storms have set their throne.

No echoes of the world afar
  Disturb it night or day,
But sun and shadow, moon and star
  Pass and repass for aye.

'Twas in the grey of early dawn,
  When first the lake we spied,
And fragments of a cloud were drawn
  Half down the mountain side.

Along the shore a heron flew,
  And from a speck on high,
That hovered in the deepening blue,
  We heard the fish-hawk's cry.

Among the cloud-capt solitudes,
  No sound the silence broke,
Save when, in whispers down the woods,
  The guardian mountains spoke.

  Through tangled brush and dewy brake,
    Returning whence we came,
We passed in silence, and the lake
    We left without a name.

EASTER ISLAND

There lies a lone isle in the tropic seas,—
A mountain isle, with beaches shining white,
Where soft stars smile upon its sleep by night,
And every noonday fans it with a breeze.
Here on a cliff, carved upward from the knees,
Three uncouth statues of gigantic height,
Upon whose brows the circling sea-birds light,
Stare out to ocean over the tall trees.

For ever gaze they at the sea and sky,
For ever hear the thunder of the main,
For ever watch the ages die away;
And ever round them rings the phantom cry
Of some lost race that died in human pain,
Looking towards heaven, yet seeing no more than they.

"LITTLE FRIEND'S" GRAVE

Build a house for "Little Friend,"
    Underneath the sunniest grass,
In a place where birds' songs blend
    On the breezes as they pass.

Dig it not with sorrow's spade,
    Use no sharp-edged tools of pain,
Nothing there must cast a shade,
    Nothing there must leave a stain.

Build the walls of hope and joy,
    Gladsome as the flowers and trees,
Else the little merry boy
    Will not rest in it at ease.

Bring no torch or other light,
    As though darkness could be there,
For a soul so pure and bright
    Will give radiance everywhere.

Build the roof of faith and love,
    Pillared on foundations deep,
That the rain of tears above
    May not mar his happy sleep.

Make no windows, as though he
    Needed peep-holes to the skies,
For the vast Eternity
    Now is open to his eyes.

Build no staircase for his feet,
    Make no door-way in the wall,
For he treads the golden street
    Where the Christ is all in all.

Only let the cross be set
　Upright in the hallowed ground,
Lest the stricken heart forget
　Where the cure of grief is found.

THE WAYSIDE CROSS

A wayside cross at set of day
Unto my spirit thus did say—

"O soul, my branching arms you see
Point four ways to infinity.

"One points to infinite above,
To show the height of heavenly love.

"Two point to infinite width, which shows
That heavenly love no limit knows.

"One points to infinite beneath,
To show God's love is under death.

"The four arms join, an emblem sweet
That in God's heart all loves will meet."

I thanked the cross as I turned away
For such sweet thoughts in the twilight grey.

THE STING OF DEATH

"Is Sin, then, fair?"
　Nay, love, come now,
Put back the hair
　From his sunny brow;
See, here, blood-red
Across his head
A brand is set,
The word—"Regret."

"Is Sin so fleet
　That while he stays,
Our hands and feet
　May go his ways?"
Nay, love, his breath
Clings round like death,
He slakes desire
With liquid fire.

"Is Sin Death's sting?"
    Ay, sure he is,
    His golden wing
    Darkens man's bliss;
And when Death comes,
Sin sits and hums
A chaunt of fears
Into man's ears.

"How slayeth Sin?"
    First, God is hid,
    And the heart within
    By its own self chid;
Then the maddened brain
Is scourged by pain
To sin as before
And more and more,
    For evermore.

PAULINE JOHNSON (1862–1913)

PAULINE JOHNSON ("Tekahionwake") was born in 1862 on the Iroquois Reservation near Brantford, Ontario, and spent her childhood and youth there. Her father was a full-blooded Indian, chief of the Six Nations Confederacy, and her mother was an English-woman. Her early home was not a primitive one, and she was reared in cultured surroundings. Her education was literary, and her poetry is in no way primitive or aboriginal. Pauline Johnson was the author of *The White Wampum* (1895); *Canadian Born* (1903); *Legends of Vancouver* (1911); and the collected edition, *Flint and Feather*, published soon after her death in 1913. She is likely to be remembered chiefly for such graceful and airy lyrics as "Shadow River," which make no claim to significance, as did her once popular and theatrical Indian poems.

SHADOW RIVER
[MUSKOKA]

A stream of silver gladness,
Of filmy sun, and opal-tinted skies;
Of warm midsummer air that lightly lies
In mystic rings,
Where softly swings
The music of a thousand wings
That almost tones to sadness.

Midway 'twixt earth and heaven,
A bubble in the pearly air, I seem
To float upon the sapphire floor. A dream
Of clouds of snow,
Above, below,
Drifts with my drifting, dim and slow,
As twilight drifts to even.

The little fern-leaf, bending
Upon the brink, its green reflection greets,
And kisses soft the shadow that it meets
With touch so fine,
The border-line
The keenest vision can't define;
So perfect is the blending.

The far fir-trees that cover
The brownish hills with needles green and gold,
The arching elms o'erhead, vine-grown and old,
Repictured are
Beneath me far
Where not a ripple moves to mar
Shades underneath, or over.

Mine is the undertone;
The beauty, strength and power of the land
Will never stir or bend at my command;
But all the shade
Is marred or made
If I but dip my paddle blade;
And it is mine alone.

O! pathless world of seeming!
O! pathless life of mine whose deep ideal
Is more my own than ever was the real!
For others Fame
And Love's red flame,
And yellow gold: I only claim
The shadows and the dreaming.

DUNCAN CAMPBELL SCOTT
(1 8 6 2——)

DUNCAN CAMPBELL SCOTT was born in Ottawa in 1862 of English and Scottish parentage and was educated in the schools of Ottawa and at Stanstead College. In 1879 he entered civil service in the Department of Indian Affairs, of which he eventually became the head. He was a friend of Archibald Lampman, with whom and Wilfred Campbell he contributed a weekly page of literary criticism to the *Toronto Globe*. After Lampman's death Scott edited his collected poems and wrote an excellent "Memoir" of his friend. His Introduction to a later volume of selections is still the best study of Lampman and reveals Scott as an intelligent and sensitive critic.

Scott's own poetry was first published in 1893 in *The Magic House and Other Poems*. It was followed by *Labour and the Angel* (1898); *New World Lyrics and Ballads* (1905); *Via Borealis* (1906); *Lines in Memory of Edmund Morris* (1915); *Lundy's Lane and Other Poems* (1916); *Beauty and Life* (1921); and *The Green Cloister* (1936). His *Collected Poems* was published in 1926.

In addition to poetry, Duncan Campbell Scott has published critical and historical material, including a biography of John Graves Simcoe, and two volumes of tales which are among the finest contributions to the art of the short story in Canadian literature. *In the Village of Viger* (1896) is an interpretation of the French-Canadian as sympathetic as Drummond's and more profound. *The Witching of Elspie* (1923) contains stories dealing with pioneer life in the Hudson Bay region.

In spite of his success in these fields, it is as one of the most conscientious artists of the school of Canadian nature poets associated with Roberts and Lampman that Duncan Campbell Scott will be best remembered. Yet he is an individual, who stands apart from any of the other members of the group—even from Lampman, whom he resembles most.

Nowhere is Scott's individualism and his traditionalism seen to better advantage than in some of the love lyrics of his first volume and in "The Piper of Arll." This ballad has had its influence on

English literature. John Masefield, in his recent book of memories, *In the Mill* (New York: Macmillan Co., 1941), tells how he

bought the Christmas number of this American *Truth*, and read it through. It had in it, with some illustrations of phantasy, a longish narrative poem by Duncan Campbell Scott, called "The Piper of Arll." This was the first poem by a living writer to touch me to the quick. It was narrative; it was delicate phantasy; it was about the sea and singing and a romantic end. I did not know it at the time, but it was a choice example of the work of the romantic poets of that decade. Its longing, its wistfulness and the perfection of some of its images made deep impressions on me. I read it till I knew it by heart; even now, I often repeat it to myself. Years later I came upon the writing of a critic who mentions it as a poem "the symbolism of which escapes me." Well, let it escape. The romantic mood and the dream may be of deep personal significance and joy, even if the author's thought elude us. I used to repeat the poem mentally. . . . . I could see Arll, the cove, the pines upon the hill; and the strange ship coming in and presently sinking down. In that mood, she could have done no other than sink, and all my years with sailors failed to make me call for a Court of Enquiry into her sinking.

THE PIPER OF ARLL

There was in Arll a little cove
Where the salt wind came cool and free:
A foamy beach that one would love,
If he were longing for the sea.

A brook hung sparkling on the hill,
The hill swept far to ring the bay;
The bay was faithful, wild or still,
To the heart of the ocean far away.

There were three pines above the comb
That, when the sun flared and went down,
Grew like three warriors reaving home
The plunder of a burning town.

A piper lived within the grove,
Tending the pasture of his sheep;
His heart was swayed with faithful love,
From the springs of God's ocean clear and deep.

And there a ship one evening stood,
Where ship had never stood before;
A pennon bickered red as blood,
An angel glimmered at the prore.

About the coming on of dew,
The sails burned rosy, and the spars
Were gold, and all the tackle grew
Alive with ruby-hearted stars.

The piper heard an outland tongue,
With music in the cadenced fall;
And when the fairy lights were hung,
The sailors gathered one and all,

And leaning on the gunwales dark,
Crusted with shells and dashed with foam,
With all the dreaming hills to hark,
They sang their longing songs of home.

When the sweet airs had fled away,
The piper, with a gentle breath,
Moulded a tranquil melody
Of lonely love and longed-for death.

When the fair sound began to lull,
From out the fireflies and the dew,
A silence held the shadowy hull,
Until the eerie tune was through.

Then from the dark and dreamy deck
An alien song began to thrill;
It mingled with the drumming beck,
And stirred the braird upon the hill.

Beneath the stars each sent to each
A message tender, till at last
The piper slept upon the beach,
The sailors slumbered round the mast.

Still as a dream till nearly dawn,
The ship was bosomed on the tide;
The streamlet, murmuring on and on,
Bore the sweet water to her side.

Then shaking out her lawny sails,
Forth on the misty sea she crept;
She left the dawning of the dales,
Yet in his cloak the piper slept.

And when he woke he saw the ship,
Limned black against the crimson sun;
Then from the disc he saw her slip,
A wraith of shadow—she was gone.

He threw his mantle on the beach,
He went apart like one distraught,
His lips were moved—his desperate speech
Stormed his inviolable thought.

He broke his human-throated reed,
And threw it in the idle rill;
But when his passion had its mead,
He found it in the eddy still.

He mended well the patient flue,
Again he tried its varied stops;
The closures answered right and true,
And starting out in piercing drops,

A melody began to drip
That mingled with a ghostly thrill
The vision-spirit of the ship,
The secret of his broken will.

Beneath the pines he piped and swayed,
Master of passion and of power;
He was his soul and what he played,
Immortal for a happy hour.

He, singing into nature's heart,
Guiding his will by the world's will,
With deep, unconscious, childlike art
Had sung his soul out and was still.

And then at evening came the bark
That stirred his dreaming heart's desire;
It burned slow lights along the dark
That died in glooms of crimson fire.

The sailors launched a sombre boat,
And bent with music at the oars;
The rhythm throbbing every throat,
And lapsing round the liquid shores,

Was that true tune the piper sent,
Unto the wave-worn mariners,
When with the beck and ripple blent
He heard that outland song of theirs.

Silent they rowed him, dip and drip,
The oars beat out an exequy,
They laid him down within the ship,
They loosed a rocket to the sky.

It broke in many a crimson sphere
That grew to gold and floated far,
And left the sudden shore-line clear,
With one slow-changing, drifting star.

Then out they shook the magic sails,
That charmed the wind in other seas,
From where the west line pearls and pales,
They waited for a ruffling breeze.

But in the world there was no stir,
The cordage slacked with never a creak,
They heard the flame begin to purr
Within the lantern at the peak.

They could not cry, they could not move,
They felt the lure from the charmed sea;
They could not think of home or love
Or any pleasant land to be.

They felt the vessel dip and trim,
And settle down from list to list;
They saw the sea-plain heave and swim
As gently as a rising mist.

And down so slowly, down and down,
Rivet by rivet, plank by plank;
A little flood of ocean flown
Across the deck, she sank and sank.

From knee to breast the water wore,
It crept and crept; ere they were ware
Gone was the angel at the prore,
They felt the water float their hair.

They saw the salt plain spark and shine,
They threw their faces to the sky;
Beneath a deepening film of brine
They saw the star-flash blur and die.

She sank and sank by yard and mast,
Sank down the shimmering gradual dark;
A little drooping pennon last
Showed like the black fin of a shark.

And down she sank till, keeled in sand,
She rested safely balanced true,
With all her upward gazing band,
The piper and the dreaming crew.

And there, unmarked of any chart,
In unrecorded deeps they lie,
Empearled within the purple heart
Of the great sea for aye and aye.

Their eyes are ruby in the green
Long shaft of sun that spreads and rays,
And upward with a wizard sheen
A fan of sea-light leaps and plays.

Tendrils of or and azure creep,
And globes of amber light are rolled,
And in the gloaming of the deep
Their eyes are starry pits of gold.

And sometimes in the liquid night
The hull is changed, a solid gem,
That glows with a soft stony light,
The lost prince of a diadem.

And at the keel a vine is quick,
That spreads its bines and works and weaves
O'er all the timbers veining thick
A plenitude of silver leaves.

AT THE CEDARS

You had two girls—Baptiste—
One is Virginie—
Hold hard—Baptiste!
Listen to me.

The whole drive was jammed
In that bend at the Cedars,
The rapids were damned
With the logs tight rammed
And crammed; you might know
The Devil had clinched them below.

We worked three days—not a budge,
"She's as tight as a wedge,
On the ledge,"
Says our foreman;
"Mon Dieu! boys, look here,
We must get this thing clear."
He cursed at the men
And we went for it then;
With our cant-dogs arow,
We just gave he-yo-ho;
When she gave a big shove
From above.

The gang yelled and tore
For the shore,
The logs gave a grind
Like a wolf's jaws behind,
And as quick as a flash,
With a shove and a crash,
They were down in a mash,
But I and ten more,
All but Isaàc Dufour,
Were ashore.

He leaped on a log in the front of the rush,
And shot out from the bind
While the jam roared behind;
As he floated along
He balanced his pole
And tossed us a song.

But just as we cheered,
Up darted a log from the bottom,
Leaped thirty feet square and fair,
And came down on his own.

He went up like a block
With the shock,
And when he was there
In the air,
Kissed his hand
To the land;
When he dropped
My heart stopped,
For the first logs had caught him
And crushed him;
When he rose in his place
There was blood on his face.

There were some girls, Baptiste,
Picking berries on the hillside,
Where the river curls, Baptiste,
You know—on the still side;
One was down by the water,
She saw Isaàc
Fall back.

She did not scream, Baptiste,
She launched her canoe;
It did seem, Baptiste,
That she wanted to die too,
For before you could think
The birch cracked like a shell
In that rush of hell,
And I saw them both sink—

Baptiste!—
He had two girls,
One is Virginie,
What God calls the other
Is not known to me.

NIGHT BURIAL IN THE FOREST

Lay him down where the fern is thick and fair.
Fain was he for life, here lies he low:
With the blood washed clean from his brow and his
   beautiful hair,
Lay him here in the dell where the orchids grow.

Let the birch-bark torches roar in the gloom,
And the trees crowd up in a quiet startled ring
So lone is the land that in this lonely room
Never before has breathed a human thing.

Cover him well in his canvas shroud, and the moss
Part and heap again on his quiet breast,
What recks he now of gain, or love, or loss
Who for love gained rest?

While she who caused it all hides her insolent eyes
Or braids her hair with the ribbons of lust and of lies,
And he who did the deed fares out like a hunted beast
To lurk where the musk-ox tramples the barren ground
Where the stroke of his coward heart is the only sound.

Haunting the tamarac shade,
Hear them up-thronging
Memories foredoomed
Of strife and of longing:
Haggard or bright
By the tamaracs and birches,
Where the red torch light
Trembles and searches,
The wilderness teems
With inscrutable eyes
Of ghosts that are dreams
Commingled with memories.

Leave him here in his secret ferny tomb,
Withdraw the little light from the ocean of gloom,
He who feared nought will fear ought never,
Left alone in the forest forever and ever.

Then, as we fare on our way to the shore
Sudden the torches cease to roar:
For cleaving the darkness remote and still

Comes a wind with a rushing, harp-like thrill,
The sound of wings hurled and furled and unfurled,
The wings of the Angel who gathers the souls from the
  wastes of the world.

AT GULL LAKE: AUGUST, 1810

Gull Lake set in the rolling prairie—
Still there are reeds on the shore,
As of old the poplars shimmer
As summer passes;
Winter freezes the shallow lake to the core;
Storm passes,
Heat parches the sedges and grasses,
Night comes with moon-glimmer,
Dawn with the morning-star;
All proceeds in the flow of Time
As a hundred years ago.

Then two camps were pitched on the shore,
The clustered teepees
Of Tabashaw Chief of the Saulteaux.
And on a knoll tufted with poplars
Two gray tents of a trader—
Nairne of the Orkneys.
Before his tents under the shade of the poplars
Sat Keejigo, third of the wives
Of Tabashaw Chief of the Saulteaux;
Clad in the skins of antelopes
Broidered with porcupine quills
Coloured with vivid dyes,
Vermilion here and there
In the roots of her hair,
A half-moon of powder-blue
On her brow, her cheeks
Scored with light ochre streaks.
Keejigo daughter of Launay
The Normandy hunter
And Oshawan of the Saulteaux,
Troubled by fugitive visions
In the smoke of the camp-fires,
In the close dark of the teepee,

Flutterings of colour
Along the flow of the prairies,
Spangles of flower tints
Caught in the wonder of dawn,
Dreams of sounds unheard—
The echoes of echo,
Star she was named for
Keejigo, star of the morning,
Voices of storm—
Wind-rush and lightning,—
The beauty of terror;
The twilight moon
Coloured like a prairie lily,
The round moon of pure snow,
The beauty of peace;
Premonitions of love and of beauty
Vague as shadows cast by a shadow.
Now she had found her hero,
And offered her body and spirit
With abject unreasoning passion,
As Earth abandons herself
To the sun and the thrust of the lightning.
Quiet were all the leaves of the poplars,
Breathless the air under their shadow,
As Keejigo spoke of these things to her heart
In the beautiful speech of the Saulteaux.

> *The flower lives on the prairie,*
> *The wind in the sky,*
> *I am here my beloved;*
> *The wind and the flower.*

> *The crane hides in the sand-hills,*
> *Where does the wolverine hide?*
> *I am here my beloved,*
> *Heart's-blood on the feathers*
> *The foot caught in the trap.*

> *Take the flower in your hand,*
> *The wind in your nostrils;*
> *I am here my beloved;*
> *Release the captive*
> *Heal the wound under the feathers.*

A storm-cloud was marching
Vast on the prairie,
Scored with livid ropes of hail,
Quick with nervous vines of lightning—
Twice had Nairne turned her away
Afraid of the venom of Tabashaw,
Twice had the Chief fired at his tents
And now when two bullets
Whistled above the encampment
He yelled "Drive this bitch to her master."

Keejigo went down a path by the lake;
Thick at the tangled edges,
The reeds and the sedges
Were gray as ashes
Against the death-black water;
The lightning scored with double flashes
The dark lake-mirror and loud
Came the instant thunder.
Her lips still moved to the words of her music,
"Release the captive,
Heal the wound under the feathers."

At the top of the bank
The old wives caught her and cast her down
Where Tabashaw crouched by his camp-fire.
He snatched a live brand from the embers,
Seared her cheeks,
Blinded her eyes,
Destroyed her beauty with fire,
Screaming, "Take that face to your lover."
Keejigo held her face to the fury
And made no sound.
The old wives dragged her away
And threw her over the bank
Like a dead dog.

Then burst the storm—
The Indians' screams and the howls of the dogs
Lost in the crash of hail
That smashed the sedges and reeds,
Stripped the poplars of leaves,

Tore and blazed onwards,
Wasting itself with riot and tumult—
Supreme in the beauty of terror.

The setting sun struck the retreating cloud
With a rainbow, not an arc but a column
Built with the glory of seven metals;
Beyond in the purple deeps of the vortex
Fell the quivering vines of the lightning.
The wind withdrew the veil from the shrine of
    the moon,
She rose changing her dusky shade for the glow
Of the prairie lily, till free of all blemish of colour
She came to her zenith without a cloud or a star,
A lovely perfection, snow-pure in the heaven of
    midnight.
After the beauty of terror the beauty of peace.

But Keejigo came no more to the camps of her people;
Only the midnight moon knew where she felt her way,
Only the leaves of autumn, the snows of winter
Knew where she lay.

AT DELOS

An iris-flower with topaz leaves,
    With a dark heart of deeper gold,
Died over Delos when light failed
    And the night grew cold.

No wave fell mourning in the sea
    Where age on age beauty had died;
For that frail colour withering away
    No sea-bird cried.

There is no grieving in the world
    As beauty fades throughout the years:
The pilgrim with the weary heart
    Brings to the grave his tears.

PART IV
VARIETIES OF ROMANTIC SENSIBILITY

ANNIE CHARLOTTE DALTON
(1865–1938)

MRS. DALTON was born in England in 1865 and came to Vancouver with her husband in 1904, where she lived and wrote until her death in 1938. Her first book of poems, *The Marriage of Music*, was published in 1910, and it was followed by half-a-dozen others, of which the most notable were *Flame and Adventure* (1924), *The Neighing North* (1931), and *Lilies and Leopards* (1936). Mrs. Dalton attempted a wide variety of forms and methods, from the traditionalism of the nineteenth century in her ambitious and not entirely successful philosophical statement of faith, *Flame and Adventure*, to the experimentalism of some of her essays in free verse. Her best work is seen in such tightly constructed and objectively imagined lyrics as those included here from her last book. They are at once genuinely traditional and boldly original. "The poems in *Lilies and Leopards*," she wrote, "are an appeal from the seen to the unseen; a plea for reasonable optimism at this time when bewilderment and pain overshadow our sense of the upward progress of Man."

LYCOSA, THE SPIDER

Hannah, offering her first-born
To her smiling Lord!—
So, this tiny toiling creature
In accord,
Offering many a little one
To the smiling Sun!

Hannah's faith was great—
O, come and see
This golden act—
This fealty!
Hannah could no more
For the boy she bore.

229

What great Lady
Could do so much?
With hidden face
But faithful clutch,
Holding her bag of eggs,
She begs.

With what patience
And conjuring skill,
She turns the tiny ball
At her will,
To the smiling Sun,
The bag she spun.

Hannah in the Temple,
Lycosa on the stones,
All their concern
For the little ones—
What more can be done
For Lord or Sun?

THE PRAYING-MANTIS

In the dark dungeons of the mind,
Strange creatures walk and breed their kind;
　　The Mantis mounts the stair,
　　With movements free as air.

The Praying-Mantis mounts the stair,
Her tiny arms upheld in prayer.
　　In chasuble and stole,
　　She stands to read my soul.

I know not what dark thing is there,
Nor why my soul must feel despair,
　　Nor why she turns away
　　And bids the Mantis slay.

In the deep dungeons of the mind,
Strange creatures walk and breed their kind;
　　With arms upheld in prayer
　　The Mantis mounts the stair.

TOM MacINNES (1867——)

THE son of the late Honorable T. R. McInnes, M.D., a senator and later a lieutenant-governor of British Columbia, Thomas Robert Edward MacInnes was born at Dresden, Ontario, in 1867 and educated at the University of Toronto, from which he was graduated in 1889. He was called to the bar in 1893.

MacInnes has served on many important commissions on the Pacific Coast. In 1896 he was secretary of the Behring Sea Claims Commission and the following years was a member of the police and customs force at Skagway in the Yukon. From 1898 to 1900 he was private secretary to his father. In 1901 he was secretary to the British Columbia Salmon Fisheries Commission. The Dominion government commissioned him in 1907 to prepare a confidential report on anti-oriental riots in British Columbia and two years later to report on Indian title to land in Canada. In 1910 he helped draw up the Canadian Immigration Act, the Anti-opium Act, and the Dominion Northwest Water Power Regulations. MacInnes lived for some time in China and is said to have been instrumental in having the old wall around the city of Canton taken down to make a road-bed for modern traffic. He now lives near Vancouver.

Tom MacInnes (he restored the family name to its original spelling) has published six books of poetry: *Lonesome Bar and Other Poems* (1909); *In Amber Lands* (1910); *The Rhymes of a Rounder* (1913); *The Fool of Joy* (1918); *Complete Poems* (1923); and *High Low Along* (1934).

AMBER LANDS

I

In a luminous valley once I awoke
    To the amber sound of lutes;
And I ate of the bread of a sylvan folk,
With elvish herbs and savory roots,
    And I drank of the innocent wines

231

Made by their maidens from mandarin fruits
Pluckt from low-lying luxurious vines
    In the somnolent heart of the valley.

And the sylvan folk have a simple creed:
To make with their hands whatever they need,
    And to live and be kind in the Sun:
To be one with the good brown Earth, and eat
Good things the Sun hath shone upon
    Till they be ripe and sweet:
And watch the flocks meanwhile that feed
    In the blue up-lands of the valley.

And aptly enough they sow and spin
In manner of antique industry,
And metals they mould and various glass
    And motley pottery,
Taught by priests of a gentle class
    In league with pale high Powers,
For whom they have builded singular towers
    In a grove of cypress trees,—
Towers of granite and bronze, wherein
Magic they make and medicine,
Or busied with their dim auguries
The hollows of space and cycles immense
They measure with intricate instruments.

But I mind how more it pleasur'd me
In the drowsy grass for hours and hours
To lie with the faintly conscious flowers,
    Far up on the slope of the valley;
Or run with the younger sylvan folk,
    So handsome and sturdy they be,
At play in a forest of maple and oak,
    A-romping healthily—
A-romping unkempt and all at their ease,
And kindly under the kindly trees
Doing whatever and ever they please
Consistent with courtesy.

O in youth I sail'd unusual seas,
And still I recall me lands like these,
Where they do whatever they please, dear Lord,
    Whatever and ever they please!

II

Roaming I met the gentle maid
Whom forest-folk and hunters call
The Chatelaine of Ronzival.
'Twas under a cliff in the everglade
Where the icy waters bubble forth;
In velvet green was she array'd
After the fashion of the North:
O gentle maid, for thy heart's ease
Venture with me far over the seas!

There is a room in Ronzival
Rich with bronze, and panell'd all
    In oak grown dull with time:
About the lancet windows there
    Masses of ivy climb:
And some few roses, fair, O fair,
Wave in the Northern summer air!

The Sun was sinking thro' the pines,
While I was guest of the Chatelaine;
Ruddily in slanting lines
Thro' each lancet window-pane
It lit the panell'd inner wall
Of that room in Ronzival,
With its bronze and quaint designs
And stilted things armorial:
O gentle maid, for thy heart's ease,
Venture with me far over the seas!

At table by a window-seat
The gentle maid sat long with me,
And shyly of her courtesy
    She bade me drink and eat;
Out of a hammer'd silver dish
She chose me cakes and comfits fine,
From a flagon twisted dragonish
    She pour'd me amber wine.

O gentle maid, our game is play'd,
The dragon is calling, calling!—
While over the cliffs in the everglade
    The lonely waters falling
Blanch at the sound, and shiver afraid,—
    Aye, 'tis the dragon calling!

With chilling breath and bitter rime
Cometh soon the winter-time:
Ah, see how she hath grown so frail,
Her form so slight, her face so pale!
I fear the gnomes of Niffelheim
    Will take her craftily,
And in a vault with marble stay'd,
Where long-forgotten saints have pray'd,
Her delicate body will be laid,
    Cover'd with greenery:
While down the ragged silver steep
Where the gnomish waters creep
Somnolent, sonorous, deep,
    With her ancient friends
Lost to thee her soul shall sleep
    Till the legend ends!
Nay, gentle maid, for thy heart's ease,
Venture with me far over the seas,
And we shall go free of their wizard hands,
Away and away in the amber lands!

ZALINKA

1

Last night in a land of triangles,
    I lay in a cubicle, where
A girl in pyjamas and bangles
    Slept with her hands in my hair.

2

I wondered if either or neither
    Of us were properly there,
Being subject to queer aberrations—
Astral and thin aberrations—
    Which leave me no base to compare:
    No adequate base to compare:
But her hands, with their wristful of bangles,
    Were certainly fast in my hair,
While the moon made pallid equations
    Thro' a delicate window there.

3

I was glad that she slept for I never
    Can tell what the finish will be:

What enamoured, nocturnal endeavor
    May end in the killing of me:
But, in the moonlit obscure
    Of that silken, somniferous lair,
Like a poet consumed with a far lust
    Of things unapproachably fair
I fancied her body of stardust—
Pounded of spices and stardust—
    Out of the opulent air.

4

Then the moon, with its pale liquidations,
    Fell across her in argentine bars,
And I thought: This is fine—but to-morrow
    What cut of Dawn's cold scimitars
Will sever my hold on this creature—
    I mean of this creature on me?
Amorous creature of exquisite aura—
    Marvel of dark glamourie.

5

What joy of folly then followed
    Is beyond my expression in rhyme:
And I do not expect you to grasp it
    When I speak of expansions of time:
Of reaching and zooming serenely
    As it were at right angles to time:
Knowing well you will think, on your level,
    This was only a dream indiscreet—
    Or experience quite indiscreet:
But little I care, in this instance,
    What you do or do not think discreet:
    O utterance futile, but sweet,
    Like a parrot I pause and repeat,
In delight of my own, and for nothing,
    To myself I repeat and repeat:

6

Last night in a land of triangles,
    I lay in a cubicle where
A girl in pyjamas and bangles
    Slept with her hands in my hair.

TO WALT WHITMAN

1

Hello there, Walt!
Out of sight on the old Highway
I hear your song:
I hear the words that you have said for me:
I, a sayer of words, sing out hello to you:
And you are not so very far ahead but you will hear
    my words also.

2

Words, Walt, words!
Your words, anybody's words, and the words of the
    rolling worlds!
But under all the one Word never uttered.

3

O comrade mine!
Accepting all, eager for all, taking no denial!
Good-will shines in you, through you, from you,
Splendid as the sun!

4

O eagle-eyed! O Titan-heart!
I look with you to the heights of old philosophies:
Looking above and beyond them, shouting ahoy
To wonders weaving out of Wonder endless in the still
    Eterne!

5

But mostly, Walt,
I watch you saunter down with huge, rejoicing tread,
Tramping America:
Noting New York and its enormity:
Swinging an axe in the Oregon forests:
Bellowing songs to the sea.

6

Your catalogs I read unedified:
Your lines that lumber humorless as Jewish genealogy:

Your divine average is not divine:
And for all your rant and brag about your States,
    who cares?
But the coming of the lilacs, Walt,
And the call of mating birds,
And the smell of June, with its berries,
And the feel of the harvest air,
And supple-bodied youth, and clean red blood, and
    the ripe, white quiver of the grown girl's breast,
And all the easy, common joys of life to be had for the
    asking,
The beautiful, bountiful flow of things in every land:
Simple, copious, unrestrained forever:
The sky and the stars and the winds of God, and the
    lovely faces behind the masque of Death:—
For chanting these my hat goes off to you,
Old stalwart out of days primeval,
Earth-born and generous!

7

Down South:
And the tide is coming in:
I watch you fishing from the edge of the old dock:
And a darky sitting by you in the sunshine:
I listen to your lazy chat:
Careless there, happy, smoking a corn-cob pipe:
Blowing blue incense up to the round blue sky:
Breathing the absolute now.

8

O but the Ocean played great tunes for you in octaves
    run too deep
For your dull-eared compatriots to hear!

9

I tell you, Walt,
The world lies sick for want of men like you!
Resistant, unconforming, singular,
Against the moulding and compression of the average:
Against the drag to the level, and the blatherskite
    commune.

10

Here's to you, Walt!
To you, and all good tramps of Adam following!
Singing at sun-up through the morning air,
Free of all stifling unions,
Striking the trail of the great companions,
Forever on their own!

THE TIGER OF DESIRE

Villanelle

Starving, savage, I aspire
    To the red meat of all the World:
I am the Tiger of Desire!

With teeth bared, and claws uncurled,
    By leave o' God I creep to slay
The innocent of all the World.

Out of the yellow, glaring day,
    When I glut my appetite,
To my lair I slink away.

But in the black, returning night
    I leap resistless on my prey,
Mad with agony and fright.

The quick flesh I tear away,
    Writhing till the blood is hurled
On leaf and flower and sodden clay.

My teeth are bared, my claws uncurled,
    Of the red meat I never tire;
In the black jungle of the World
    I am the Tiger of Desire!

FRANCIS SHERMAN (1871–1926)

FRANCIS SHERMAN was born in Fredericton, New Brunswick, and was educated at the collegiate school there, where he came under the influence of the famous schoolmaster, George R. Parkin, and at the University of New Brunswick. As a young man he was well acquainted with Charles G. D. Roberts, Theodore Goodridge Roberts, and Bliss Carman, and something of the spirit of Roberts and Carman is found in his poetry. It was the peculiar sensibility and precise technique of the Pre-Raphaelite school and particularly of his acknowledged master, William Morris, that played the most important part in shaping his style. Sherman's verse, which is not great in quantity but distinguished in quality, was published in the following little books and brochures: *Matins* (1896); *In Memorabilia Mortis* (1896), six sonnets in memory of William Morris; *A Prelude* (1897); *The Deserted City* (1899); and *A Canadian Calendar: XII Lyrics* (1900). All these but the first were privately printed in limited editions, and all but the last were published in Boston or Cambridge; *A Canadian Calendar* was published in Havana.

Sherman had a distinguished career as a banker, and in 1899 he was transferred to Havana, where he performed a useful service to Canadian business. In 1915 he enlisted as a private and won his commission in France. He died in 1926. With the publication in 1935 of *The Complete Poems of Francis Sherman*, edited with a Memoir by Lorne Pierce and a Foreword by Sir Charles G. D. Roberts, Sherman's position in Canadian letters was secure. He stands with Marjorie Pickthall as the best Canadian representative of certain aspects of late-nineteenth-century romanticism—she of Celtic mysticism, and he of Pre-Raphaelite sensibility. In addition to the two valuable introductory articles in the *Complete Poems*, R. H. Hathaway's "Francis Sherman: Canadian Poet," in *Willison's Monthly*, March, 1927, and Lorne Pierce's *Three Fredericton Poets* (1933)—Roberts, Carman, and Sherman—offer some useful information and criticism, though the criticism is mainly appreciative.

THE FOREIGNER

He walked by me with open eyes,
And wondered that I loved it so;
Above us stretched the gray, gray skies;
Behind us, footprints on the snow.

Before us slept a dark, dark wood.
Hemlocks were there, and little pines
Also; and solemn cedars stood
In even and uneven lines.

The branches of each silent tree
Bent downward, for the snow's hard weight
Was pressing on them heavily;
They had not known the sun of late.

(Except when it was afternoon,
And then a sickly sun peered in
A little while; it vanished soon
And then they were as they had been.)

There was no sound (I thought I heard
The axe of some man far away)
There was no sound of bee, or bird,
Or chattering squirrel at its play.

And so he wondered I was glad.
—There was one thing he could not see;
Beneath the look these dead things had
I saw Spring eyes agaze at me.

BETWEEN THE BATTLES

Let us bury him here,
Where the maples are red!
He is dead,
And he died thanking God that he fell with
    the fall of the leaf and the year.

Where the hillside is sheer,
Let it echo our tread
Whom he led;
Let us follow as gladly as ever we followed
    who never knew fear.

Ere he died, they had fled;
Yet they heard his last cheer
Ringing clear,—
When we lifted him up, he would fain have
  pursued, but grew dizzy instead.

Break his sword and his spear!
Let this last prayer be said
By the bed
We have made underneath the wet wind in the
  maple trees moaning so drear:

"O Lord God, by the red
Sullen end of the year
That is here,
We beseech Thee to guide us and strengthen
  our swords till his slayers be dead!"

JOHN McCRAE (1872–1918)

APPEARING anonymously in *Punch* on December 8, 1915, "In Flanders Fields" caught the mood of dedication and determination which a few English soldier-poets, notably Rupert Brooke and Herbert Asquith, had expressed in the first years of the Great War, and became, after Brooke's "1914," the most famous of all British poems of patriotism and sacrifice. Its sureness of feeling and freedom from complexity is in marked contrast to the bitterness, pity, and conflicting ironies of the later war poems of Siegfried Sassoon and Wilfred Owen or to the disillusioned complexities of some of the poetry of the second World War.

John McCrae was born in 1872 in Guelph, Ontario, and was educated at the University of Toronto, where he had a distinguished career in general science and later in medicine. He was attached to the staff of McGill University and the Royal Victoria Hospital, Montreal. When the war broke out, he joined the Royal Army Medical Corps and proceeded overseas. He served with great distinction in France until his death from pneumonia in January, 1918.

In the same year a selection of McCrae's verses was edited with a Memoir by the poet's friend, Sir Andrew Macphail. It consisted of only twenty-nine brief poems, but their formal perfection and strength of feeling assure them an honored place in Canadian literature.

IN FLANDERS FIELDS

In Flanders fields the poppies blow
Between the crosses, row on row,
   That mark our place; and in the sky
   The larks, still bravely singing, fly
Scarce heard amid the guns below.

We are the Dead. Short days ago
We lived, felt dawn, saw sunset glow,
   Loved and were loved, and now we lie,
     In Flanders fields.

Take up our quarrel with the foe:
To you from failing hands we throw
  The torch; be yours to hold it high.
  If ye break faith with us who die
We shall not sleep, though poppies grow
  In Flanders fields.

THE DYING OF PÈRE PIERRE

  ". . . . with two other priests; the same night he died, and was buried by the shores of the lake that bears his name."—CHRONICLE

"Nay, grieve not that ye can no honour give
  To these poor bones that presently must be
But carrion; since I have sought to live
  Upon God's earth, as He hath guided me,
I shall not lack! Where would ye have me lie?
  High heaven is higher than cathedral nave:
Do men paint chancels fairer than the sky?"
  Beside the darkened lake they made his grave,
Below the altar of the hills; and night
  Swung incense clouds of mist in creeping lines
That twisted through the tree-trunks, where the light
  Groped through the arches of the silent pines:
And he, beside the lonely path he trod,
Lay, tombed in splendour, in the House of God.

J. E. H. MacDONALD
(1873 – 1932)

BORN in Durham, England, in 1873, J. E. H. MacDonald was one of the leading modern painters of Canada, a member of the well-known "Group of Seven," and principal of the Ontario College of Art. He died in 1932, and the following year his poems, many of which had appeared in the *Canadian Forum*, were published in a volume entitled *West by East. J. E. H. MacDonald: A Biography and Catalogue of His Work*, by E. R. Hunter, appeared in 1940.

THE HANGING

*"It has been decided that the law must be
allowed to take its course."*—DAILY PAPER

THE LAW SPEAKS:

*I bind the Soul that fathered me;
I am the Law, and resolute
Against the growing of the Soul,
I hang, behead, electrocute.*

I take my course. How fine the day!
And all are here by duty stirred,
Hangman and prisoner, warden and press,
And Jesus with the Holy Word.

I am the Law. May order rule!
My warrant let the warden read,
Then all with proper decency
Will to our lifted stage proceed.

How fine the day! The happy sun
Beams into corridor and square
To cheer our prisoner and bless
The purpose of our altar there.

Our footsteps on the sunny stones
Beat to the pulse of earth and star;
The law that drives yon budding tree
Condemned our prisoner at its bar.

Let Jesus hold his trembling arm
And stand beside him to the end
(He loves these opportunities
To function as experienced friend).

Now, hangman, use your cunning well,
And hide his face that none may see
The anguish of his tortured soul.
I take my course, let these things be.

Come, Jesus, speak your little prayer
And, when "Deliver us" is said,
Then, hangman, draw the gliding bolt
And give our brother air to tread.

"Our Father," sound the gracious words,
"Thy will be done"—and all the rest—
(I hope our poor delivered friend
Had time to note the subtle jest).

He shoots into the opened dark,
His soul is torn through narrow ways.
I take my course. I only see
A straightened rope that trembling sways.

I bind the Soul that fathered me;
I am the Law, and resolute
Against the growing of the Soul,
I hang, behead, electrocute.

GEORGE HERBERT CLARKE
(1873———)

PROFESSOR CLARKE, until his retirement in 1943, was head of the English department at Queen's University and is an editor of the *Queen's Quarterly*. He was born in England in 1873 and was educated in Canada at Woodstock College and McMaster University. He is the author of *The Hasting Day* (1930) and *Halt and Parley* (1934). The title poem of the latter volume won acclaim when it appeared in the *Atlantic Monthly*. It is a good example of this poet's elegant traditionalism and of the search for spiritual values that informs his best verse.

Professor Clarke is the compiler of two anthologies of war poetry, one devoted to World War I and the recent *New Treasury of War Poetry* (1943).

HALT AND PARLEY

Good Toll-Gate keeper, kindle a light!
The Sun has fallen: full sudden the Night:
(He seemeth some ancient anchorite
Who broodeth, and heedeth us not.)

              He heeds.

Stay by the Gate and tell your needs!
Sir, we would learn the lawful toll.
How many travellers?

              Body and Soul.

How long have you journeyed together thus?
All Day, and nothing shall sunder us.

How have you fared? Was the roadway rough?
Some miles were stony and steep enough.

But why have you toiled and suffered so?
And whither is it that you would go?

246

Our goal is a vision that vanisheth.
To pause is to perish: devouring Death
Would slow our pulses and choke our breath . . . .

Tollman, teach us your name! A sage
Are you, acquaint with our pilgrimage?

No sage, yet mayhap wiser than Man,
Torn with a doubt since Time began:
Man the afraid, infirm, impure!
Yet how he can love and how endure,—
Endure to the end and arise again,
Victorious victim of passion and pain . . . .

Motley the breed that mount to my Gate:
They fear their fate, yet they face their fate.
Of Radiant Heat and Primal Slime
Engendered, hither they creep and climb,—
Ether and earth, perverse, sublime! . . . .

The Ongoer made me His Deputy here:
Who payeth may pass, though he reckon it dear,—
His quittance from clumsy, cumbering gear.

You are Death?

                 I am Death, Devourer and Foe
Or Friend and Deliverer: how may ye know? . . . .

Slowly the Gate swings for entrance—and end:
The shrouded way waits, unposted, unkenned;
Time's phantasies fade: the Reals impend . . . .

Let the toll be taken!

                 Nay, gallantly dare
The dark passage, Soul! Body's paid the full fare—
Poor clod—while you've parried and parleyed out there.

ARTHUR STRINGER (1874——)

ARTHUR STRINGER was born in 1874 in London, Ontario, and educated at the collegiate institute there and at the University of Toronto. After a year at Oxford he became a journalist, at first on the *Montreal Herald* and later with the American Press. In 1901 he gave up his regular position, living for a time on a fruit farm in Ontario and for a time on the wheat-growing plains of Alberta. He traveled extensively in southern Europe and the Mediterranean. He has published *Watchers of Twilight* (1894); *Pauline and Other Poems* (1895); *Epigrams* (1896); *The Woman in the Rain and Other Poems* (1907), his best book; *Irish Poems* (1911); and, more recently, *The Old Woman Remembers and Other Irish Poems* (1938). He has also published many popular novels and one important contribution to the development of realism in the Canadian novel, his trilogy of farm life in the West: *The Prairie Wife* (1916), *The Prairie Mother* (1919), and *The Prairie Child* (1921).

A useful study of Arthur Stringer by Victor Lauriston was published in the "Makers of Canadian Literature Series" in 1941. It contains a complete bibliography.

THE KNIGHT ERRANT

He rode at dusk down woodlands strange,
　　Where stood all bathed in fire
A great dark Tower whose shadow gloomed
　　The Valley of Desire.

Alluring glowed that sun-lit Tower,
　　But dark the way, and long;
And where the walls seemed pearl and gold
　　The gates stood doubly strong.

Life lay with all its wrongs to right,
　　And all its deeds undone;

Earth held full many a height to storm,
But he must take this one.

We knew that castle of delight
Was death to him who knocks,
Where roses screened the granite walls
And lilies hid the locks.

We told him how ten thousand men
Had failed and fallen there
"Her eyes," he sang, "are like the stars;
Like ripened wheat her hair!"

We laughed our laugh, for we ourselves
Of old had heard these things.
But hearkens he to any man,
The youth who fights and sings!

He, watching there each casement dark,
By dawn and dreary dusk,
Lay siege unto those mystic walls
Of lily, rose, and musk;

And saw by night, from turrets dim,
Some dubious signal start;
—*We* knew each sign, we who had sought
The fortress of her heart—.

In loneliness and gloom and cold
His hungry youth went past.
"Lo, all ye tribe of Puny Things,
How one great love can last!"

The pitying stars shone over him:
Still flamed his sword on high.
"Her mouth," he sang, "is like the rose,
And white her soul, say I!"

But lo, he beat the dark gates down,
And there his fortress lay
Four lonely walls wherein all life
Had fallen to decay.

Each old retainer, night by night,
In silence crept from her;
And one by one her vassals died,
For all her musk and myrrh.

Starved aspirations, hopes, regrets,
    From her white body stole,
And left her there a woman dead,
    And with an empty soul.

Four walls, she stood, from whence the last
    Embattled rose had blown;
"I yield," she gasped, with goodly art,
    "Take all that is your own!"

Beside that castle grim he wept—
    We heard him in our sleep—
" 'Tis not, O God, the life I gave,
    And the tares that I must reap.

"Of battered, not of rusting swords
    Thy knights, I know, are made;—
Oh, 'tis not, God, that in this fight
    You broke me as a blade!

"But ah, so empty lies this thing,
    Why barred she not each door
And sent me singing through the Dusk
    Of my grey Dreams once more!"

She laughed her laugh, and swept the blood
    From off her granite stair,
For down the wood a strange youth sang:
    "Like golden sheaves her hair!"

The pitying stars shone over him,
    He shook his sword on high.
"Her mouth," he sang in turn, "is red,
    But white her soul, say I!"

WAR

From hill to hill he harried me;
    He stalked me day and night;
He neither knew nor hated me;
    Nor his nor mine the fight.

He killed the man who stood by me,
    For such they made his law;
Then foot by foot I fought to him,
    Who neither knew nor saw.

I trained my rifle on his heart;
  He leapt up in the air.
The screaming ball tore through his breast,
  And lay embedded there.

Lay hot embedded there, and yet
  Hissed home o'er hill and sea
Straight to the aching heart of one
  Who'd wronged not mine nor me!

SOUR WINE

I met the wife who'd left me bed,
  The wife I'd loved so true,
Wid a faded shawl on her ould head
  And a scowl that'd stab ye through.

She eased her barrow of turf and stood
  Wide-beamed in her rain-soaked clogs—
Yet wanst we'd kissed as lovers could,
  And then fought like cats and dogs!

"You're lookin' your worst, you mangy cur,"
  Says she, the damned ould cat.
"May you blister in hell," I answered her
  And let it go at that.

ROBERT W. SERVICE (1876———)

BORN in Lancashire, England, in 1876 and educated in Scotland at the University of Glasgow, Robert W. Service came to Canada as a young man. For five years he wandered back and forth along the Pacific Coast, working at various jobs from the Far North to as far south as Mexico. Later he served as a bank clerk in British Columbia and the Yukon. He worked as a war correspondent for the *Toronto Star* during the Balkan War of 1912–13 and the first World War and then for two years was an ambulance driver in France.

Service is the author of the following books of verse: *Songs of a Sourdough* (1907), *Ballads of a Cheechako* (1909), *Rhymes of a Rolling Stone* (1912), *Rhymes of a Red Cross Man* (1916), *Ballads of a Bohemian* (1921), and *Bar-Room Ballads* (1940). *The Complete Poems of Robert Service* was published in 1941.

THE SHOOTING OF DAN McGREW

A bunch of the boys were whooping it up in the Malamute saloon;
The kid that handles the music-box was hitting a jag-time tune;
Back of the bar, in a solo game, sat Dangerous Dan McGrew,
And watching his luck was his light-o'-love, the lady that's known as Lou.

When out of the night, which was fifty below, and into the din and the glare,
There stumbled a miner fresh from the creeks, dog-dirty, and loaded for bear.
He looked like a man with a foot in the grave and scarcely the strength of a louse,
Yet he tilted a poke of dust on the bar, and he called for drinks for the house.
There was none could place the stranger's face, though we searched ourselves for a clue;

252

But we drank his health, and the last to drink was Dangerous Dan
McGrew.

There's men that somehow just grip your eyes, and hold them
hard like a spell;
And such was he, and he looked to me like a man who had lived
in hell;
With a face most hair, and the dreary stare of a dog whose day is
done,
As he watered the green stuff in his glass, and the drops fell one by
one.
Then I got to figgering who he was, and wondering what he'd do,
And I turned my head—and there watching him was the lady that's
known as Lou.

His eyes went rubbering round the room, and he seemed in a kind
of daze,
Till at last that old piano fell in the way of his wandering gaze.
The rag-time kid was having a drink; there was no one else on the
stool,
So the stranger stumbles across the room, and flops down there
like a fool.
In a buckskin shirt that was glazed with dirt he sat, and I saw
him sway;
Then he clutched the keys with his talon hands—my God! but
that man could play.

Were you ever out in the Great Alone, when the moon was awful
clear,
And the icy mountains hemmed you in with a silence you most
could *hear;*
With only the howl of a timber wolf, and you camped there in
the cold,
A half-dead thing in a stark, dead world, clean mad for the muck
called gold;
While high overhead, green, yellow and red, the North Lights
swept in bars?—
Then you've a haunch what the music meant . . . . hunger and
night and the stars.

And hunger not of the belly kind, that's banished with bacon
and beans,
But the gnawing hunger of lonely men for a home and all that
it means;

For a fireside far from the cares that are, four walls and a roof
above;
But oh! so cramful of cosy joy, and crowned with a woman's love—
A woman dearer than all the world, and true as Heaven is true—
(God! how ghastly she looks through her rouge,—the lady that's
known as Lou.)

Then on a sudden the music changed, so soft that you scarce could
hear;
But you felt that your life had been looted clean of all that it once
held dear;
That someone had stolen the woman you loved; that her love was a
devil's lie;
That your guts were gone, and the best for you was to crawl away
and die.
'Twas the crowning cry of a heart's despair, and it thrilled you
through and through—
"I guess I'll make it a spread misere," said Dangerous Dan McGrew.

The music almost died away . . . . then it burst like a pent-up
flood;
And it seemed to say, "Repay, repay," and my eyes were blind
with blood.
The thought came back of an ancient wrong, and it stung like a
frozen lash,
And the lust awoke to kill, to kill . . . . then the music stopped with
a crash,
And the stranger turned, and his eyes they burned in a most pe-
culiar way;
In a buckskin shirt that was glazed with dirt he sat, and I saw him
sway;
Then his lips went in in a kind of grin, and he spoke, and his voice
was calm,
And "Boys," says he, "you don't know me, and none of you care
a damn;
But I want to state, and my words are straight, and I'll bet my
poke they're true,
That one of you is a hound of hell . . . . and that one is Dan Mc-
Grew."

Then I ducked my head, and the lights went out, and two guns
blazed in the dark,
And a woman screamed, and the lights went up, and two men lay
stiff and stark.

Pitched on his head, and pumped full of lead, was Dangerous Dan
  McGrew,
While the man from the creeks lay clutched to the breast of the
  lady that's known as Lou.

These are the simple facts of the case, and I guess I ought to know.
They say that the stranger was crazed with "hooch," and I'm not
  denying it's so.
I'm not so wise as the lawyer guys, but strictly between us two—
The woman that kissed him and—pinched his poke—was the lady
  that's known as Lou.

THEODORE GOODRIDGE ROBERTS
(1877——)

A YOUNGER brother of C. G. D. Roberts, Theodore Goodridge
Roberts was born in Fredericton, New Brunswick, in 1877. He
was educated at the Fredericton Collegiate School and for a time at
the University of New Brunswick. He has had a varied career as
journalist, war correspondent, and novelist in Canada, the West
Indies, England, and France. He served as a captain at the front
during World War I and was appointed an official government
correspondent. He has written a number of novels and romances
of adventure. His poetry was collected in 1934 in a modest volume
entitled *The Leather Bottle*. The two poems included here are representative of the vivid imagery and perfection of form ("The Blue
Heron") and the human interest and romance ("The Lost Ship-
mate") characteristic of his best verse.

THE LOST SHIPMATE

Somewhere he failed me, somewhere he slipped away—
Youth, in his ignorant faith and his bright array.
The tides go out; the tides come flooding in;
Still the old years die and the new begin;
But Youth?—
Somewhere we lost each other, last year or yesterday.

Somewhere he failed me. Down at the harbour-side
I waited for him a-little, where the anchored argosies ride.
I thought he came—the steady "trade" blew free—
I thought he came—'twas but the shadow of me!
And Youth?—
Somewhere he turned and left me, about the turn of the tide.

Perhaps I shall find him. It may be he waits for me,
Sipping those wines we knew, beside some tropic sea;

256

The tides still serve, and I am out and away
To search the spicy harbours of yesterday
For Youth,
Where the lamps of the town are yellow beyond the lamps
   on the quay.

Somewhere he failed me, somewhere he slipped away—
Youth, in his ignorant heart and his bright array.
Was it in Bados? God, I would pay to know!
Was it on Spanish Hill, where the roses blow?
Ah, Youth!
Shall I hear your laughter to-morrow, in painted Olivio?

Somewhere I failed him. Somewhere I let him depart—
Youth, who would only sleep for the morn's fresh start.
The tides slipped out, the tides washed out and in,
And Youth and I rejoiced in their wastrel din.
Ah, Youth!
Shall I find you south of the Gulf?—or are you dead in my
   heart?

THE BLUE HERON

In a green place lanced through
With amber and gold and blue;
A place of water and weeds
And roses pinker than dawn,
And ranks of lush young reeds,
And grasses straightly withdrawn
From graven ripples of sands,
The still blue heron stands.

Smoke-blue he is, and grey
As embers of yesterday.
Still he is, as death;
Like stone, or shadow of stone,
Without a pulse or breath,
Motionless and alone
There in the lily stems:
But his eyes are alive like gems.

Still as a shadow; still
Grey feather and yellow bill:
Still as an image made
Of mist and smoke half hid
By windless sunshine and shade,
Save when a yellow lid
Slides and is gone like a breath:
Death-still—and sudden as death!

KATHERINE HALE

KATHERINE HALE (Mrs. John Garvin) was born in Galt, Ontario, and educated there and in private schools in Toronto. She studied singing in New York and wrote musical and literary criticism for the *Toronto Mail and Empire*. She has lectured widely on Canadian literature and has given readings and folk-song recitals in the United States and England as well as in Canada. She has been a leader in the activities of women's clubs in Toronto and in the Canadian Authors' Association. In addition to several volumes of verse, of which the best are *Morning in the West* (1923) and *The Island and Other Poems* (1934), she has published *Canadian Cities of Romance* (1922), *Legends of the St. Lawrence* (1925), and a study of Isabella Valancy Crawford in the "Makers of Canadian Literature Series."

NORTHERN GRAVEYARDS

Stony fields and lonely roads,
　　Meagre hamlets, very lean,
And most prosperous graveyards
　　Lying all between.

Each few miles a graveyard,
　　With its crouching column
And its urns and headstones,
　　Very dark and solemn.

But with what an accent!
　　Yellow, purple, red,
Lie the votive offerings
　　To this public dead.

Close beside the railway,
　　Where the smoke drifts high,
These are decked in garlands
　　For the passerby.

Even in the winter,
    Breaking through the snow
Immortelles beguile us,
    When the train runs slow.

They are strangely cheerful,
    All these plots of ground
That have lost the loneliness
    Of the living. Here abound

In a comradeship increasing
    Those who in their hour
Reaped a dreary harvest,
    Missed a magic flower.

Over them the smoke-wreaths,
    Snow, and whispering grass,
And the voice of neighbours,
    Sighing as they pass;

While the urns of iron
    And the barbarous vases
Chant a willing ritual
    To forgotten faces.

So they sleep together,
    And their shades may say:
"Wave to us, O restless traveller!
    We are glad to stay."

LOUISE MOREY BOWMAN
(1 8 8 2———)

MRS. BOWMAN was born in 1882 in Sherbrooke, Quebec, of Puritan New England stock, and was educated privately and at Dana Hall, Wellesley, Massachusetts. She is the best representative in Canadian letters of the school of feminine imagists which flourished in the twenties under the aegis of Amy Lowell. Her poems were published in a number of the best American literary periodicals and won the admiration of Miss Lowell and Harriet Monroe, the founder of *Poetry*. She is the author of three books of verse: *Moonlight and Common Day* (1922); *Dream Tapestries* (1924), which was given the David Prize by the Quebec government for the best poetry of the year; and *Characters in Cadence* (1938). The virtues of Mrs. Bowman's poems are the clarity of the images they present and the sensitiveness of the impressionism. But the emotion is diffuse rather than concentrated—and often somewhat self-consciously that of a lady, though of a lady sensitive, refined, and subtle in her appreciation of the aesthetic patterns to be discerned in flowers, gardens, drawing-rooms, and people.

SEA LAVENDER

My Puritan Grandmother!—I see her now,
With placid brow,
Always so sure
That no things but the right things shall endure!
Sombrely neat, so orderly and prim,
Always a little grim,
Austere but kind . . . .
Smooth-banded hair and smoothly-banded mind.

But let me whisper it to you to-day—
I know it now—
That deep in her there was a flame at play.
Beneath that brow

The blue-grey eyes sought beauty, found it too
Most often by the ocean's passionate blue.
Her sea-beach treasures—shells and coloured weed
Gathered and hoarded with glad human greed—
They warm my heart to-day with insight new.
How vividly I see her, frail and old,
A tiny, black-clothed figure on the beach,
Compactly wrapped against the sea-wind's cold,
Patiently waiting till waves let her reach
Some sandy strip, where purple, amber, green,
Her lacy sea-weed treasures could be seen.
(She pressed and mounted them—frail tangled things!
Handled by her, fit to trim fairies' wings.)

So I recall her,
Searching salt-sea pools
For Beauty's shadow.
All her rigid rules,
And cold austereness with a storm-tossed child,
Melt into airs of evenings, warm and mild.
And I find revelation, sweet indeed,
In her dear treasures of sea shells and weed.

MARJORIE PICKTHALL
(1883–1922)

VARIOUS aspects of the aesthetic movement of the eighties and nineties—the eroticism of Rossetti, the mysticism of Francis Thompson, the sterile passion of Ernest Dowson, and the activism of Kipling—were reflected in curious combinations in the poetry of C. G. D. Roberts and Bliss Carman. Another literary movement near the turn of the century was the "Celtic Twilight"—the impingement of aestheticism upon the romantic material lying dormant in the folk tales and legends of ancient Ireland and in the Irish temperament itself. The early poetry of W. B. Yeats, the stories and poems of Fiona MacLeod, and some of Masefield's sea ballads were the instruments through which this movement entered into Canadian poetry in the work of a talented young woman, Marjorie L. C. Pickthall, author of *The Drift of Pinions* (1913); *The Lamp of Poor Souls* (1917); *The Woodcarver's Wife and Other Poems* (1922), with an Introduction by Isabel Ecclestone Mackay; and *Complete Poems* (1936).

Marjorie Pickthall was born in London, England, in 1883 and was brought by her parents to Canada when she was seven years old. She was educated at Bishop Strachan School, Toronto. While still in her teens she began contributing poems and short stories to some of the leading periodicals in Canada, England, and the United States. Her work came to the attention of Dr. Pelham Edgar, Dr. Lorne Pierce, and Sir Andrew MacPhail, who in 1913 arranged for the publication of her first book. She served for a time as a librarian in Victoria College, Toronto. Visiting in England when the first World War broke out, she remained there to undertake war work. She returned to Canada in 1920, making her home in Vancouver until her untimely death in 1922. In addition to her poems, she also wrote *The Bridge* (1921), a novel, and *Angel's Shoes* (1923), short stories.

The poetry of Marjorie Pickthall is romantic and literary. From Celtic mythology, as rediscovered by poets of the Irish Renaissance, and the medievalism of William Morris she created a dream world of ineffable beauty into which the imagination escapes from the world

263

of limited opportunities and sordid values. That this was a dramatization of her own life's experience accounts for the unmistakable note of sincerity heard in her work—and perhaps for its technical excellence. E. K. Brown has listed the qualities of her art as "fine observation of nature, pious meditation, Celtic mistiness, fevered patriotism, [and] psychological analysis," yet in spite of their rather mixed nature they add up to the presentation of a personality of charm and integrity. The poems have an intensity and mastery that lift them above the level of ordinary romantic feminine verse.

The best modern study of Marjorie Pickthall is the essay "Dream Gardens" in Mr. W. E. Collin's *The White Savannahs*, and a more personal appreciation will be found in Lorne Pierce's *Marjorie Pickthall: A Book of Remembrance*.

THE BRIDEGROOM OF CANA

"There was a marriage in Cana of Galilee. . . . . And both Jesus was called and His disciples, to the marriage."

Veil thine eyes, O belovéd, my spouse,
Turn them away,
Lest in their light my life withdrawn
Dies as a star, as a star in the day,
As a dream in the dawn.

Slenderly hang the olive leaves
Sighing apart;
The rose-and-silver doves in the eaves
With a murmur of music bind our house.
Honey and wine in thy words are stored,
Thy lips are bright as the edge of a sword
That hath found my heart,
That hath found my heart.

Sweet, I have waked from a dream of thee,—
And of Him:
He who came when the songs were done.
From the net of thy smiles my heart went free
And the golden lure of thy love grew dim.
I turned to them asking, "Who is He,
Royal and sad, who comes to the feast
And sits Him down in the place of the least?"
And they said, "He is Jesus, the carpenter's son."

Hear how my harp on a single string
Murmurs of love.
Down in the fields the thrushes sing
And the lark is lost in the light above,
Lost in the infinite, glowing whole,
As I in thy soul,
As I in thy soul.

Love, I am fain for thy glowing grace
As the pool for the star, as the rain for the rill.
Turn to me, trust to me, mirror me
As the star in the pool, as the cloud in the sea.
Love, I looked awhile in His face
And was still.

The shaft of the dawn strikes clear and sharp;
Hush, my harp.
Hush, my harp, for the day is begun,
And the lifting, shimmering flight of the swallow
Breaks in a curve on the brink of morn,
Over the sycamores, over the corn.
Cling to me, cleave to me, prison me
As the mote in the flame, as the shell in the sea,
For the winds of the dawn say, "Follow, follow
Jesus Bar-Joseph, the carpenter's son."

PÈRE LALEMENT

I lift the Lord on high,
Under the murmuring hemlock boughs, and see
The small birds of the forest lingering by
And making melody.
These are mine acolytes and these my choir,
And this mine altar in the cool green shade,
Where the wild soft-eyed does draw nigh
Wondering, as in the byre
Of Bethlehem the oxen heard Thy cry
And saw Thee, unafraid.

My boatmen sit apart,
Wolf-eyed, wolf-sinewed, stiller than the trees.
Help me, O Lord, for very slow of heart
And hard of faith are these.
Cruel are they, yet Thy children. Foul are they,
Yet wert Thou born to save them utterly.

Then make me as I pray
Just to their hates, kind to their sorrows, wise
After their speech, and strong before their free
Indomitable eyes.

Do the French lilies reign
Over Mont Royal and Stadacona still?
Up the St. Lawrence comes the spring again,
Crowning each southward hill
And blossoming pool with beauty, while I roam
Far from the perilous folds that are my home,
There where we built St. Ignace for our needs,
Shaped the rough roof tree, turned the first sweet sod,
St. Ignace and St. Louis, little beads
On the rosary of God.

Pines shall Thy pillars be,
Fairer than those Sidonian cedars brought
By Hiram out of Tyre, and each birch-tree
Shines like a holy thought.
But come no worshippers; shall I confess,
St. Francis-like, the birds of the wilderness?
O, with Thy love my lonely head uphold.
A wandering shepherd I, who hath no sheep;
A wandering soul, who hath no scrip, nor gold,
Nor anywhere to sleep.

My hour of rest is done;
On the smooth ripple lifts the long canoe;
The hemlocks murmur sadly as the sun
Slants his dim arrows through.
Whither I go I know not, nor the way,
Dark with strange passions, vexed with heathen charms,
Holding I know not what of life or death;
Only be Thou beside me day by day,
Thy rod my guide and comfort, underneath
Thy everlasting arms.

RESURGAM

I shall say, Lord, "Is it music, is it morning,
Song that is fresh as sunrise, light that sings?"
When on some hill there breaks the immortal warning
Of half-forgotten springs.

I shall say, Lord, "I have loved you, not another,
Heard in all quiet your footsteps on my road,
Felt your strong shoulder near me, O my brother,
Lightening the load."

I shall say, Lord, "I remembered, working, sleeping,
One face I looked for, one denied and dear.
Now that you come my eyes are blind with weeping,
But you will kiss them clear."

I shall say, Lord, "Touch my lips, and so unseal them;
I have learned silence since I lived and died."
I shall say, Lord, "Lift my hands, and so reveal them,
Full, satisfied."

I shall say, Lord, "We will laugh again to-morrow,
Now we'll be still a little, friend with friend.
Death was the gate and the long way was sorrow.
Love is the end."

QUIET

Come not the earliest petal here, but only
Wind, cloud, and star,
Lovely and far,
Make it less lonely.

Few are the feet that seek her here, but sleeping
Thoughts sweet as flowers
Linger for hours,
Things winged, yet weeping.

Here in the immortal empire of the grasses,
Time, like one wrong
Note in a song,
With their bloom, passes.

AUDREY ALEXANDRA BROWN
(1904———)

BORN at Nanaimo, British Columbia, in 1904, Audrey Alexandra Brown has been an invalid for the greater part of her life. She has published two books of poetry, *A Dryad in Nanaimo* (1931) and *The Tree of Resurrection and Other Poems* (1937), and an autobiographical work, *The Log of a Lame Duck* (1936).

The quality of Miss Brown's best work has been described by L. A. Mackay (*Canadian Forum*, June, 1932): "Allied with vivid and even luscious description is a strong and delicate poignancy of feeling, a dignified tragic sensitiveness. The merit . . . . lies in the measured and quiet melody of the lines rather than in their force, in the reserved justness, not the surprise, of the expression." She continues the tradition of nineteenth-century romanticism and is a not unworthy successor to Marjorie Pickthall.

THE REED

This is the song of the reed:
It grew by a stream,
In the fair and pleasant land of Arcady:
That land that's bounded by a placid sea,
Stretching away and away for evermore,
Stirred by no oar,
Broken by never a glimpse of golden shore.

The reed was one of many: but it grew tall,
Greener, more slenderly delicate than all:
Lissom and straight,
With a glimmer of morning dew about its stalk;
It heard the timid feet of the oread pass,
Dancing with shadows in the tender grass:
It heard the trees confer in whispered talk,
And the shy sweet throstle sing to his nesting mate
Early and late.

It fell on a noon
With the daisies first in bud, and a broad white moon
Over the hilltop, full in the face of day,
Pan with the cloven foot came by that way:
And the heat was strong on the upper irised meadow,
Tremulous-bright on the tawny-burning grass—
So Pan forbore to pass,
But flung himself down on a twisted alder root,
Half in, half out of shadow.

Down by his side his flute
Slipped unregarded, while as one in a dream
He heard the endless murmur of the stream,
Clear silver, quaintly set with emerald weeds,
Wimpling in drowsy tones among the reeds.
Over the surface of the tranquil river
He saw the mayflies weave their flitting dance,
Retreat, advance:
And through a maze of interwoven stems
He saw the turquoise dragonflies a-quiver,
Like lovely living gems.

Pan listened and beheld, and the blended sound,
The tapestry of color wrapped him round:
He heard the cricket's thin unceasing quarrel,
He heard the wind among the crimson sorrel,
The beat of tiny, half-transparent wings:
And all these things
Slowly and surely, with miraculous art,
Fashioned a web of music in his heart.

He took his pipes and blew:
Dew-clear and honey-sweet the melody grew:
Softly at first: no wind among the reeds
Walks lighter bearing precious violet-seeds
Or silky down from the tall thistleweeds:
Behold, it grew:
Sweeter and clearer, sweeter yet he blew—
And in his strain the listening alders heard
The faint unhurried murmur of the stream
Rapt in its wistful dream:
They heard the note of song the cricket weaves,
They heard the sighing of their own sad leaves
Plaintively stirred:

The rainbow-quiver of the mayfly's wing,
The gnat's shrill trumpeting.

Sweeter and yet more clear:
Lo, as he played the stream was still to hear:
The thoughtful rushes, necklaced round with dew,
Nearer and nearer drew:
In the thin coppice underneath the hill
The cradled wind lay still,
And the shy oread stayed
Her rapid footsteps in the green wild glade,
To listen, unafraid.

About, around,
His pipes wove song from threads of silver sound,
Airily-exquisite, ambrosial-sweet:
Fainter and farther—suddenly blithe and fleet
As chords of elfin laughter lightly flung
On the breathless air when all the world was young:
Tenderer now,
Like the thrush's plaintive note from an empty nest
On the white hawthorn-bough:
And then
Suddenly—suddenly—suddenly high and clear
As the song of marching men:
Suddenly full of exultant wild unrest
Like the bugles blown from a leaguered town at dawn—
The pipes were still, the quaint musician gone.

The reed yet grows by the stream
In the shepherdess-land of pleasant Arcady,
Where the golden river seeks for the shoreless sea,
And the knotted hazels dream.
Pluck it, hollow it, shape it as you will
Into an ivory flute for a poet's blowing—
It has heard the feet of the wind on the purple hill,
It has heard the breath of the dawn in the iris meadow,
The breeze with all its linnets westward going,
And the shy oread singing to her shadow:
But most of all—
Sweetest of all sweet things by stream or shore,
Sweetest of all sweet things since time began,
It has heard the miracle-melodies of Pan,
And it is a reed no more.

It is an instrument for a poet's hand—
And whoso first shall set its music ringing,
He shall awake the drowsy ears of the land,
And all the world shall hearken to his singing!

KING PHILIP'S MEN

. . . . The *Estrella* and the *Rosa de Dios*, flying with the rest of the Armada,
were separated therefrom and driven upon the Orkneys by a great wind that
arose a little ere dusk. . . . . When therefore the captain of the *Rosa de Dios*
perceived that all hope was gone, he called his company together and spoke
to them, saying: "Men of Spain and servants of King Philip, God hath
ordained that from this our voyage there shall be no returning. Wherefore
we will first make our prayer as Christians, and afterward die like men."

> At dusk they heard the roar
>   Of all the ocean hurled
> Upon the iron shore
>   Of half the world.
>
> Through the wan even-gloam
>   With whipped and straining breath
> Blind-eyed across the foam
>   They looked on death.
>
> Then said their captain—"Shriven
>   We drive upon the dawn;
> Turn we to thoughts of heaven,
>   For earth is gone.
>
> "Fair lips that praise our fame—
>   New April in the vine—
> Pomegranate flowers like flame,
>   And golden wine—
>
> "Bird-song and ivory rose—
>   All fruit of all delight,
> God hath ordained shall close
>   For us to-night:
>
> "Ay, and the bitter past,
>   The evil-starred campaign
> End for us here at last,
>   O men of Spain!
>
> "The great red death of day
>   Rushes upon our ships;

Keep courage—we will pray
  With steadfast lips

"That God, who made us men,
  Grant us like men to die:
Then will we rise, and then
  Will lay life by.

"Not with dishonoring fear,
  Though the deep thunder rolls
And the black verge is near,
  Yield we our souls:

"We, who have dared the flood,
  The rapier, and the flame,
Remember that high blood
  From whence we came:

"Not flinching from the wave
  Render we up our breath;
But turn to face our grave,
  Dauntless in death!"

THE ISLAND

Eastward lies the Island,
In a bay of raw sapphire streaked with shoals;
The tide rolls,
Beating itself to pieces in the jaws
Of broken-fanged reefs as white as bone;
Spray splinters on stone
Of the sharply-rising waterless soilless highland:
Such is the Island.

There no man lives nor may, but there each year
The seals heavily
Drag themselves up the smooth rock from the sea,
Their soft eyes confident, their hides sleek—
Coming without haste, without fear,
To the citadel they seek.
Here, these unbefriending wastes among,
Yearly are born their young:
Here and thus
Yearly however temporarily
The solitude is populous
With the stupid gentle people of the sea.

Along the road that rounds the bay is a slope;
Halfway down the slope to the sea is a house—
Built so cunningly into the slope-stair,
Screened so darkly by fir and the fir boughs,
You might pass and pass and never know it was there.
In that house there lives a lady
Whose glassed wall looks steadfastly
Down the wild fall of rock to the sea
And the roaring reef and the spume flying
And ever and evermore
About the shore
The gulls crying, the gulls wheeling and crying.

I have seen her once: she was strange and beautiful—tall,
With milk-white hair and a dead-white face; she went
Sumptuous in green brocade and golden roses:
I looked, I was not content
To look and pass; my heart said, "Winter closes—
What will you do, O lady, when outside
Is only the far country white and wide
And the listening firs at the door, and ceaselessly
The cannonading sea?"

What will you do, O lady? Night and day
The sound of the mad surf that never lulls
Is in your heart, and the cry of the mad gulls.
Do they say true, the gossips, when they say
Whisperingly
That a white seal haunts the Island
When the grey seals come up from the sea?

PART V

MODERN POETRY: THE
NATIVE TRADITION

E. J. PRATT (1883——)

EDWIN J. PRATT was born at Western Bay, Newfoundland, in 1883, and was educated at Methodist College, St. John's, and at Victoria College of the University of Toronto, where he is now professor of English. He is the author of eleven volumes of poetry: *Newfoundland Verse* (1923), *The Witches' Brew* (1925), *Titans* (1926), *The Iron Door* (1928), *The Roosevelt and the Antinoe* (1930), *Verses of the Sea* (1930), *Many Moods* (1932), *The Titanic* (1935), *The Fable of the Goats and Other Poems* (1937), *Brébeuf and His Brethren* (1940), and *Dunkirk* (1941).

Pratt began in the lyrics and shorter narratives of *Newfoundland Verse* with personal impressions of the sea and the harsh life of the rock-bound coast he was familiar with in boyhood; and in his second book, the delightful *Witches' Brew*, he allowed his fancy to roam in a quasi-Rabelaisian world of spontaneous revelry. This poem is great, and sometimes learned, fun, and it is nothing more. As Mr. W. E. Collin put it in his brilliant chapter on Pratt in *The White Savannahs:* "This chante-fable makes no demands on us, it simply invites us to a rollicking ecumenical stag party." With *Titans*, which was published in England, Pratt began to attract a wider critical notice. His energy and sustained narrative skill, his deeply felt perception of the sea, and the bold geographical sweep of his imagination were clearly shown in the two little epics that made up the book—"The Cachalot," a miniature *Moby Dick* that tells in rushing decasyllables the story of the hunting of a mighty whale king, and "The Great Feud," a longer poem in a similar verse form telling the story of a gargantuan war to extinction between the mighty and exotic beasts of the Paleolithic age. The poem is a parable of the suicidal waste of war, presented here as a subhuman and meaningless struggle, and it is all the more effective because the poet nowhere stops to explain or to moralize. Later, under the stress of tragic world events, Pratt was to return to a similar theme and tell in verse that had gained in ease and variety if not in strength a second and more explicit parable, "The Fable of the Goats."

These were Pratt's poems of fantasy and imagination. In his other

277

poems, while still concerned with energy and heroic action, he at once narrows and exalts the stage to the specific and the human.

In *The Roosevelt and the Antinoe* and *The Titanic*, the sea poetry of his earliest volume is combined with a spaciousness of narrative sweep that his fantastic "epics" had revealed as peculiarly genial to his temperament. But the material is contemporary and human, and the method is largely that of realism. Nowhere in modern English poetry—except in the best of Masefield—is the art of the novelist more skilfully demonstrated; yet what gives these poems significance is the conception of courage and devotion to duty as virtues natural to the commonest humanity.

In the volumes of shorter poems published during the thirties, besides poems of the sea, there are many lyrics, some of them experimental in form, which testify to Pratt's concern with the politics of peace and democracy. In these he speaks as a humanitarian and a liberal, though the pity and irony of man's inhumanity to man, sharpened by the weapons science has put into his hands, provoke the poet to a bitterness that gives a new kind of strength to his art.

In 1940, in his longest and most ambitious poem, *Brébeuf and His Brethren*, Pratt turned, almost for the first time, to a purely Canadian theme. The story of the heroic French priests, martyred in their efforts to bring Christianity to the Hurons and the Iroquois, is in itself of epic quality, and firsthand accounts written with the noblest severity exist in the monumental *Jesuit Relations*. Abandoning the rushing tetrameters of his most characteristic poems in favor of a quietly moving blank verse, Pratt fills his canvas with subdued autumn colors and presents his characters in a series of pictures that show them heroic, stoical, God-intoxicated, and yet human. That *Brébeuf* is at once a Christian poem and a heroic narrative that does honor to our French compatriots is of great significance.

The most recent of Pratt's poems, the little epic *Dunkirk*, is a return to popular poetry. In some ways this is the most remarkable of all Pratt's works, because it is so eminently successful on several different levels. The dangers of writing a popular patriotic poem on a theme that is of immediate and stirring interest are obvious. The poet may be tempted to express a vicarious and unearned intensity. *Dunkirk*, because of its modesty of scope and unassuming frankness, avoids this error with the adroitest success. It is the sort of poem that might have come from John Masefield at the height of the Laureate's powers and is in a sense a counterpart to Masefield's little prose epic of the last war, *Gallipoli*. One agrees with the reviewer in the June, 1942, issue of *Poetry* that "it is the best poem so far to come out of the present war."

THE CACHALOT

I

A thousand years now had his breed
Established the mammalian lead;
The founder (in cetacean lore)
Had followed Leif to Labrador;
The eldest-born tracked all the way
Marco Polo to Cathay;
A third had hounded one whole week
The great Columbus to Bahama;
A fourth outstripped to Mozambique
The flying squadron of de Gama;
A fifth had often crossed the wake
Of Cortez, Cavendish and Drake;
The great grandsire—a veteran rover—
Had entered once the strait of Dover,
In a naval fight, and with his hump
Had stove a bottom of Van Tromp;
The grandsire at Trafalgar swam
At the *Redoubtable* and caught her,
With all the tonnage of his ram,
Deadly between the wind and water;
And his granddam herself was known
As fighter and as navigator,
The mightiest mammal in the zone
From Baffin Bay to the Equator.
From such a line of conjugate sires
Issued his blood, his lumbar fires,
And from such dams imperial-loined
His Taurian timbers had been joined,
And when his time had come to hasten
Forth from his deep sub-mammary basin,
Out on the ocean tracts, his mamma
Had, in a North Saghalien gale,
Launched him, a five-tone healthy male,
Between Hong Kong and Yokohama.
Now after ninety moons of days,
Sheltered by the mammoth fin,
He took on adolescent ways
And learned the habits of his kin;
Ransacked the seas and found his mate,
Established his dynastic name,

Reared up his youngsters, and became
The most dynamic vertebrate
(According to his Royal Dame)
From Tonga to the Hudson Strait.
And from the start, by fast degrees,
He won in all hostilities;
Sighted a hammerhead and followed him,
Ripped him from jaw to ventral, swallowed him;
Pursued a shovelnose and mangled him;
Twisted a broadbill's neck and strangled him;
Conquered a rorqual in full sight
Of a score of youthful bulls who spurred
Him to the contest, and the fight
Won him the mastery of the herd.

Another ninety moons and Time
Had cast a marvel from his hand,
Unmatched on either sea or land—
A sperm whale in the pitch of prime.
A hundred feet or thereabout
He measured from the tail to snout,
And every foot of that would run
From fifteen hundred to a ton.
But huge as was his tail or fin,
His bulk of forehead, or his hoists
And slow subsidences of jaw,
He was more wonderful within.
His iron ribs and spinal joists
Enclosed the sepulchre of a maw.
The bellows of his lungs might sail
A herring skiff—such was the gale
Along the wind-pipe; and so large
The lymph-flow of his active liver,
One might believe a fair-sized barge
Could navigate along the river;
And the islands of his pancreas
Were so tremendous that between 'em
A punt would sink; while a cart might pass
His bile-duct to the duodenum
Without a peristaltic quiver.
And cataracts of red blood stormed
His heart, while lower down was formed
That fearful labyrinthine coil

Filled with the musk of ambergris;
And there were reservoirs of oil
And spermaceti; and renal juices
That poured in torrents without cease
Throughout his grand canals and sluices.
And hid in his arterial flow
Were flames and currents set aglow
By the wild pulses of the chase
With fighters of the Saxon race.
A tincture of an iron grain
Had dyed his blood a darker stain;
Upon his coat of toughest rubber
A dozen cicatrices showed
The place as many barbs were stowed,
Twisted and buried in his blubber,
The mute reminders of the hours
Of combat when the irate whale
Unlimbered all his massive powers
Of head-ram and of caudal flail,
Littering the waters with the chips
Of whale-boats and vainglorious ships.

II

Where Cape Delgado strikes the sea,
A cliff ran outward slantingly
A mile along a tossing edge
Of water towards a coral ledge,
Making a sheer and downward climb
Of twenty fathoms where it ended,
Forming a jutty scaur suspended
Over a cave of murk and slime.
A dull reptilian silence hung
About the walls, and fungus clung
To knots of rock, and over boles
Of lime and basalt poisonous weed
Grew rampant, covering the holes
Where crayfish and sea-urchins breed.
The upper movement of the seas
Across the reefs could not be heard;
The nether tides but faintly stirred
Sea-nettles and anemones.
A thick festoon of lichens crawled

From crag to crag, and under it
Half-hidden in a noisome pit
Of bones and shells a kraken sprawled.
Moveless, he seemed, as a boulder set
In pitch, and dead within his lair,
Except for a transfixing stare
From lidless eyes of burnished jet,
And a hard spasm now and then
Within his viscous centre, when
His scabrous feelers intertwined
Would stir, vibrate, and then unwind
Their ligatures with easy strength
To tap the gloom, a cable length;
And finding no life that might touch
The mortal radius of their clutch,
Slowly relax, and shorten up
Each tensile tip, each suction cup,
And coil again around the head
Of the mollusc on its miry bed,
Like a litter of pythons settling there
To shutter the Gorgonian stare.

But soon the squid's antennæ caught
A murmur that the waters brought—
No febrile stirring as might spring
From a puny barracuda lunging
At a tuna's leap, some minor thing,
A tarpon or a dolphin plunging—
But a deep consonant that rides
Below the measured beat of tides
With that vast, undulating rhythm
A sounding sperm whale carries with him.
The kraken felt that as the flow
Beat on his lair with plangent power,
It was the challenge of his foe,
The prelude to a fatal hour;
Nor was there given him more than time,
From that first instinct of alarm,
To ground himself in deeper slime,
And raise up each enormous arm
Above him, when, unmeasured, full
On the revolving ramparts, broke

The hideous rupture of a stroke
From the forehead of the bull.
And when they interlocked, that night—
Cetacean and cephalopod
No Titan with Olympian god
Had ever waged a fiercer fight;
Tail and skull and teeth and maw
Met sinew, cartilage, and claw,
Within those self-engendered tides,
Where the Acherontic flood
Of sepia, mingling with the blood
Of whale, befouled Delgado's sides.
And when the cachalot out-wore
The squid's tenacious clasp, he tore
From frame and socket, shred by shred,
Each gristled, writhing tentacle,
And with serrated mandible
Sawed cleanly through the bulbous head;
Then gorged upon the fibrous jelly
Until, finding that six tons lay
Like Vulcan's anvil in his belly,
He left a thousand sharks his prey,
And with his flukes, slow-labouring, rose
To a calm surface where he shot
A roaring geyser, steaming hot,
From the blast-pipe of his nose.
One hour he rested, in the gloom
Of the after-midnight; his great back
Prone with the tide and, in the loom
Of the Afric coast, merged with the black
Of the water; till a rose shaft, sent
From Madagascar far away,
Etched a ripple, eloquent
Of a freshening wind and a fair day.

Flushed with the triumph of the fight,
He felt his now unchallenged right
To take by demonstrated merit
What he by birth-line did inherit—
The lordship of each bull and dam
That in mammalian water swam,
As Maharajah of the seas
From Rio to the Celebes.

And nobly did the splendid brute
Leap to his laurels, execute
His lineal functions as he sped
Towards the Equator northwards, dead
Against the current and the breeze;
Over his back the running seas
Cascaded, while the morning sun,
Rising in gold and beryl, spun
Over the cachalot's streaming gloss,
And from the foam, a fiery floss
Of multitudinous fashionings,
And dipping downward from the blue,
The sea-gulls from Comoro flew,
And brushed him with their silver wings;
Then at the tropic hour of noon
He slackened down; a drowsy spell
Was creeping over him, and soon
He fell asleep upon the swell.

SILENCES

There is no silence upon the earth or under the earth like the silence
    under the sea;
No cries announcing birth,
No sounds declaring death.
There is silence when the milt is laid on the spawn in the weeds and
    fungus of the rock-clefts;
And silence in the growth and struggle for life.
The bonitoes pounce upon the mackerel,
And are themselves caught by the barracudas,
The sharks kill the barracudas
And the great molluscs rend the sharks,
And all noiselessly—
Though swift be the action and final the conflict,
The drama is silent.

There is no fury upon the earth like the fury under the sea.
For growl and cough and snarl are the tokens of spendthrifts who
    know not the ultimate economy of rage.
Moreover, the pace of the blood is too fast.
But under the waves the blood is sluggard and has the same tem-
    perature as that of the sea.

There is something pre-reptilian about a silent kill.

Two men may end their hostilities just with their battle-cries.
"The devil take you," says one.
"I'll see you in hell first," says the other.
And these introductory salutes followed by a hail of gutturals and
    sibilants are often the beginning of friendship, for who would not
    prefer to be lustily damned than to be half-heartedly blessed?
No one need fear oaths that are properly enunciated, for they be-
    long to the inheritance of just men made perfect, and, for all we
    know, of such may be the Kingdom of Heaven.
But let silent hate be put away for it feeds upon the heart of the
    hater.
Today I watched two pairs of eyes. One pair was black and the
    other grey. And while the owners thereof, for the space of five
    seconds, walked past each other, the grey snapped at the black
    and the black riddled the grey.
One looked to say—"The cat,"
And the other—"The cur."
But no words were spoken;
Not so much as a hiss or a murmur came through the perfect
    enamel of the teeth; not so much as a gesture of enmity.
If the right upper lip curled over the canine, it went unnoticed.
The lashes veiled the eyes not for an instant in the passing.
And as between the two in respect to candour of intention or eter-
    nity of wish, there was no choice, for the stare was mutual and
    absolute.
A word would have dulled the exquisite edge of the feeling,
An oath would have flawed the crystallization of the hate.
For only such culture could grow in a climate of silence,—
Away back before the emergence of fur or feather, back to the un-
    vocal sea and down deep where the darkness spills its wash on
    the threshold of light, where the lids never close upon the eyes,
    where the inhabitants slay in silence and are as silently slain.

THE OLD EAGLE

A light had gone out from his vanquished eyes;
His head was cupped within the hunch of his shoulders;
His feathers were dull and bedraggled; the tips
Of his wings sprawled down to the edge of his tail.
He was old, yet it was not his age
Which made him roost on the crags
Like a rain-drenched raven
On the branch of an oak in November.

Nor was it the night, for there was an hour
To go before sunset. An iron had entered
His soul which bereft him of pride and of realm;
Had struck him to-day: for up to noon
That crag had been his throne.
Space was his empire, bounded only
By forest and sky and the flowing horizons.
He had outfought, outlived all his rivals,
And the eagles that now were poised over glaciers
Or charting the coastal outlines of clouds
Were his by descent: they had been tumbled
Out of their rocky nests by his mate,
In the first trial of their fledgling spins.

Only this morning the eyes of the monarch
Were held in arrest by a silver flash
Shining between two peaks of the ranges—
A sight which galvanized his back,
Bristled the feathers on his neck,
And shot little runnels of dust where his talons
Dug recesses in the granite.
Partridge? Heron? Falcon? Eagle?
Game or foe? He would reconnoitre.
Catapulting from the ledge,
He flew at first with rapid beat,
Level, direct: then with his grasp
Of spiral strategy in fight,
He climbed the orbit
With swift and easy undulations,
And reached position where he might
Survey the bird—for bird it was;
But such a bird as never flew
Between the heavens and the earth
Since pterodactyls, long before
The birth of condors, learned to kill
And drag their carrion up the Andes.

The eagle stared at the invader,
Marked the strange bat-like shadow moving
In leagues over the roofs of the world,
Across the passes and moraines,
Darkening the vitriol blue of the mountain lakes.
Was it a flying dragon? Head,

Body and wings, a tail fan-spread
And taut like his own before the strike;
And there in front two whirling eyes
That took unshuttered
The full blaze of the meridian.
The eagle never yet had known
A rival that he would not grapple,
But something in this fellow's length
Of back, in the plated glistening shoulders,
Had given him pause. And did that thunder
Somewhere in his throat not argue
Lightning in his claws? And then
The speed—was it not double his own?
But what disturbed him most, angered
And disgraced him was the unconcern
With which this supercilious bird
Cut through the aquiline dominion,
Snubbing the ancient suzerain
With extra-territorial insolence,
And disappeared.

So evening found him on the crags again,
This time with slattern shoulders
And nerveless claws.
Dusk had outridden the sunset by an hour
To haunt his unhorizoned eyes.
And soon his flock flushed with the chase
Would be returning, threading their glorious curves
Up through the crimson archipelagoes
Only to find him there—
Deaf to the mighty symphony of wings,
And brooding
Over the lost empire of the peaks.

COME AWAY DEATH

Willy nilly, he comes or goes, with the clown's logic,
Comic in epitaph, tragic in epithalamium,
And unseduced by any mused rhyme.
However blow the winds over the pollen,
Whatever the course of the garden variables,
He remains the constant,
Ever flowering from the poppy seeds.

There was a time he came in formal dress,
Announced by Silence tapping at the panels
In deep apology.
A touch of chivalry in his approach,
He offered sacramental wine,
And with acanthus leaf
And petals of the hyacinth
He took the fever from the temples
And closed the eyelids,
Then led the way to his cool longitudes
In the dignity of the candles.

His mediaeval grace is gone—
Gone with the flame of the capitals
And the leisured turn of the thumb
Leafing the manuscripts,
Gone with the marbles
And the Venetian mosaics,
With the bend of the knee
Before the rose-strewn feet of the Virgin.
The *paternosters* of his priests,
Committing clay to clay,
Have rattled in their throats
Under the gride of his traction tread.

One night we heard his footfall—one September night—
In the outskirts of a village near the sea.
There was a moment when the storm
Delayed its fist, when the surf fell
Like velvet on the rocks—a moment only;
The strangest lull we ever knew!
A sudden truce among the oaks
Released their fratricidal arms;
The poplars straightened to attention
As the winds stopped to listen
To the sound of a motor drone—
And then the drone was still.
We heard the tick-tock on the shelf,
And the leak of valves in our hearts.
A calm condensed and lidded
As at the core of a cyclone ended breathing.
This was the monologue of Silence
Grave and unequivocal.

What followed was a bolt
Outside the range and target of the thunder,
And human speech curved back upon itself
Through Druid runways and the Piltdown scarps,
Beyond the stammers of the Java caves,
To find its origins in hieroglyphs
On mouths and eyes and cheeks
Etched by a foreign stylus never used
On the outmoded page of the Apocalypse.

From *DUNKIRK*

IN THE SKIES

The world believed the trap was sprung,
And no Geneva words or signatures of mercy
Availed the quarry on the sands.
The bird's right to dodge the barrels on the wing,
The start for the hare,
The chance for the fox to cross his scent,
For the teeth to snap at the end of the chase,
Did not belong to this tally-ho.

The proffered sword disclaimed by the victor,
The high salute at the burial of a foe
Wrapped in the folds of his flag,
The wreath from the skies,
Were far romantic memories.
As little chivalry here
As in the peregrines chasing the carriers,
As in the sniff of the jackals about a carcass!
Here over the dunes
The last civil rag was torn from the body of war—
The decencies had perished with the Stukas.

*   *   *

From Dover to Dunkirk,
From Dunkirk to Ramsgate,
And back to the dunes.
Power boats of the enemy
Were driving torpedoes into transports and colliers,
Lifting the engines clear from their beds,
Blowing the boilers, sheering the sterns,

And the jettisoned loads gathered up from the sea
Were transferred to other decks
And piled in steep confusion
On the twisted steel of the listed destroyers,
On the rough planks of the barges,
Into the hatches of the freighters,
Jammed against bulkheads and riddled ventilators,
On the coils of the cables,
On quarterdecks and in the fo'c'sles,
On the mess-tables and under them.
"Was that roar in the North from the *Rodney?*
We hope to God it was."
Drip of the leadlines on the bows—
"Two fathoms, sir, four feet, three and a half."
"Wake up, you dead end. You're not on the feathers now.
Make room for this 'ere bloke."
"Stiff as cement 'e is." "Git a gate on,
Or the Stukas 'll be raisin' boils on your necks."
"Ahoy, skipper, a can of petrol."
"Compass out of gear—Give us the line to Ramsgate."
"Follow the skoots."

The great birds, carrying under their wings
The black distorted crosses,
Plunged, straightened out,
Laid their eggs in air,
Hatched them in fountains of water,
In craters of sand,
To the leap of flame,
To the roar of avalanche.

And in those hours,
When Death was sweating at his lathe,
When heads and legs and arms were blown from their trunks,
When the seventh day on the dunes became the eighth,
And the eighth slumped into the dawn of the ninth,
When the sand's crunch and suck under the feet
Were sounds less to be endured than the crash of bombs
In that coma and apathy of horror—
It was then that the feel of a deck,
The touch of a spar or a halyard,
Was like a hold on the latch of the heart of God.
It's the Navy's job!

It's their turn now,
From the Beach to the ports.
Let the Stukas break their bloody necks on the Mole;
Let the fires scorch the stars—
For now, whether on the burnished oak of the cabins,
Or on the floor-boards of the punts,
Or in the cuddies of the skiffs,
Sleep at last has an even game with Death.

The blessed fog—
Ever before this day the enemy,
Leagued with the quicksands and the breakers—
Now mercifully masking the periscope lenses,
Smearing the hair-lines of the bomb-sights,
Hiding the flushed coveys.
And with it the calm on the Channel,
The power that drew the teeth from the storm,
The peace that passed understanding,
Soothing the surf, allaying the lop on the swell.
Out of the range of the guns of Nieuport,
Away from the immolating blasts of the oil-tanks,
The flotillas of ships were met by flotillas of gulls
Whiter than the cliffs of Foreland;
Between the lines of the Medway buoys
They steamed and sailed and rowed,
Back to the roadsteads, back to the piers
Inside the vigilant booms,
Back to the harbours,
Back to the River of London, to England,
Saved once again by the tread of her keels.

LLOYD ROBERTS (1884——)

T HE eldest son of C. G. D. Roberts, Lloyd Roberts was born in
Fredericton, New Brunswick, in 1884. He has had a varied
career as author and newspaper correspondent. He published
a volume of verse, *England Over Seas*, in 1914, and in 1923 *The
Book of Roberts*, an intimate prose narrative glorifying the literary
achievements of the Roberts family under the leadership of its chieftain, Sir Charles, whose own poetry has served as a model for much
of his son's verse. The best of this appears in a more recent volume,
I Sing of Life: Selected Poems of Lloyd Roberts (1937).

DEAD DAYS

The haws cling to the thorn,
Shrivelled and red;
The limbs long dead
Clutch at a leaf long torn—
It taps all day on the spikes
As the spume licks over the dikes.

The reeds creak in the dawn
By the dead pond;
Dry tongues respond
From grasses yellow and drawn;
And ever scourged by the wind,
The alders clatter and grind.

Vines furred with the frost
String from the wall:
Their bones recall
Summer leaves long lost,
Cricket and fly and bee
And their low melody.

No bird wails to the waste
Of scentless snow,
Where streaming low
The steel-blue shadows haste;
But through the hard night
The dead moon takes flight.

KENNETH LESLIE (1892——)

KENNETH LESLIE was born in Pictou, Nova Scotia, in 1892, and was educated at the universities of Dalhousie, Nebraska, and Harvard. He is now editor of the *Protestant* (New York) and is active in democratic and anti-Fascist organizations. He has published four collections of poetry: *Windward Rock* (1934), *Such a Din!* (1935), *Lowlands Low* (1936), and *By Stubborn Stars* (1938). The last was winner of the Governor-General's Annual Literary Award for Poetry in 1938.

The quality which lends distinction to the best poems of Kenneth Leslie is wholeness. The details of experience are fused in the heat of imagination and expressed in a language that utilizes the idioms and rhythms of popular speech as well as of formal poetry. This applies particularly to such a poem as "The silver herring throbbed thick in my seine," where by the subtlest suggestion the rhythm of the sea and the rhythm of rowing are identified with the rhythm of life itself and of love. These fourteen lines have a richness of implication and an intensity of feeling that recall D. H. Lawrence. The other three sonnets are not far inferior. They are taken from the sequence of love poems, *By Stubborn Stars*. Included in the same volume were two remarkable longer poems, "Fifth Columnist," a dramatic vignette of the Spanish civil war, and "Cobweb College," a wise and witty essay on poetry and education, dedicated to Robert Frost and showing, in a wholly admirable way, the influence of that poet.

LOWLANDS LOW

What can be better than to let the screen of years
fold up and leave a boy,
a fireplace and a man there singing?
The last light dying from the coals, the last note dying
in the ears of the song-captured idolater . . . .
remembering days that shall not be again

294

except this way, remembering,
letting the image enter well-used doors,
the smell of Harris tweed and English leather,
the smell of "Old Chum" smoking,
the clean aroma of a man.
No words to hint the quality of his voice,
the salt-edge in it, the sweet and vibrant sorrow.

No way to hint the quality of his eyes,
set bold and challenging, yet queerly shy,
dark mirrors of a boy's unslaked delight
in all things various and strange,
in all the heaped-up helping life had served him.

His song, *The Lowlands Low*, not mouthed from a book
but taken alive and terrible from the sea . . . .
to remember the thickening in my throat
when "his shipmates picked him up and on the deck he died,"
the brave boy, the betrayal, the irreparable loss,
my father's eyes half-closed upon the last long note,
"and they sank him in the Lowlands Low!"

The screen of years unfolds again
and pushes this strange semblance of myself
into this strange semblance of my city.
He, too, is gone the way of the sea
and is lost in the Lowlands Low . . . .
and I am left here with no token, no watch or knife or book
by which to call him back,
but I remember here in my throat his song,
remembering.

COBWEB COLLEGE

An Antinomian Parable written for Robert Frost

A batch of freshmen came to Cobweb College;
the Spider looked them over, frowned and said,
"These boys are ghosts of boys, cracked wide with knowledge,
their dreams dried out and left the dreamers dead.
There's not a meal among them, no illusion
to sharpen up my tooth on, no romance
for me to ridicule to red confusion,
no creed on which to slake my poison lance.

I've drawn their blood too many generations
and spoiled the breed. Their fathers, when I wrapped them
in causal web and silken strong equations,
would lunge and writhe, grimacing when I snapped them
with categoried claws. These modern schools
condition them until they yearn to yield;
their wills are like the blown pigskin that drools
November muck around a soggy field.
They murmur, 'Say, Professor, skip the prodding,
just dish it out, the ifs, the ands, the buts!
who'd question fifty million miles of wadding
engendered through the ages in your guts?
Welcome the warm cocoon of cosy thought
through which we gain the world but lose surprise!
we'll answer by your book, old man, but not
pretend amazement,'
　　　　　　　　　　thus the pampered flies
and those who hope for pampering . . . . the rest
nursing a schoolboy grudge within the core
of mangy-bearded justice are at best
a thin and scanty ration for my store."

So modernly at his wits' end to find
food for his pattern-maw: as when old cries
were battle banners for the foolish blind;
or wisdom knelt before the prattling wise;
or doddering knights clanked forth as to a feast
and opened old wounds for an empty tomb
while on their heads the stupefying East
poured her unholy oil to their sure doom;
or as when that rough sheepherd whose wild head
ached noisily pulled from the pasture mire
her heavy brogues and herded kings instead
and burned two kingdoms in her fagots' fire;
or as when hare-brained Shelley turned the tack,
unwigged the judge, lifted the felon bard
out of his cage onto the judge's sack
and placed the moral guardian under guard;
('twas Shelley solved it) he would find a poet
and pen him just beyond the edge of knowledge
(tether him well but never let him know it)
to be a milch-fly for old Cobweb College.

"Come, then, quaint poet, feed them hints of God
my hounds of two-plus-two-are-four will chew!
Cast over them your old divining rod
and draw their deep springs to my sultry view!"
Thus came the Ageless One to Cobweb College
and said,
        "It is incumbent upon me
to be the thing that I was dreamed to be;
the word I say and live will not divide;
it must be born complete."
                His voice cross-grained,
he said it sitting on a class-room table,
not lotus-seated but legs swinging free,
a very Yankee Buddha (if a Buddha),
leaving it once to look abstractedly
out of the open window at the sky,
smiling to welcome in the coming storm,
the quick low murmur and the sudden dark,
his voice the thunder's texture and his hands
its muscled wind, veined lightning. The storm broke.
"Lately we hear much talk about selection.
I'll dip some random uses of that word
out of the pot where words boil up in deeds:
'What is your selection for the Derby?'
'The new headmaster is a good selection.'
'Out of these evils I select the least.'
'The most important thing you learn at college
is how to live your life selectively,
to recognize the seal of excellence,
the caste-mark of those persons one should know,
the hallmark of those books that one should read.'
Easy to note the part selection plays;
yet here's the antiphon, the song's recoil:
(what we forget is that it works two ways)
the seed is chosen by and chooses soil.
Not difficult to choose things ready made
and marked with price-tags, plainly stamped and signed
or guaranteed by cliques and claques of critics;
but making things is more than choosing things.
It is the hardened artery of the soul
that delves in *objets d'art*, jostling the good
and bad of artists' and no-artists' leavings

conducted by a melancholy dealer
who wears upon his one and only eye
a disc of gold and rubs his hands to hear
the dry voice of a dowager exlaim:

'What a pretty crucifix,
Only seventeen and six!
Just the thing I want to fill
that bit of wall-space . . . . what a thrill!'

Here is a simple parable of life:
The bark upon a tree is wood; it peels
year after year while holding to its form,
its form tradition, and its peeling off
the yielding of tradition to the sap
of new creation . . . . so we have the tree.
Now teach the bark its business with steel bands
and twist those bands until they choke the sap . . . .
steel bands for the pharisee, for him
no living tree but stark unbending branches
on which to nail the Life that loves through death . . . .
steel bands for the graceless scholar; he
tallies three kinds of grace, A, B, and C,
snuffing the living flame with adjectives
saying 'how quaint, how quite Wordsworthian!'
The slowed-up poetry of speculation,
the Martha role of keeping things in order,
the retail merchant sorting and arranging
the world's goods on his hierarchic shelves . . . .
there is a deeper thing on which these bud,
a passion that is too much in the blood,
too moving in the marrow of the loin,
too much the chosen itself to mould a coin
whose metal face would blind the human face
and shut it from the inner holy place.
Rather than moulds invisible in the air
into which petals pour selective milk
I seem to sense a partnered agony
of creature and creator in the rose,
and in each act of mine there dwells a host
of that same pair, a host with the strange power
of swinging wide the door for them to enter
or slamming it against them, I that host."

There was a frantic scurrying in their minds,
a rush to find appropriate pigeonholes
for all this tangle; nothing seemed to fit.
The Spider sidled in with a quick squeak
and a suggestion born of sudden fear
that rather than a lecture once a week
a better plan would be one once a year.

The Ageless One heard (not the interjection)
the scurrying to and fro within their minds;
yet he went on in that most sublime faith
that ever life goes seeking for its own
leaving the indexed husks .... here in this very room
might brood a boy with hunger strong enough
to smell the truth. Now there began to sprout
in Doctor Spider's brain a horrible doubt ....
What gender was this animal? What ilk?
Gin for his tender babes if this was milk!
"The hundredth sheep was not a select sheep,
but just a sheep that happened to be lost.
Mary would have loved her Son as much
had he been but the unrepentant thief.
Do lovers tally points of excellence
as if they were self-breeding animals?
(I speak of breeding; it involves selection.)
You may breed long legs thus, even long heads,
but love is neither bred nor educated.
Love knows no grammar, yet the stiffest lock,
the dullest door, may open to his knock.
Tradition, once as subtle as the film
that wraps unfelt the living nerve and vein,
begins to choke the vein and lull the nerve
to liking it; the film is wire now
and coalesces to a band of steel
so that a good professor is a blacksmith
or combination smith and spi— ...."
                              The Spider
dwindled with a squeak until his gown
seemed hung in mid-air on a wire hanger,
his mortar sagged upon a shrunken peg.
The storm had passed beyond the folded hills,
only its curious echo in this room,
this man's rough voice its far threat of thunder.

"From soil somehow the poet's word
and from that word the spreading tree
where swells all fruit, sings every bird,
whose strong trunk is philosophy,
whose branches thrust in legal maze,
whose leaves are myriad windows green
sifting the one to many ways,
tinting the unseen to the seen.
Your teachers list the birds and fruit,
the trunk and branches of the tree;
but they forget about the root,
because the root they cannot see.
Yet have the roots a ray to find
their road between the stones and clay;
like Raftery, the singing blind,
better than day they know the day!"

Four Sonnets from *BY STUBBORN STARS*

I

The silver herring throbbed thick in my seine,
silver of life, life's silver sheen of glory;
my hands, cut with the cold, hurt with the pain
of hauling the net, pulled the heavy dory,
heavy with life, low in the water, deep
plunged to the gunwale's lips in the stress of rowing,
the pulse of rowing that puts the world to sleep,
world within world endlessly ebbing, flowing.
At length you stood on the landing and you cried,
with quick low cries you timed me stroke on stroke
as I steadily won my way with the fulling tide
and crossed the threshold where the last wave broke
and coasted over the step of water and threw
straight through the air my mooring line to you.

II

A warm rain whispers, but the earth knows best
and turns a deaf ear, waiting for the snow,
the foam of bloom forgotten, the rolling crest
of green forgotten and the fruit swelling slow.
The shearing plow was here and cut the mould

and shouldered over the heavy rain-soaked lands,
letting the hot breath out for the quiet cold
to reach deep down with comfort in its hands.
The sap is ebbing from the tips of the trees
to the dry and secret heart, hiding away
from the blade still green with stubborn memories;
down in the roots it closes the door of clay
on grief and growing and this late warm rain
babbling false promises in the pasture lane.

III

Day slipped out of the web of her fog-wet gown
and buried her bright face in the pale sheen
of the maple leaves and pushed her fingers down
in the damp moss under the deeper green
of the darkling spruce and found a cool mind
and turned and looked back through the lucent panes
of maple leaves at the sky she had left behind
and traced each pointed leaf and its intricate veins.
Lying there she shook with a sudden mirth
and waited awhile without breathing a breath
and nestled closer into the hollow earth
and knew a bliss that would have welcomed death,
knowing she could not deeper drink delight,
and she dreamed there of shadow and of night.

IV

My love is sleeping; but her body seems
awake within itself, secure from ills
of consciousness; her veins are buried streams,
her flanks are ghostly vales, her breasts are hills
of some far planet finding its sure way
beyond the orbit of this night of fears,
beyond the burnished darkness of this day;
my love is sleeping out of reach of tears.
How can her limbs dance motionless, what makes
her lips curve smiling to a crescent moon,
what does her hand reach out for, what dawn breaks
beneath her eyelids, to her ears what tune?
I shall not sleep, nor seek that yonder land
where her hand yearns, but not to touch my hand.

ARTHUR S. BOURINOT (1893——)

ARTHUR S. BOURINOT was born in Ottawa in 1893. He was the son of Sir John G. Bourinot, one of the most distinguished of Canadian scholars, author of many works on constitutional history and of one classic monograph, his presidential address before the Royal Society, *Canada's Intellectual Strength and Weakness* (1893). The poet was educated at Ottawa Collegiate and the University of Toronto. He served overseas during the first World War and returned with the rank of captain. He is the author of more than a dozen books of verse, of which the following are the most notable: *Laurentian Lyrics* (1915); *Poems* (1921); *Lyrics from the Hills* (1923); *Selected Poems* (1915–35), with an Introduction by Sir Andrew MacPhail; *Rhymes of the French Regime* (1937); *Under the Sun* (1939); and *What Far Kingdom* (1941). A distinguishing feature of Bourinot's verse is its craftsmanship and control. He has set himself to interpret the historical background and the natural setting of the Ottawa Valley and the Laurentian Hills. In his last two books his themes are drawn from a wider range and his technique has become at once more experimental and more austere. In 1939 he was awarded the Governor-General's Annual Literary Award for Poetry. His most recent work is a narrative poem on the Canadians at Dieppe (1943).

THE INDIAN

Standing by the shore of the great bitter water
When the Sun god rose from his rest
In the dark tepees of the east,
I looked out over the great lake of bitter water
White with the manes of galloping stallions
And farther than arrows can reach
Over the bitter water
Swam great white birds
Arching white feathered necks

302

Shaking their plumage,
Swimming, swimming towards me.
Nearer and nearer they came,
And soon,
Canoes were the birds,
Burdened like squaws,
Carrying huge blankets of white.
And the wind was their friend
Blowing them close to the shore,
Blowing them close. Then they stopped
And a great noise came over the bitter water,
Louder than the noise of the thunder bird
When he flaps his great black wings,
Shadowing the land,
And the mountains tremble
And the Great Turtle moves in his sleep
And the earth shakes.
And fire I saw
Like the lightning,
And I covered my eyes
Lest blindness should come
As it comes from the fire and smoke in the tepee.
And shouting I ran to the trees
And sheltered myself
Calling my brothers to come.
And quickly they ran
And gathered about me
And we lay on our old mother earth,
Trembling, looked out on the broad bitter water.

Braves we saw
With pale white faces,
Eyes as blue as the skies
When the snows are here
And hair like the veins
That run through the rocks
On the shore of the great inland water.
And they carried the thunder in their hands
And silver they wore on their heads
And their voices were soft,
Soft were their words when they called to us.
And slowly we walked to the shore
Our bows in our hands,

Our quivers of arrows ready for use.
But soft were their words
And they came bringing gifts,
Trinkets and beads for our squaws
And shiny things for the children,
Hatchets and hoes for the boys and the braves.
And our hearts were great with happiness
And brothers we called them
And passed the pipe of peace.
The pale faces from over the bitter water
Laughed at us and wondered
As we sat and smoked our pipes of stone
Contented and happy.

Many suns they were with us
And happy we were.
Came the time when the pumpkins were yellow,
Red corn in the clearing was tasselled
And sweet.
They hoisted their sails on their mighty canoes,
Sailed away to the east,
Vanished from sight,
Were lost on the bitter water.
And two of our brothers went with them
And now they are gone
Sad are our hearts
And empty our days;
And often we go to the shore
But nothing we see,
No sail on the water
To gladden our sight,
No sound of the thunder;
Only the great lake of the bitter water
And the white gulls wheeling
And crying.
And sad and bitter are our hearts
As the bitter water.
Will they come again,
The great spirits,
Bringing us gifts
As they promised,
Bringing our brothers
With tales to tell

Of the great white father
Who dwells in his wigwam
Beyond the bitter water?
We are lonely for our brothers,
We are waiting to hear
The tales they'll tell us
When they return
With the pale faces
From over the bitter water.
Oh hasten, little brothers,
We are waiting,
We are waiting,
We are lonely
And our pipes
Are empty.

UNDER THE PINES

All is still
Under the Pines,
All is still.
Still as the heart of Eve
When fear first came
And the flush
Of shame
Mantled her cheek
And the sword of flame
Flashed
In the garden of the Lord.
All is still
Under the Pines,
All is still.

W. W. E. ROSS (1894——)

BORN at Peterborough, Ontario, in 1894, W. W. Eustace Ross was educated at the University of Toronto. He is a scientist by profession and is on the staff of the Dominion weather bureau at Toronto. His poems have appeared chiefly in the *Dial* and in *Poetry* and have been discriminatingly praised by the American poet, Marianne Moore. Ross has published two small volumes of verse, *Laconics* (1930), in which stripped statement and sharply objective images have been used to interpret a northern and strictly Canadian scene, and *Sonnets* (1932), more conventional in form, though perhaps less so in spirit. The sonnets show the influence of their author's classical and medieval reading. The characteristic note of Ross's poetry is its simplicity and freshness. Experience is presented with a directness and unself-conscious naïveté that reveals objects set free from the hiding scale of habit. It is as though the poet, and hence his reader, were looking at a fish, a meadow, or a train for the first time and with a childlike eagerness that instinctively rejects whatever is nonessential or derivative.

THE DAWN; THE BIRDS

The dawn; the birds'
tumultuous clamour
grows as the light
gradually
makes more distinct
the rocks, the trees,
picking out each
from among the grey.

The clamour grows
and noises mingle—
of water slapping
along the rocks—

all the sounds
of the dawn, the early
morning, all
the early sounds.

And more distinct
the rocks, the trees,
and brighter now
the early lighting—
when suddenly
all these sounds cease—
a strange silence
and then the sun!

THE DIVER

I would like to dive
Down
Into this still pool
Where the rocks at the bottom are safely deep,

Into the green
Of the water seen from within,
A strange light
Streaming past my eyes—

Things hostile,
You cannot stay here, they seem to say;
The rocks, slime-covered, the undulating
Fronds of weeds—

And drift slowly
Among the cooler zones;
Then, upward turning,
Break from the green glimmer

Into the light,
White and ordinary of the day,
And the mild air,
With the breeze and the comfortable shore.

Three Spiritual Sonnets

ON THE SUPERNATURAL

We must affirm the supernatural
However doubtfully we have looked upon
Its bare existence in the time that's gone,
For it is ever near and ever real;
As we shall find. We love the natural.
The human reason seated on a throne,
Creator of kingdoms for itself alone,
Is conscious of no zone ethereal.
But to an end with all this lower view,
The cause illusory, vain and yet employed;—
Angels there are and kindly daemons too,
Their throng, removed from faulty human sight,
In the unseen worlds as we should know in spite
Of natural explanation thin and void.

THE STREAM OF LIFE

Angelic figures gliding in the stream
Of life, with a celestial sky above,
Show forth, embody the great rule of love
There underneath the illuminating beam
That through this spiritual zone doth gleam,
Making, itself, those mobile natures move—
Though none against the benign current strove—
Through the bright regions where fair spirits teem;
Where all is life and motion that employs
The energies ever of the creative light
That gleams and shows each heavenly nature young,—
The living light, mild, active, in the night
Even, of earth, most steadily fills with joys
Minds where a lasting melody is sung.

ON ANGELS

Angels, as well as birds, on silent wing
Proceeding through the upper, open air,
Under the full intense celestial glare,
Perceive the true form of each earthly thing;

Birdlike the eye they deftly, subtly fling
Into the distance. Steadily they stare
Unhindered by the circumambient glare,—
Angels as well as birds can sweetly sing.
They too are known to hover above a nest
Wherein the swathéd soul of man doth lie
Soft-hidden deep in matter as in wool,
And theirs, too, the prerogative of rest,—
To soothe at times in manner wonderful,
With kind and piercing glance of soul and eye.

A DEATH

Often in times before
He wandered through that wood.
He entered it once more.
His path was red with blood.

Some mystery there must be—
Solution is not known.
He entered carelessly,
At set of sun, alone.

Mysterious things were seen
In the shadow of the night,
And leaves no longer green
In the feeble failing light;

While spirits from the tomb
Gathered around his way—
"You too will come to us soon,
And you have come today."

No signs of life were seen
But signs of death were known.
The night came down between.
The hunter was alone.

His side was wet with blood
In the bitter chilling air,
And he lay with side all bare
In that murderous dark wood.

IF ICE

If
ice shall melt if
thinly the fresh
cold clear   water
running   shall make
grooves in the sides
of the ice;
if life return
           after death,
or depart not at death,
then shall buds
burst into   may-
leafing, the blooms of may
appear like stars
on the brown dry
           forest-bed.

LEO COX (1898——)

BORN in London in 1898 and educated in England, Leo Cox served with the Canadian Expeditionary Force during the first World War. As a poet, he is a careful craftsman who has interpreted, particularly in a large number of finely shaped sonnets, the scenery and traditional life of the St. Lawrence River region in Lower Quebec. He is the author of three chapbooks: *Sheepfold* (1926), *The Wind in the Field* (1932), and *River without End* (1937). A volume of selected poems, *North Star*, appeared in 1941. He has been actively interested in the work of the Canadian Authors' Association.

LABRADOR NIGHT

To-night our ship is anchored where
Sand-silvered is the shore,
To find at Havre St. Pierre
Black gold of Labrador.

The pioneer's first night on land,
Unsteady from the seas,
Was not more still than this, the sand
And stars the same as these. . . . .

This cycle of the selfsame wind,
Cooled in far hills of snow,
And charged with balsam, makes the mind
At one with his of long ago.

So little travelled is the street
With grasses overgrown,
There may be traces of his feet
By weed and flower and stone.

And all the houses face the sea—
Mother of gain and loss—
And every heart in piety
Is turned toward a cross.

BIRCH-WOOD

I wandered down the dying afternoon,
Calling my spirit back from land and sky—
It had crept out when I stood mountain-high—
I might have lost it in that survey soon;
Came down to the cool wood's leaf-floored vault
Whence all the green and birds had fled
Leaving stillness and some gold instead,
And braced my soul for the birches' sweet assault.
Their dazzling columns swiftly closed me round,
And struck me silver wounds in ghostly number,
Out-generalled me without a move or sound,
Till all else faded to a birch-tree'd slumber;
And when I did reluctantly escape,
All things took on their dead, familiar shape. . . . .

RAYMOND KNISTER
(1 9 0 0 – 1 9 3 2)

THE tragic death by drowning of Raymond Knister at the age of thirty-two cut off one of the most significant talents among the younger generation of Canadian writers. Born at Blenheim, Ontario, in 1900, Knister worked for many years on an Ontario farm. He lived for a time in the middle western states of the United States and was on the staff of the well-known literary magazine, *The Midland*. He contributed farm poems to *Poetry* and to such advance-guard magazines as *This Quarter* and *Transition*. He wrote two novels, *White Narcissus* and *My Star Predominant*, the latter concerned with the life of Keats, and edited with an excellent critical introduction a useful anthology, *Canadian Short Stories*. He was one of the first critics to welcome the new-poetry movement in Canada.

THE PLOUGHMAN

All day I follow
Watching the swift dark furrow
That curls away before me,
And care not for skies or upturned flowers,
And at the end of the field
Look backward
Ever with discontent.

A stone, a root, a strayed thought
Has warped the line of that furrow—
And urge my horses round again.

Sometimes even before the row is finished
I must look backward;
To find, when I come to the end
That there I swerved.

Unappeased I leave the field,
Expectant, return.

The horses are very patient.
When I tell myself
This time
The ultimate unflawed turning
Is before my share,
They must give up their rest.

STABLE TALK

We have sweat our share;
The harrow is caught full of sod-pieces,
The bright disks are misted yellow in the wet.
Hear tardy hesitant drops from the eaves!
Let the rain work now.

We can rest today.
Let the dozy eye,
The one raised hip
Give no hint to the hours.

We are not done with toil:
Let rain work in these hours,
Wind in the night's hours,
We with the sun together
Tomorrow.

FEED

For Danny whistling slowly
"Down in Tennessee"
A fat white shoat by the trough
Lifts his snout a moment to hear,
Among the guzzling and slavering comrades,
Squeezing and forcing:
And begins to feed again.
Whenever a certain note comes
He will raise his jaws
His unturning eyes,
Then lean again to scoop up the swill.

THE HAWK

Across the bristled and sallow fields,
The speckled stubble of cut clover,
Wades your shadow

Or against a grimy and tattered
Sky
You plunge

Or you shear a swath
From trembling tiny forests
With the steel of your wing—

Or make a row of waves
By the heat of your flight
Along the soundless horizon.

CHANGE

I shall not wonder more, then,
But I shall know.

Leaves change, and birds, flowers,
And after years are still the same.

The sea's breast heaves in sighs to the moon,
But they are moon and sea forever.

As in other times the trees stand tense and lonely,
And spread a hollow moan of other times

You will be you yourself,
I'll find you more, not else,
For vintage of the woeful years.

The sea breathes, or broods, or loudens,
Is bright or is mist and the end of the world;
And the sea is constant to change.

I shall not wonder more, then,
But I shall know.

ELISE AYLEN

THE poems of Elise Aylen (Mrs. D. C. Scott) were published in 1930 in a volume entitled *Roses of Shadow* with an introduction by Duncan Campbell Scott. "Poetry," wrote Dr. Scott, "sometimes impresses by its volume and sometimes by its intensity; sometimes by the wealth of its content and the breadth of its appeal; sometimes by the strength of its effect within narrow limits: it is to the last in kind of these classes that Miss Aylen's poems belong." The "Ode" included here is a later poem. It appeared originally in the *London Mercury*.

ODE

Here where a new life stirs and broods,
In reaching plain or closing woods,
    By river or wayside
    What god has lived or died?

Did prophet ever, god-intent,
To these rough hills make long ascent,
    And lonely at the even
    Watch and speak with Heaven?

By the chill pine-held northern lake
Cowed in the wind the thin reeds shake,
    But not upon these reeds
    Breathed Pan his sorrows' needs.

Not here the wind-lured Psyche slept,
Not here Demeter searched and wept,
    In her sore wandering,
    Bare-footed, sorrowing.

Rude from the garth, in regions far,
Of old the Volsungs met for war;
   Keen to a distant sky
   Rang Brynhild's battle-cry.

And where the low moon at the even
Drooped lotus-like on the still heaven,
   In paths all blossom-hung
   Walked Krishna bringing song.

Where Dana keeps her ancient mood,
Bound by pale seas in bitter flood,
   By a grey coast and drear
   Fled the swan sons of Lir.

Through our grim pines what god has strayed,
At some wood-spring his thirst allayed,
   Or held strange tryst undaunted
   In hollows spirit-haunted?

Was there god-head, dusk and eerie,
Star-begotten on the prairie,
   Where by the lodge-fire yet
   Wild hearts may not forget?

Sad remnant of the haggard bands
Who hopeless rove the outmost lands,
   And wait in night and storm
   For some lost wizard form.

You who have known the lonely earth,
In sombre ways of death and birth
   Stark from a heart unscanned
   Give gods unto the land.

The dark wind sweeps the mournful plain,
And through the far waste comes again
   An echo thinly heard,
   Red scream of Thunderbird.

Vague whisperings from a misty age
When heaven was earth's heritage,
   While vision lingered yet
   In sunrise or sunset.

Gauntly in a world withdrawn
Kuloskap strode across the dawn,
    And from a sullen shore
    Darkly, in evil hour,

On the waves where hoarse gulls darted
Flung his kettle, and departed;
    Left lonely the long sand—
    Went god thus from the land?

The forests breathe their ancient word,
The rooted hills in rest unstirred
    Give answer silently,
    Instinct with mystery.

While strangely to the northern skies,
From lake to lake the wild loon cries,
    Shrill from its hidden bed,
    Alone, uncomforted.

EARLE BIRNEY (1904——)

EARLE BIRNEY was born in Calgary in 1904 and educated at the universities of British Columbia and Toronto. He has done postgraduate work at the universities of California and London and has taught English at the University of Utah and at University College, Toronto. He is now a captain in the Canadian army overseas.

Literary editor of the *Canadian Forum* from 1936 to 1940, Birney has had, in addition to his academic and literary work, a diversity of experience in the rough-and-tumble life of the workaday world. He has been newsboy, butcher's boy, farm laborer, bank clerk, ditch-digger, mosquito-control foreman, mountain guide, house-painter, door-to-door canvasser, chainman, logger, and sailor! Hence, in his poetry learning and craftsmanship apply themselves to a body of material that is rooted in the direct experience of active and difficult living.

David and Other Poems (1942) marked the advent in Canadian literature of poetry on a high level of intensity that combined a cosmopolitan sensibility and a modern technique with a thoroughly Canadian pride in what is excellent and unique in Canadian life. The spaciousness, clarity, and exacting strength of the mountains and forests of British Columbia are felt as a stern controlling force, not without moral significance, and they provide in "David" more than a vivid backdrop for the tragic action. They are the forces of strength, immutability, and truth against which youth in its candor and pride measures itself. Though the climax is failure, it is a tragic one, endured with a full knowledge of what has been lost.

Birney's poetry, like the recent work of Dorothy Livesay and Anne Marriott, is "Canadian" in the only way that is worth anything, implicitly and inevitably; and along with pride in the best elements of Canadian life there is found a sense of shame and anger at all that is servile and corrupt. Out of this comes the wry satire on the bedraggled Anglophilistinism of the Toronto slums in "Anglosaxon Street." "Hands" and "Dusk on English Bay" are the most subtle and powerful expressions of a Canadian's reactions to the second World War that have yet appeared. They present a significant contrast to the patriotic poems of some of the writers of an older generation.

DAVID

I

David and I that summer cut trails on the Survey,
All week in the valley for wages, in air that was steeped
In the wail of mosquitoes, but over the sunalive weekends
We climbed, to get from the ruck of the camp, the surly

Poker, the wrangling, the snoring under the fetid
Tents, and because we had joy in our lengthening coltish
Muscles, and mountains for David were made to see over,
Stairs from the valleys and steps to the sun's retreats.

II

Our first was Mount Gleam. We hiked in the long afternoon
To a curling lake and lost the lure of the faceted
Cone in the swell of its sprawling shoulders. Past
The inlet we grilled our bacon, the strips festooned

On a poplar prong, in the hurrying slant of the sunset.
Then the two of us rolled in the blanket while round us the cold
Pines thrust at the stars. The dawn was a floating
Of mists till we reached to the slopes above timber, and won

To snow like fire in the sunlight. The peak was upthrust
Like a fist in a frozen ocean of rock that swirled
Into valleys the moon could be rolled in. Remotely unfurling
Eastward the alien prairie glittered. Down through the dusty

Skree on the west we descended, and David showed me
How to use the give of shale for giant incredible
Strides. I remember, before the larches' edge,
That I jumped a long green surf of juniper flowing

Away from the wind, and landed in gentian and saxifrage
Spilled on the moss. Then the darkening firs
And the sudden whirring of water that knifed down a fern-hidden
Cliff and splashed unseen into mist in the shadows.

III

One Sunday on Rampart's arête a rainsquall caught us,
And passed, and we clung by our blueing fingers and bootnails
An endless hour in the sun, not daring to move
Till the ice had steamed from the slate. And David taught me

How time on a knife-edge can pass with the guessing of fragments
Remembered from poets, the naming of strata beside one,
And matching of stories from schooldays. . . . . We crawled astride
The peak to feast on the marching ranges flagged

By the fading shreds of the shattered stormcloud. Lingering
There it was David who spied to the south, remote,
And unmapped, a sunlit spire on Sawback, an overhang
Crooked like a talon. David named it the Finger.

That day we chanced on the skull and the splayed white ribs
Of a mountain goat underneath a cliff, caught tight
On a rock. Around were the silken feathers of kites.
And that was the first I knew that a goat could slip.

IV

And then Inglismaldie. Now I remember only
The long ascent of the lonely valley, the live
Pine spirally scarred by lightning, the slicing pipe
Of invisible pika, and great prints, by the lowest

Snow, of a grizzly. There it was too that David
Taught me to read the scroll of coral in limestone
And the beetle-seal in the shale of ghostly trilobites,
Letters delivered to man from the Cambrian waves.

V

On Sundance we tried from the col and the going was hard.
The air howled from our feet to the smudged rocks
And the papery lake below. At an outthrust we balked
Till David clung with his left to a dint in the scarp,

Lobbed the iceaxe over the rocky lip,
Slipped from his holds and hung by the quivering pick,
Twisted his long legs up into space and kicked
To the crest. Then grinning, he reached with his freckled wrist

And drew me up after. We set a new time for that climb.
That day returning we found a robin gyrating
In grass, wing-broken. I caught it to tame but David
Took and killed it, and said, "Could you teach it to fly?"

VI

In August, the second attempt, we ascended The Fortress.
By the forks of the Spray we caught five trout and fried them

Over a balsam fire. The woods were alive
With the vaulting of mule-deer and drenched with clouds all the
   morning,

Till we burst at noon to the flashing and floating round
Of the peaks. Coming down we picked in our hats the bright
And sunhot raspberries, eating them under a mighty
Spruce, while a marten moving like quicksilver scouted us.

VII

But always we talked of the Finger on Sawback, unknown
And hooked, till the first afternoon in September we slogged
Through the musky woods, past a swamp that quivered with frog-
   song,
And camped by a bottle-green lake. But under the cold

Breath of the glacier sleep would not come, the moonlight
Etching the Finger. We rose and trod past the feathery
Larch, while the stars went out, and the quiet heather
Flushed, and the skyline pulsed with the surging bloom

Of incredible dawn in the Rockies. David spotted
Bighorns across the moraine and sent them leaping
With yodels the ramparts redoubled and rolled to the peaks,
And the peaks to the sun. The ice in the morning thaw

Was a gurgling world of crystal and cold blue chasms,
And seracs that shone like frozen saltgreen waves.
At the base of the Finger we tried once and failed. Then David
Edged to the west and discovered the chimney; the last

Hundred feet we fought the rock and shouldered and kneed
Our way for an hour and made it. Unroping we formed
A cairn on the rotting tip. Then I turned to look north
At the glistening wedge of giant Assiniboine, heedless

Of handhold. And one foot gave. I swayed and shouted.
David turned sharp and reached out his arm and steadied me
Turning again with a grin and his lips ready
To jest. But the strain crumbled his foothold. Without

A gasp he was gone. I froze to the sound of grating
Edge-nails and fingers, the slither of stones, the lone
Second of silence, the nightmare thud. Then only
The wind and the muted beat of unknowing cascades.

VIII

Somehow I worked down the fifty impossible feet
To the ledge, calling and getting no answer but echoes
Released in the cirque, and trying not to reflect
What an answer would mean. He lay still, with his lean

Young face upturned and strangely unmarred, but his legs
Splayed beneath him, beside the final drop,
Six hundred feet sheer to the ice. My throat stopped
When I reached him, for he was alive. He opened his grey

Straight eyes and brokenly murmured "over . . . . over."
And I, feeling beneath him a cruel fang
Of the ledge thrust in his back, but not understanding,
Mumbled stupidly, "Best not to move," and spoke

Of his pain. But he said, "I can't move. . . . . If only I felt
Some pain." Then my shame stung the tears to my eyes
As I crouched, and I cursed myself, but he cried,
Louder, "No, Bobbie! Don't ever blame yourself.

I didn't test my foothold." He shut the lids
Of his eyes to the stare of the sky, while I moistened his lips
From our water flask and tearing my shirt into strips
I swabbed the shredded hands. But the blood slid

From his side and stained the stone and the thirsting lichens,
And yet I dared not lift him up from the gore
Of the rock. Then he whispered, "Bob, I want to go over!"
This time I knew what he meant and I grasped for a lie

And said, "I'll be back here by midnight with ropes
And men from the camp and we'll cradle you out." But I knew
That the day and the night must pass and the cold dews
Of another morning before such men unknowing

The ways of mountains could win to the chimney's top.
And then, how long? And he knew . . . . and the hell of hours
After that, if he lived till we came, roping him out.
But I curled beside him and whispered, "The bleeding will stop.

You can last." He said only, "Perhaps. . . . . For what? A wheel-
    chair,
Bob?" His eyes brightening with fever upbraided me.
I could not look at him more and said, "Then I'll stay
With you." But he did not speak, for the clouding fever.

I lay dazed and stared at the long valley,
The glistening hair of a creek on the rug stretched
By the firs, while the sun leaned round and flooded the ledge,
The moss, and David still as a broken doll.

I hunched to my knees to leave, but he called and his voice
Now was sharpened with fear. "For Christ's sake push me over!
If I could move. . . . . Or die. . . . ." The sweat ran from his fore-
      head,
But only his head moved. A kite was buoying

Blackly its wings over the wrinkled ice.
The purr of a waterfall rose and sank with the wind.
Above us climbed the last joint of the Finger
Beckoning bleakly the wide indifferent sky.

Even then in the sun it grew cold lying there. . . . . And I knew
He had tested his holds. It was I who had not. . . . . I looked
At the blood on the ledge, and the far valley. I looked
At last in his eyes. He breathed, "I'd do it for you, Bob."

IX

I will not remember how nor why I could twist
Up the wind-devilled peak, and down through the chimney's empty
Horror, and over the traverse alone. I remember
Only the pounding fear I would stumble on It

When I came to the grave-cold maw of the bergschrund . . . . reeling
Over the sun-cankered snowbridge, shying the caves
In the névé . . . . the fear, and the need to make sure It was there
On the ice, the running and falling and running, leaping

Of gaping greenthroated crevasses, alone and pursued
By the Finger's lengthening shadow. At last through the fanged
And blinding seracs I slid to the milky wrangling
Falls at the glacier's snout, through the rocks piled huge

On the humped moraine, and into the spectral larches,
Alone. By the glooming lake I sank and chilled
My mouth but I could not rest and stumbled still
To the valley, losing my way in the ragged marsh.

I was glad of the mire that covered the stains, on my ripped
Boots, of his blood, but panic was on me, the reek
Of the bog, the purple glimmer of toadstools obscene
In the twilight. I staggered clear to a fire waste, tripped

And fell with a shriek on my shoulder. It somehow eased
My heart to know I was hurt, but I did not faint
And I could not stop while over me hung the range
Of the Sawback. In blackness I searched for the trail by the creek

And found it. . . . . My feet squelched a slug and horror
Rose again in my nostrils. I hurled myself
Down the path. In the woods behind some animal yelped.
Then I saw the glimmer of tents and babbled my story.

I said that he fell straight to the ice where they found him,
And none but the sun and incurious clouds have lingered
Around the marks of that day on the ledge of the Finger,
That day, the last of my youth, on the last of our mountains.

SLUG IN WOODS

For eyes he waves greentipped
taut horns of slime. They dipped,
hours back, across a reef,
a salmonberry leaf.
Then strained to grope past fin
of spruce. Now eyes suck in
as through the hemlock butts
of his day's ledge there cuts
a vixen chipmunk. Stilled
is he—green mucus chilled,
or blotched and soapy stone,
pinguid in moss, alone.
Hours on, he will resume
his silver scrawl, illume
his palimpsest, emboss
his diver's line across
that waving green illim-
itable seafloor. Slim
young jay his sudden shark;
the wrecks he skirts are dark
and fungussed firlogs, whom
spirea sprays emplume,
encoral. Dew his shell,
while mounting boles foretell
of isles in dappled air
fathoms above his care.

Azygous muted life,
himself his viscid wife,
foodward he noses cold beneath his sea.
So spends a summer's jasper century.

ANGLOSAXON STREET

Dawndrizzle ended,   dampness steams from
blotching brick and   blank plasterwaste.
Faded housepatterns,   hoary and finicky,
unfold stuttering,   stick like a phonograph.
Over the eaves and   over dank roofs
peep giraffetowers,   pasted planless
against grey sky,   great dronecliffs
like cutouts for kids,   clipped in two dimensions. . . . .

Here is a ghetto   gotten for goyim,
O with care denuded   of nigger and kike.
No coonsmell rankles,   reeks only cellarrot,
attar of carexhaust,   catcorpse and cookinggrease.
Imperial hearts   heave in this haven.
Cracks across windows   are welded with slogans;
There'll Always Be An England   enhances geraniums,
and *V*'s for a *Victory*   vanquish the housefly.

Ho! with climbing sun,   heading from cocoons,
go bleached beldames,   garnished in bargainbasements,
festooned with shoppingbags,   farded, flatarched,
bigthewed Saxonwives,   stepping over buttrivers,
waddling back to suckle   smallfry, wienerladen.

Hoy! with sunslope,   shrieking over hydrants,
flood from learninghall   the lean fingerlings,
Nordic, nobblecheeked,   not all clean of nose,
leaping Commando-wise   into leprous lanes.

What! after whistleblow,   spewed from wheelboat,
after daylong doughtiness,   dire handplay
in sewertrench or sandpit,   come Saxonthegns,
Junebrown Jutekings,   jawslack for meat.

Sit after supper   on smeared doorsteps,
not humbly swearing   hatedeeds on Huns,
profiteers, politicians,   pacifists and Jews.

Then by twobit magic   to muse in movie,
unlock picturehoard,   or lope to alehall,
soaking bleakly   in beer, skittleless.

Home again to hotbox   and humid husbandhood,
in slumbertrough adding   sleepily to Anglekin.
Alongside in lanenooks   carling and leman
caterwaul and clip,   careless of Saxonry,
with moonglow and haste   and a higher heartbeat.

Slumbers now slumtrack,   unstinks, cooling,
waiting brief for milkhind,   mornstar and worldrise.

DUSK ON ENGLISH BAY

The lighting rooms perfect a chequerboard
Across apartment boxes. Through the popcorn
Reek, hotdogs and chips, the air lets fall
A rain of quiet coolness on the flesh. The calling
Bathers trot the footpocked sand on legs
Unsexed by distance, waving arms severed
With twilight. From the whitening ribs of the raft divers
Flash cream arcs across the expiring
Sunset, and are quenched. Beyond the bay the files
Of regimented lamps are pulsing evenly
On the long tamed whale of Point Grey. The evening
Star detaches and floats into the chartreuse heavens,
An arrested rocket. The moon, behind a row
Of moons along the promenade, contracts and yellows
Upward. Night's dissolvent eats into the west,
Browning the stippled mauve, the copper sulphate,
Paling and paling the opal, melting the latest
Speck of robin's eggshell into the Gulf of Georgia,
And ever over the Pacific pursuing tomorrow's
Sun. But tomorrow's sun is clean escaped
And rushes down through Asian skies, garish
With burst of shell and unarrested rocket,
And burns on Libyan sands, by bombs
Cratered and red with libations poured to the guns.
Past Narvik's blanching hulks tomorrow's sun
Is flying, over the Mediterranean's smudged
Embattled sharks, and the sailors quenched, and is climbing
To stricken dawn in England, widening his light

On limbs unsexed and severed, and the rain of iron
Cooling the flesh, and the stench of the flesh cooled,
While the flame untamed probes the tenement ruins.
Speeding and soaring he comes, the Atlantic sighting,
And there is no Joshua can brake his flight, nor
Any clutch of ours can hold this precious night.

HANDS

In the amber morning by the inlet's high shore
My canoe drifts and the slim trees come bending
Arching the palms of their still green hands
Juggling the shimmer of ripples.
                                   Too bewildering
Even in the dead days of peace was this manumission,
The leaves' illogical loveliness. Now am I frustrate,
Alien. Here is the battle steeped in silence,
The fallen have use and fragrantly nourish the quick.
My species would wither, away from the radio's barkings,
The headline beating its chimpanzee breast, the nimble
Young digits at levers and triggers. Lithe are these balsam
Fingers, gaunt as a Jew's in Poland, but green,
Green, not of us, our colours are black and red.
Cold and unskilled is the cedar, his webbed claws
Drooping over the water shall focus no bombsight
Nor suture the bayoneted bowel, his jade tips
Alert but to seadew and air and the soundless touch
Of the light winked by the wind from the breathing ocean,
Inept to clutch the parachute cord, the uniformed
Throat, the mud by the Thames in ebbing agony.
These alders cupping their womanish palms, pulsing
To the startled light when the long unpredictable swell
Reaches from the grey heart of the far Pacific,
Are not of my flesh. Their hands speak for Brutus,
And signal sedition to the poet interned and the lover
Suppressed; they render nought unto Caesar.
                                   My fingers
Must close on the paddle. Back to the safe dead
Wood of the docks, the whining poles of the city,
And to hands the extension of tools, of the militant typewriter,
The self-filling patriot pen, back to the paws

Clasping warmly over the bomber contract,
Applauding the succulent orators, back to the wrinkled
Index weaving the virtuous sock, pointing the witch hunt,
While the splayed fist thrusts at the heart of hereafter.
We are gloved with steel, and a magnet is set us in Europe.
We are not of these woods, we are not of these woods,
Our roots are in autumn, and store for no spring.

CHARLES BRUCE (1906——)

SINCERITY and a forthright solidity of feeling are characteristic of Charles Bruce's poems of the Nova Scotia countryside and seacoast, qualities which are well illustrated in his remarkable "Words Are Never Enough," which was awarded first prize in a Dominion-wide competition. Charles Bruce was born in 1906 at Port Shoreham, Nova Scotia, and was educated in the country school there and at Mount Allison University, Sackville, New Brunswick. He is a newspaperman by profession and is at present head of the Canadian Press Bureau in Toronto. He has published *Wild Apples* (privately printed, 1927); *Tomorrow's Tide* (1932); and *Personal Record* (1942), an impressive statement of faith in the heroism with which the common people of Britain carry on the war.

WORDS ARE NEVER ENOUGH

These are the fellows who smell of salt to the prairie,
Keep the back country informed of crumbling swell
That buckles the international course off Halifax
After a night of wind:
Angus Walters and Ben Pine, carrying on for Tommy Himmelman
    and Marty Welch,
Heading up the tough men who get into the news,
Heading up the hard men of Lunenburg and Gloucester,
Keeping the cities bordered with grass and grain
Forever mindful that something wet and salt
Creeps and loafs and marches round the continent,
Careless of time, careless of change, obeying the moon.

Listen to little Angus, squinting at the *Bluenose:*
"The timber that'll beat her still grows in the woods."
Yes, these are the fellows who remind you again of the sea.

But one town or two
Are never enough to keep the salt in the blood.

I haven't seen Queensport Light over the loom of Ragged Head
   in years,
And never a smell of rollers coming up the bay from Canso;
No one ever heard of Queensport outside of a bait report,
No one ever saw the name of Ragged Head anywhere.

Off that obscure beach Will Bruce and George McMasters
Set their herring nets, and went farther out for mackerel.
The mackerel never ran; but in July
Fat herring tangled in wet twine were silver-thick,
And the flat low in the water as we hauled around
To head back for the huts;
In full daylight now,
After the grey dusk of a windless morning,
After the bay, gently stirring in half darkness,
Tipped down again to blush at the sun's rim.

Cleaning fish is a job you would balk at;
But nothing is mean with gulls hovering down,
Sun brighter than life on glistening eelgrass,
The bay crawling again in a quickening south-west wind.

There was always time after the wash-barrels were empty,
After hand-barrows were lugged up the beach to the hut,
And herring lay behind handwrought staves, clean with salt.

Time to lie on warm stone and listen
While the sting went out of crooked fingers and thighs ceased
   to ache;
Time to hear men's voices, coming quietly through a coloured
   cloth of sound
Woven in the slap of water on fluent gravel.

Their talk was slow and quiet, of fish and men
And fields back on the hill with fences down,
Hay to be made through long hot days with never a splash on
   the oilskins
Or the lift of water awake under half-inch pine.

The mackerel never ran; and if the herring
Had been only a story, a legend for midnight telling,
These would have launched their flats and tended the empty nets.

I know it now, remembering now the calm;
Remembering now the lowering care that lifted
From a face turned to the wind off Ragged Head.

These are the fellows who keep the salt in the blood.
Knowing it fresh in themselves, needful as hope,
They give to the cities bordered with woods and grass
A few homesick men, walking an alien street;
A few women, remembering misty stars
And the long grumbling sigh of the bay at night.

Words are never enough; these are aware
Somewhere deep in the soundless well of knowing
That sea in the flesh and nerves and the puzzling mind
Of children born to the long grip of its tide
Must always wash the land's remotest heart.
These are the fellows who keep the salt in the blood.

IMMEDIATES

Immediates? Let us take for text
The bite of salt through sodden wool,
And place a running headrope next
Ink by the pen or bucketful.

A cent for haddock, two for cod;
Weather a chance, and wind a guess—
But no allegiance to the god
Of unavailing bitterness.

Here on the roofless beach they know
The fallibility of plan,
That justice and injustice grow
Not from the system but the man.

An ageless land and sea conspire
To smooth the imperfect mould of birth;
While freezing spray and drying fire
Translate the inexplicit earth:

"Get understanding first of these:
The open cut, the healing scar;
Before you flick prophetic keys
To tell us what immediates are."

ALTERNATIVE

Immediates? Well we have birth and sickness and death,
And hunger for whispering water and good white bread.
Immediates? Fireside warmth and a caught breath
At flowering stars, and a friendly body in bed.

There are times when the eye of the spirit can see it all,
But voice and pencil are never enough to enrich
The man next door with a flame. They are only a scrawl
On the edge of a picture, one note on the pipes, one stitch

In a seam so woven that fabric and thread are one.
It is good to look at this hour and then set free
Protest and studied invective; granted and done;
There is virtue, too, in a gray and dragonish sea.

DOROTHY LIVESAY (1909——)

DOROTHY LIVESAY was born in Winnipeg in 1909. She was educated at the University of Toronto and the Sorbonne in Paris. Her first poems were published in a small brochure entitled *Green Pitcher* (1928) and, like the first work of many young poets, were not without echoes of her early enthusiasms. Miss Livesay went to school to poets most like herself, sensitive women poets who were developing a modern technique—the poets who could help her most: Emily Dickinson, Elinor Wylie, and H. D. The successful assimilation of these "influences" in a series of lyrics that combine emotion and wit in an individual and personal, yet thoroughly feminine, way gives its significance to a greater part of the volume of poems, *Signpost*, published in 1932. The personal lyrics deal with nature, love, and death. What lends them a special distinction is the freshness, simplicity, and clarity of the impressions and the childlike intensity and honesty of the feeling. A sense of country things and a knowledgeable appreciation of sunshine, water, growing things, and animals are responsible for the charm of the nature poems. These qualities are combined in the longer dramatic poem, "City Wife."

In Paris, Miss Livesay wrote a dissertation, *The Influence of French Symbolism on Modern English Poets*, and while her interest in the background and technique of modernist poetry was growing she was also acquiring experience in left-wing social and political activity. The development of Miss Livesay's poetry has been well summarized by Professor E. K. Brown, in the Canadian issue of *Poetry: A Magazine of Verse:* "From a mood of delicate introspection and a concern with refined patterns, Dorothy Livesay passed first to deliberately simple verse, packed with social exhortation and invective and addressed to an unsophisticated audience; and then to a combination of social concern with elaborate modes of expression which suited her individuality, but now the expression was suppled and purged." The best examples of these two stages in Dorothy Livesay's verse are, of the first, the pantomimic representation of the soul-killing destructiveness of labor on the assembly line, "Day and

334

Night," which was featured in the first issue of the *Canadian Poetry Magazine*, and, of the second, the elegy on Federico García Lorca, the Spanish poet put to death by Franco's men in September, 1936. Her latest verse, as illustrated in "Prelude for Spring" and "Poem," shows a development in the direction of intensity of feeling and originality of expression. An ecstatic impressionism has become the servant of genuine spiritual experience. A collection of her recent poems is to appear in 1943.

There is a useful essay on Dorothy Livesay in W. E. Collin's *The White Savannahs* (1936).

CITY WIFE

Almost before the sun has touched the fields
Horses and cart are waiting patiently
Inside the yard, until their driver comes
To swing with iron hand the heavy gate
As if it were the night he pushes back:
Only to show where slow the daylight comes
With silent footsteps over silent roads.
The gate swings back: one movement, and I watch
The cart, the horses and the man alone,
Absorbed in the day ahead, which means to him
Only the day between concession lines.
I watch: the image of these quiet things
Is graven on my heart. He will not turn;
The horses will not turn, but go their way
Soberly, steadily, up and over the hill
Until there is nothing left to see but hill
And nothing left to hear but silentness
Now that the horse, the cart, the man, are gone.
I know by heart what farmers do in spring.
I know by heart the things I ought to do;
And yet, forgetting all, I stand and dream.

Springs came before like this. Last year the crows
Made all the morning echo with their songs,
Just as to-day. Sun must have been as bright,
Wind as caressing as this country wind.

NOTE: A "city" girl, among farm people, is one who, reared in the towns, comes to make her home in the country.

Yet never, it seems, have I half understood
The music and the singing festival
That cries to be expressed, of early spring.
It is delight simply to stand entranced
Caught in the aery, golden web of dream
The sun spins, while every sense is lost
Within the enchanted pattern of the spring.

Springs came before like this, I say again,
But never before with me, in any year,
Has spring been knowledge laid into my heart;
Knowledge of wind and sun on open fields,
Of silence brooding on some nest of woods.
Why should I know how springs came long ago,
Lost as I am in this? Only I feel
No more is morning like a gleaming knife
Coming to pierce my sleep. Instead it is
Dream into changing dream, until at last
There comes reality—the scarlet sun.
Or say it is song into song, perhaps, until
Harshly the song of the crow breaks over all.

Jet crows beating their tireless wings,
Fighting northward where the snow still clings:
Strong crows breaking into strident song—
And now I remember how the winter was long.

So are my days kindled from quiet thought,
Serenity, to unexpected fire:
So is my mind a little open space
Free for all varying winds to stop and rest.
So is my heart a wider, new-ploughed field
Waking to hear the slow feet treading there.
Yes, I come always to this memory
Of feet going and coming over the land,
The man plodding behind the persistent team
For all the day, but coming at last to me,
At last to the house, and the meal and the quietness.
Is it to me he comes, or to the barn
Where in the golden gloom the horses stamp
And munch the hay he shakes down from the loft?
Is it to me? . . . . But why this heavy doubt,
When everywhere the world cries out in faith:
When every single leaf on every tree
Holds yet a different light against the sky?

Oh, I have followed where the first bare maple
Suddenly turned to gold, where deeper still
There flamed in red a different maple tree
Boldly against the sober evergreens:
And even further I plunged, until too soon
The other end of the wood was reached, and broke
Into a line of pale wild cherry trees
Too lovely to be startled by a sound,
Too young to be enchanted by the wind.

*　　*　　*

I ran from there, thinking I could not turn
But only follow the swiftly-curving road
Until I saw that silence was swinging back,
A golden pendulum above the wood—
No! the spring sweetness was too much: a voice
Seemed to cry loud and louder: Turn! Turn once—
As long ago one thought he heard a voice
And could not move until he called her name:
The name of all names surely loveliest,
Of lost, forever lost, Eurydice.

> *How many of us have learned, with Orpheus,*
> *Not to look back at loveliness:*
> *Not to look back, lest any evil chance*
> *Should tell us how life vanishes . . . .*

In soberness I walked the road again
Seeming to hear lost ecstasy fall back,
Ever receding as I travelled on.
The road ran through a group of thin young birch
Shining like silver arrows in the sun:
And lombardies, without their summer leaves,
Were free to feel the wind. The road then turned;
Leaving the wood, it ran between two fields.
I found delight again watching the elms
That grew beside snake fences in a row,
Or even stooping in the wayside grass
To see if purple violets were in bloom.

> *Jet crows beating their tireless wings,*
> *Jet crows flying and crying:*
> *How long before they all return,*
> *Afraid of the keen wind's sighing?*

But even so, in my little house,
Even if autumn comes
Will not the dark fall faster then
When my love comes?

Will not the dark bring quietness
And make him forget the land,
Make him forget the harvesting
Of the strong land?

I am not frightened of the earth,
But I have flung myself
Deep in a field of grass and dust
And known myself:

Yet for such long, long hours he ploughs,
Intent on his horses' step;
If I come near he does not know
Nor hear *my* step . . . .

> *Jet crows cawing and cawing above,*
> *Crows in the sky:*
> *Is it a song they shout—*
> *Or a warning cry?*

I may not end my song; evening is here,
And spring is possessing once more the field of my heart.
I must be silent again, as the elm at the gate
Which broods till the time of leaves.—If I speak, will
    he look,
Will he open his eyes and gaze suddenly into my face,
Starting the fire of my joy, and the sweet unrest?

I hear no answer in the quiet elm,
Still and enduring. Even as the tree, I wait
Till over the hill the horses slowly climb.

PRELUDE FOR SPRING

These dreams abound:
Foot's leap to shore
Above the sound
Of river's roar—
Disabled door
Banged and barricaded.

Then on, on
Furrow, fawn
Through wall and wood
So fast no daring could
Tear off the hood
Unmask the soul pursued.

Slash underbrush
Tear bough and branch
Seek cover, rabbits' burrow—
Hush!

He comes. Insistent, sure
Proud prowler, this pursuer comes
Noiseless, no wind-stir
No leaf-turn over;
Together quiet creeps on twig,
Hush hovers in his hands.

How loud heart's thump—
Persistent pump
Sucks down, down sap
Then up in surge
(Axe striking stump).

How breezy breath—
Too strong a wind
Scatters a stir
Where feathers are,
Bustles a bough.

How blind two eyes
Shuttling to-fro
Not weaving light
Nor sight . . . .
In darkness flow.

(Only the self is loud;
World's whisperless.)

Dive down then, scuttle under:
Run, fearless of feet's thunder.
Somehow, the road rolls back in mist
Here is the meadow where we kissed
And here the horses, galloping
We rode upon in spring . . . .

O beat of air, wing beat
Scatter of rain, sleet
Resisting leaves,
Retarding feet

And drip of rain, leaf drip
Sting on cheek and lip
Tearing pores
With lash of whip

And hoof's away, heart's hoof
Down greening lanes, with roof
Of cherry blow
And apple puff—

O green wet, sun lit
Soaked earth's glitter!
Down mouth, to munch
Up hoof, to canter

Through willow lanes
A gold-shaft shower,
Embracing elms
That lack leaf-lustre

And copse' cool bed
All lavendered
With scentless, sweet
Hepatica—

Till side by side
In fields' brown furrow
Swathe sunlight over
Every shadow!

But still
On heart's high hill
And summit of
A day's delight
Still will he swoop
From heaven's height
Soaring unspent,
Still will he stoop to brush
Wing tip on hair,
Fan mind with fear.

And now the chill
Raw sun
Goes greener still—
The sky
Cracks like an icicle:

Frozen, foot-locked
Heart choked and chafed
Wing-battered and unsafe,
Grovel to ground!
A cry
Lashes the sky—

These dreams abound.

FOR FEDERICO GARCÍA LORCA

When veins congeal
And gesture is confounded
When pucker frowns no more
And voice's door
Is shut forever

On such a night
My bed will shrink
To single size
Sheets go cold
The heart hammer
With life-loud clamor
While someone covers up the eyes.

Ears are given
To hear the silence driven in
Nailed down.
And we descend now down from heaven
Into earth's mould, down.

*While you—
You hold the light
Unbroken.*

When you lived
Day shone from your face
Now the sun rays search
And find no answering torch.

If you were living now
This cliffside tree
With its embracing bough
Would speak to me.

If you were speaking now
The waves below
Would be the organ stops
For breath to blow.

And if your rigid head
Flung back its hair
Gulls in a sickle flight
Would circle there.

> *You make the flight*
> *Unshaken.*

You are alive!
O grass flash emerald sight
Dash of dog for ball
And skipping rope's bright blink
Lashing the light!

High in cloud
The sunset fruits are basketed
And fountains curl their plumes
On statue stone.
In secret thicket mould
Lovers defend their hold
Old couples hearing whisperings
Touch in a handclasp, quivering.

For you sang out aloud
Arching the silent wood
To stretch itself, tiptoe,
Above the crowd . . . .

> *You hold the word*
> *Unspoken.*

You breathe. You be!
Bare, stripped light
Time's fragment flagged
Against the dark.

You dance. Explode
Unchallenged through the door
As bullets burst
Long deaths ago, your breast.

And song outsoars
The bomber's range
Serene with wind-
Maneuvered cloud.

Light flight and word
The unassailed, the token!

POEM

Night's soft armor welds me into thought
Pliant and all engaging; warm dark,
No scintillations to distract
Nor any restless ray, moon-shot.
I am still of all but breathing—
No throbbing eye, no pulse; and a hushed heart.

* * *

Sometimes at rest, the bones assume
World's weight, hold us dumb
We cannot lift a finger, flick
An eyelash, wag a tongue;
Breath is the only fluctuation in
Death's posture, stony, dumb.

Then is all sound fled
Flown from the fluted ear
Wind in the heavy head
Can find no corridor

And then is sight so bound
Lids petrified to earth
Only one light is found—
Imagination's going forth!

Only the heaven sent
Pulse of the universe
Beats through the buried heart
Its steady course.

MARY ELIZABETH COLMAN

MARY ELIZABETH COLMAN lives in Vancouver and works as a librarian. She has contributed poetry to a number of Canadian magazines and to the Canadian number of *Poetry* (Chicago). A "Ryerson Chapbook," *The Immigrants*, appeared in 1929 and another, *For This Freedom Too*, in 1942. Here a social awareness of the issues at stake in the struggles of our time seeks to justify itself by searching for philosophical, and ultimately religious, values. The undertaking is ambitious, and it leads in some of Miss Colman's poems to diffuseness and vagueness, but when, as in "Answer," thought, imagery, and emotion suddenly fuse, the result is poetry at once strange and completely convincing, a small but genuine achievement.

ANSWER

Hungry unnumbered since the birth of time
Question the dusty sky
In vain: no answer there.

Gone, gone, as darkness floods the day,
Fled, sped, unsatisfied—
Ashes to ashes; dust to dust.

(The scabbard falls, yet the bright sword
Guardian no longer
Speeds, speeds to the Horseman's hand.)

Still time arrogant, invincible, is armed with death;
Still the unregarding worlds roll on;
The universe expands—is dumb.

With no stone hunger be fed, but quickening bread
When tall-sceptered time at last
Is whipped, stripped, done and dead.

FLORIS CLARK McLAREN

BORN in Skagway, Alaska, and now living in Victoria, British Columbia, Floris McLaren found the subjects of her early verse in the Arctic landscapes and wintry weather of the primitive Northwest. In her first volume, *Frozen Fire* (1937), she was content to suggest the feel of her country in precise and objective images. Her recent lyrics have a richness of implication that goes beyond the isolated and individual austerities of the Arctic poems. The wood and the stream of the two poems included here exist in a metaphysical as well as a natural landscape.

WHO HAS GONE THROUGH THE WOOD

Is there no landmark: no north-growing moss:
No cairn, no dipper-star, no color of dawn:
Only pale end of night succeeding dark?

Surely we saw that split-top pine last night
But in the other direction: do trees move
Striding across the forest in the dark:
Do mountains play cat-corner so we go
Stumbling bewildered toward identical hills
Through similar thickets?

Here are signs that another has come this way:
A broken mullein spike, a trodden leaf,
A pressed-down hollow of moss where he lay to rest. . . . .
Or did we rest here? Was this the trickle of stream
Where we wet our handkerchiefs in the afternoon?
There are snapped-off twigs,
There are other footprints here
Joining and crossing: are they all our own?
Confusion come full circle: the hidden fear
Crouched in the thicket:
The thunder, the mounting stormheads, the copper sky.

Wind in the cracking trees: the dangerous air
Hurls javelin branches. Cower from the sharp-edged rain
Hide from the wind: hide where?

If this were fire exploding from pine to pine
We could run together, run from the terror, find
Safety perhaps: a stream or the edge of the wood:
The shared perception incredibly heightened: the focused
Experience suddenly clear: the shattering fire-flash of vision.
But this is not terror. This is only fear:
Fear and the cold uncertainty that sends us
Hopelessly calling through the trees
Shielding our heads with our arms
Numb, separate, lost.

With the spend wind, the reaffirming sun,
The after-peace of storm, pause momently
In the pulsing forest: ask again
The unanswered question.

Now has the light changed?

Sun over storm wrack: litter of broken boughs
Not prism-edged but every leaf defined
In clean perspective:
Here is the trail waist-deep in windfall now:
Move the heaped branches slowly tediously
Make a new path around this prostrate tree
Root-spread against the sky.
Go wary where the swamp-edge sucks your feet
Presently reach the safe the hard-packed ground.

In this towering trunk of time blind circles go
Narrowing back to the center, the constant heart;
And see against the sky the needles stirred
By rhythmic high air currents, the future flowing
From pattern to pattern. This is all we know.
Lay your ear to the resin-beaded bark
To hear the slow rings growing.

NO MORE THE SLOW STREAM

No more the slow stream spreading clear in sunlight
Lacing the swamp with intricate shining channels
Patterned by wind and the dipping tall marsh grasses:

No more the mica glint in the sliding water
The bright-winged flies and the muskrat gone like a shadow
No more the curved trout breaking concentric silver:

Now the basalt cliffs and the yellow foam in the eddies
Now the strong brown water boiling deeply from under
Now the log abutment left where the bridge has fallen:

O the slow stream lovely, lovely no more in sunlight:
The flotsam of quiet lives turned over and over,
The dark destructive flood; and the plan the promise
Spun in the current, swept toward no visible ocean.

ANNE MARRIOTT (1913——)

ANNE MARRIOTT was born in Victoria, British Columbia, in 1913, and was educated at private schools there. Her poems have appeared in a number of periodicals and in three chapbooks: *The Wind Our Enemy* (1939); *Calling Adventurers* (1941), being the verse choruses from *Payload*, a documentary radio drama about the Canadian North; and *Salt Marsh and Other Poems* (1941).

Combining the imagists' method of presenting significant detail in sharp, concrete flashes with the more expansive sweep of the poet of social revolt, Miss Marriott has presented, in "The Wind Our Enemy," one of the most effective expressions of the tragedy of drought on the prairie that Canadian literature has to offer. It is interesting to compare Miss Marriott's method—a method involving bulk and variety—with that of Mr. Laight in "Soliloquy" (p. 355) and of Miss Colman in "Answer" (p. 344). In the two short poems the effect is gained by concentration, the former illustrating the power of a conventional form and familiar images, the latter of a subtle, original, and even difficult approach. Of Miss Marriott's poems, some are skilfully-seen imagist pictures in which raw colors and jagged shapes give strength and solidity to the pattern, while others, like "Prairie Graveyard," continue, with an objectivity that produces a note of sardonic irony, the social criticism implicit in "The Wind Our Enemy." *Calling Adventurers*, dealing with a theme more romantic in appeal, was honored with the Governor-General's Award in 1941.

THE WIND OUR ENEMY

I

Wind
flattening its gaunt furious self against
the naked siding, knifing in the wounds
of time, pausing to tear aside the last
old scab of paint.

Wind
surging down the cocoa-coloured seams
of summer-fallow, darting in about
white hoofs and brown, snatching the sweaty cap
shielding red eyes.

Wind
filling the dry mouth with bitter dust
whipping the shoulders worry-bowed too soon,
soiling the water pail, and in grim prophecy
greying the hair.

II

The wheat in spring was like a giant's bolt of silk
Unrolled over the earth.
When the wind sprang
It rippled as if a great broad snake
Moved under the green sheet
Seeking its outward way to light.
In autumn it was an ocean of flecked gold
Sweet as a biscuit, breaking in crisp waves
That never shattered, never blurred in foam.
That was the last good year. . . . .

III

The wheat was embroidering
All the spring morning,
Frail threads needled by sunshine like thin gold.
A man's heart could love his land,
Smoothly self-yielding,
Its broad spread promising all his granaries might hold.
A woman's eyes could kiss the soil
From her kitchen window,
Turning its black depths to unchipped cups—a silk crepe dress—
(Two-ninety-eight, Sale Catalogue)
Pray sun's touch be gentleness,
Not a hot hand scorching flesh it would caress.
But sky like a new tin pan
Hot from the oven
Seemed soldered to the earth by horizons of glare. . . . .

The third day he left the fields. . . . .

Heavy scraping footsteps
Spoke before his words, "Crops dried out—everywhere—"

IV

They said, "Sure, it'll rain next year!"
When that was dry, "Well, next year anyway."
Then, "Next—"
But still the metal hardness of the sky
Softened only in mockery.
When lightning slashed and twanged
And thunder made the hot head surge with pain
Never a drop fell;
Always hard yellow sun conquered the storm.
So the soon sickly-familiar saying grew,
(Watching the futile clouds sneak down the north)
"Just empties goin' back!"
(Cold laughter bending parched lips in a smile
Bleak eyes denied.)

V

Horses were strong so strong men might love them,
Sides groomed to copper burning the sun,
Wind tangling wild manes, dust circling wild hoofs,
Turn the colts loose! Watch the two-year-olds run!
Then heart thrilled fast and the veins filled with glory
The feel of hard leather a fortune more sweet
Than a girl's silky lips. He was one with the thunder,
The flying, the rhythm, of untamed, unshod feet!

But now—

It makes a man white-sick to see them now,
Dull—heads sagging—crowding to the trough—
No more spirit than a barren cow.
The well's pumped dry to wash poor fodder down,
Straw and salt—and endless salt and straw—
(Thank God the winter's mild so far)
Dry Russian thistle crackling in the jaw—
The old mare found the thistle pile, ate till she bulged,
Then, crazily, she wandered in the yard,
Saw a water-drum, and staggering to its rim,
Plodded around it—on and on in hard,
Madly relentless circle. Weaker—stumbling—
She fell quite suddenly, heaved once and lay.
(Nellie the kids' pet's gone, boys.
Hitch up the strongest team. Haul her away.

Maybe we should have mortgaged all we had
Though it wasn't much, even in good years, and draw
Ploughs with a jolting tractor.
Still—you can't make gas of thistles or oat-straw.)

VI

Relief.
"God, we tried so hard to stand alone!"

Relief.
"Well, we can't let the kids go cold."
They trudge away to school swinging half-empty lard-pails,
to shiver in the schoolhouse (unpainted seven years),
learning from a blue-lipped girl
almost as starved as they.

Relief cars.
"Apples, they say, and clothes!"
The folks in town get their pick first,
Then their friends—
"Eight miles for us to go so likely we
won't get much—"
"Maybe we'll get the batteries charged up and have
the radio to kind of brighten things—"

Insurgents march in Spain

Japs bomb Chinese

Airliner lost

"Maybe we're not as badly off as some—"
"Maybe there'll be a war and we'll get paid to fight—"
"Maybe—"
"See if Eddie Cantor's on to-night!"

VII

People grew bored
Well-fed in the east and west
By stale, drought-area tales,
Bored by relief whinings,
Preferred their own troubles.
So those who still had stayed
On the scorched prairie,
Found even sympathy
Seeming to fail them
Like their own rainfall.

"Well—let's forget politics,
Forget the wind, our enemy!
Let's forget farming, boys,
Let's put on a dance to-night!
Mrs. Smith'll bring a cake.
Mrs. Olsen's coffee's swell!"

The small uneven schoolhouse floor
Scraped under big work-boots
Cleaned for the evening's fun,
Gasoline lamps whistled.
One Hungarian boy
Snapped at a shrill guitar,
A Swede from out north of town
Squeezed an accordion dry,
And a Scotchwoman from Ontario
Made the piano dance
In time to "The Mocking-Bird"
And "When I grow too Old to Dream,"
Only taking time off
To swing in a square dance,
Between ten and half-past three.

Yet in the morning
Air peppered thick with dust,
All the night's happiness
Seemed far away, unreal
Like a lying mirage,
Or the icy-white glare
Of the alkali slough.

VIII

Presently the dark dust seemed to build a wall
That cut them off from east and west and north,
Kindness and honesty, things they used to know,
Seemed blown away and lost
In frantic soil.
At last they thought
Even God and Christ were hidden
By the false clouds.
—Dust-blinded to the staring parable,
Each wind-splintered timber like a pain-bent Cross.
Calloused, groping fingers, trembling

With overwork and fear,
Ceased trying to clutch at some faith in the dark,
Thin sick courage fainted, lacking hope.
But tightened, tangled nerves scream to the brain
If there is no hope, give them forgetfulness!
The cheap light of the beer-parlour grins out,
Promising shoddy security for an hour.
The Finn who makes bad liquor in his barn
Grows fat on groaning emptiness of souls.

IX

The sun goes down. Earth like a thick black coin
Leans its round rim against the yellowed sky.
The air cools. Kerosene lamps are filled and lit
In dusty windows. Tired bodies crave to lie
In bed forever. Chores are done at last.
A thin horse neighs drearily. The chickens drowse,
Replete with grasshoppers that have gnawed and scraped
Shrivelled garden-leaves. No sound from the gaunt cows.
Poverty, hand in hand with fear, two great
Shrill-jointed skeletons stride loudly out
Across the pitiful fields, none to oppose.
Courage is roped with hunger, chained with doubt.
Only against the yellow sky, a part
Of the jetty silhouette of barn and house
Two figures stand, heads close, arms locked,
And suddenly some spirit seems to rouse
And gleam, like a thin sword, tarnished, bent,
But still shining in the spared beauty of moon,
As his strained voice says to her, "We're not licked yet!
It must rain again—it *will!* Maybe—soon—"

X

Wind
in a lonely laughterless shrill game
with broken wash-boiler, bucket without
a handle, Russian thistle, throwing up
sections of soil.

God, will it never rain again? What about
those clouds out west? No, that's just dust, as thick
and stifling now as winter underwear.
No rain, no crop, no feed, no faith, only
wind.

PRAIRIE GRAVEYARD

Wind mutters thinly on the sagging wire
binding the graveyard from the gouged dirt road,
bends thick-bristled Russian thistle,
sifts listless dust
into cracks in hard grey ground.
Empty prairie slides away
on all sides, rushes toward a wide
expressionless horizon, joined
to a vast blank sky.

Lots near the road are the most expensive
where heavy tombstones lurch a fraction
tipped by splitting soil.
Farther, a row of aimless heaps
names weather-worn from tumbled sticks
remember now the six thin children
of a thin, shiftless home.

Hawk, wind-scouring, cuts
a pointed shadow on the drab scant grass.

Two graves apart by the far fence
are suicides, one with a grand
defiant tombstone, bruising at the heart
"Death is swallowed up in victory."
(And may be, God's kindness being more large
than man's, to this, who after seven years
of drought, burned down his barn,
himself hanged in it.)
The second, nameless, set around
with even care-sought stones
(no stones on this section)
topped with two plants, hard-dried,
in rust-thick jam tins in the caked drab pile.

A gopher jumps from a round cave,
springs furtively, spurts under fence, is gone.
Wind raises dead curls of dust and whines
under its harsh breath on the limp dragged wires,
then leaves the graveyard stiff with silence, lone
in the centre of the huge lone land and sky.

FREDERICK E. LAIGHT
(1915———)

FREDERICK E. LAIGHT was born in Regina, Saskatchewan, in 1915, where he now lives. He is the author of several one-act plays and has contributed poetry to many Canadian magazines. The sonnet included here gives powerful expression to the sense of desperation that the years of drought and economic depression made familiar in the prairie provinces.

SOLILOQUY

I have seen tall chimneys without smoke,
   And I have seen blank windows without blinds,
   And great dead wheels, and motors without minds,
And vacant doorways grinning at the joke.

I have seen loaded wagons creak and sway
   Along the roads into the North and East,
   Each dragged by some great-eyed and starving beast
To God knows where, but just away—away.

And I have heard the wind awake at nights
   Like some poor mother left with empty hands,
   Go whimpering in the silent stubble lands
And creeping through bare houses without lights.

These comforts only have I for my pain—
   The frantic laws of statesmen bowed with cares
   To feed me, and the slow, pathetic prayers
Of godly men that somehow it shall rain.

PART VI

MODERN POETRY: THE
COSMOPOLITAN TRADITION

F. R. SCOTT (1899——)

THE son of Archdeacon Frederick George Scott, F. R. Scott was born in Quebec City in 1899. He was educated at Bishop's University, Oxford, and McGill, where he is now professor of constitutional law. A former Rhodes Scholar and Guggenheim Fellow, he has a distinguished reputation as a writer on Canada's economic and social problems. His best-known work is *Canada Today* (1938). F. R. Scott's first poems were published with those of A. M. Klein and Leo Kennedy in the *McGill Fortnightly Review* (1926–27), and he was largely responsible for the publication of the group anthology, *New Provinces* (1936). Scott's best work is in the field of light satire, but the directness and intensity of his love poems and the sense of social responsibility in his more recent poems are indications of the variety and complexity of his interests. Recently he has been one of the leading figures in the group of Montreal poets responsible for the mimeographed little magazine, *Preview*.

There is an essay on F. R. Scott in W. E. Collin's *The White Savannahs* (1936), though it is less satisfactory than some of the others in the book.

DEDICATION

From those condemned to labour
For profit of another
We take our new endeavour.

For sect and class and pattern
Through whom the strata harden
We sharpen now the weapon.

Till power is brought to pooling
And masses share in ruling
There will not be an ending
Nor any peace for spending.

CONFLICT

When I see the falling bombs
Then I see defended homes.
Men above and men below
Die to save the good they know.

Through the wrong the bullets prove
Shows the bravery of love.
Pro and con have single stem
Half a truth dividing them.

Between the dagger and the breast
The bond is stronger than the beast.
Prison, ghetto, flag and gun
Mark the craving for the One.

Persecution's cruel mouth
Shows a twisted love of truth.
Deeper than the rack and rope
Lies the double human hope.

My good, your good, good we seek
Though we turn no other cheek.
He who slays and he who's slain
Like in purpose, like in pain.

Who shall bend to single plan
The narrow sacrifice of man?
Find the central human urge
To make a thousand roads converge?

TOURIST TIME

This fat woman in canvas knickers
Gapes seriously at everything.
We might be a city of the dead
Or cave men
Instead of simple town folk.
We have nothing to show
That can't be seen better somewhere else,
Yet for this woman the wonder ceases not.

Madam, the most extraordinary thing in this town
Is the shape of your legs.

O communication!
O rapid transit!

THE CANADIAN AUTHORS MEET

Expansive puppets percolate self-unction
Beneath a portrait of the Prince of Wales.
Miss Crotchet's muse has somehow failed to function,
Yet she's a poetess. Beaming, she sails

From group to chattering group, with such a dear
Victorian saintliness, as is her fashion,
Greeting the other unknowns with a cheer—
Virgins of sixty who still write of passion.

The air is heavy with "Canadian" topics,
And Carman, Lampman, Roberts, Campbell, Scott
Are measured for their faith and philanthropics,
Their zeal for God and King, their earnest thought.

The cakes are sweet, but sweeter is the feeling
That one is mixing with the *literati;*
It warms the old and melts the most congealing.
Really, it is a most delightful party.

Shall we go round the mulberry bush, or shall
We gather at the river, or shall we
Appoint a poet laureate this Fall,
Or shall we have another cup of tea?

O Canada, O Canada, Oh can
A day go by without new authors springing
To paint the native maple, and to plan
More ways to set the selfsame welkin ringing?

HARDEST IT IS

Your touch is a torch,
A bruise, the spirit broken,
Slow movement under an arch,
The sea's interminable motion.

Pressure slackens, too long extended,
Pressure quickens, infinitely withheld,
    Between hard and harder lies the ecstasy.
    Hardest it is to touch yet have and hold.

ROBERT FINCH (1900——)

PROFESSOR of French at University College, Toronto, an accomplished musician and painter, Robert Finch is one of the group of poets introduced in the anthology of modern Canadian verse, *New Provinces*, in 1936. Of the contributors to this volume, Finch is the most elegant and the least sensuous. His verse is not without feeling, but the feeling is so carefully husbanded and so fastidiously winnowed that one is impressed with its delicacy and precision rather than with its abundance and strength. What is expressed most intensely is an aesthetic emotion—an emotion which rises from the effort to compel an order upon experience. Finch's poems are interesting for more than their subject matter. They illustrate excellently a quality that has not often appeared in Canadian literature—the quality of "dandyism." Their perfection of form and the precision with which visual patterns express a subtle but definite idea make poems like "Egg-and-Dart" and "The Sisters" an original and valuable achievement.

SCROLL-SECTION

You who practise the four elegant occupations
tea music calligraphy and checkers
follow me over the snow in search of plum blossom.

Leave kingdom breakers
to juggle nations,
and care's broad
cloud
to the white hare that with mortar and pestle
sits in the moon by the cassia tree,
leave your lacquer trestle
of puppets, your aviary
of pets in petrified wood,

your malachite lion with its ball of brocade,
your clique to scribble the past
on dust,
and with no inlaid saddle,
no jewelled bridle,
follow me over the snow in search of plum blossom.

The leaping salmon rainbows the cataracts,
the dragon in chase of a pearl skips space
and the phoenix, alighting, first selects a place
to arrange its tail. Emulate in a degree these agreeable
    acts.

Silent though peach and plum
a path is trod to them.
Every rustic talent
till seen is silent.
Even the hollow bamboo
has leaves that droop.

Come back over the snow,
set up
wrist-rests, paint in ink
mountains trees creepers clouds
gorges rivers cascades
the brink
of wind, monasteries in mist,
beauties that have no best,
that through your purpose a longing be learned,
    earned,
the seal of your mind borrowed and not returned.

THE SISTERS

There are two sisters, one is a rose,
And no one knows what the other is.
The first says go and the other goes
Or come and she comes, or that, or this,

And sometimes not a word is said,
Yet always the rose on her balcony
Smiles down in lace at the thin bread
And up in grace at the guests for tea.

Invisible fingers pour and pass,
Unerringly the curate glides
On invisible feet, while as through glass
The Visible Presence of Rose presides

In a hat of shadow, a dress of light,
A shawl let fall from the silver sport
Of weaving rain; the fragrant sight
Is ever and never the same in sort,

For Rose reblooms each day that blooms,
Each hour that opens on time's tree
Finds her unchanged and still she comes
A new rose to another tea.

What deft tool of delicate mettle
Daily remoulds the casual smooth
Coral of each imperial petal
Into this maxim of fadeless youth?

Declared unique, a rose as due
Receives a ribbon and a name.
The name dies with the rose. The blue
Ribbon fades on the sapped stem.

TRAIN WINDOW

The dark green truck on the cement platform
is explicit as a paradigm.
Its wheels are four black cast-iron starfish.
Its body, a massive tray of planking,
ends in two close-set dark green uprights
crossed with three straight cross-pieces, one
looped with a white spiral of hose.

The truck holds eleven cakes of ice,
each cake a different size and shape.
Some look as though a weight had hit them.
One, solid glass, has a core of sugar.
They lean a transitory Icehenge,
in a moor of imitation snow
from the hatchet's bright wet-sided steel.

Five galvanized pails, mottled, as if
of stiffened frosted caracul, three
with crescent lids and elbowed spouts,
loom in the ice, their half-hoop handles
linking that frozen elocution
to the running chalk-talk of powder-red
box-cars beyond, while our train waits here.

WORDS

There are words that can only be said on paper.
It is fortunate they are few. All others shrink
On paper to the thinness of dried ink
And fade at the mind into forgotten vapour.

There are words that can only be said once
And have all been said before that fact is plain.
In a sense no word can ever be said again
And none can be said again in the same sense.

There are words that have to be said or written,
Answers and questions, times to be observed,
But most words die in a cause they have not served
Or bite forever what never should be bitten.

And then there are the words that are left unsaid
And the undetectable words used in their stead.

EGG-AND-DART

This never-ended searching for the eyes
Wherein the unasked question's answer lies;
This beating, beating, beating of the heart
Because a contour seems to fit the part;
The long, drear moment of the look that spoils
The little bud of hope; the word that soils
The pact immaculate, so newly born;
The noisy silence of the old self-scorn;
These, and the sudden leaving in the lurch;
Then the droll recommencement of the search.

OVER

It is over, the ceaseless search is over,
Souls may collide but not like bodies mate,
After collision they must separate,
Minds are not twins as Calais is to Dover.

Searching was half the world while searching lasted,
Finding was all the world created new,
Losing was hardest to believe come true,
But search, find, loss, not one of them is wasted

That shed this timeless moonlit week on week
In an uncumulative series. Frost
Could not quietlier gild and geld the fall.

There is no search when nothing is left to seek,
Nothing to find when what was found is lost,
Nothing to lose when what is lost was all.

MARCUS ADENEY (1900——)

MARCUS ADENEY was born in London, England, in 1900, and spent his youth in Ontario. He has traveled widely and studied music in England and on the European continent. He is a distinguished cellist and has written music criticism for the *Toronto Saturday Night*. At present he is an editor of the *Canadian Review of Music and Art*. In 1931 he was awarded a valuable prize by the Graphic Press, of Ottawa, for a novel of life in Paris, Ontario. *Mansong* is an ambitious philosophical poem that has occupied Mr. Adeney for a number of years.

From *MANSONG*

CHORAL

We the proper ancients speak not out of turn;
Grant us a hearing, O ye gods that lived and died
Time-bound as men, as nature and as knowing;
You who fulfilled an hour, a year, an age
Of mortal need always in mortal fashion,
                                        Hear us now.

Here at the chalky road's end, where the turf
Leads merely seaward; where the white gulls plead
Eternal hungers, and the wind-drift is
Breath of an alien element, O return
From fields immortal; bless these asphodels,
                                        Be latest guests.

This is no ceremonial, gravely precedent;
No ritual utterance greets you from mansoul.
Only the ruffled surface of our thought, as these sere stems
Obedient to each gust of idle wind,
Offers its presents to eternity.
                                        O bear with us.

We who planned hugely to feast but picnic here
At the cliff's edge where the clean chalk crumbles;
And the land of our desire by night falls seaward,
Though concrete walls were built to stop erosion—
Built solidly by men of property,

　　　　　　　　　　　　　　　Behold our loss.

And know: we love not less for our divorce
(In luxury of pride swift undertaken)
From every self but this, the social man;
Only—desire runs crying down the wind,
With gulls' cries desolate, hungry for its own,

　　　　　　　　　　　　　　　Be then not strange.

We who would serve made service a disgrace;
And fortune, with its ills, our only good.
There was no gift that One who lives by giving
Might offer the so needy; and the loving
Were fearfully denied by love's own creatures,

　　　　　　　　　　　　　　　Accept these names.

Accept these tokens also. Who as children
Gave only treasures where sweet joy commanded,
Now proffer intrinsic worth, again unknowing.
Men may declare
In a less troubled age our customs value,

　　　　　　　　　　　　　　　Bear with us still.

And let it be not said that we were fools
Wholly; though a world of goods we squandered
Mainly to satisfy a trampled urge. Reaction
Ruled, pompous, everywhere, of dark necessity;
We were not blind, who stumbled, but depressed,

　　　　　　　　　　　　　　　Be patient, then.

.　.　.　.　.　.　.　.　.　.　.　.　.　.　.　.

For we were torn between the hour and knowing,
Between the word and life's so sweet emergence,
Between our grief retributive and love;
Nor had our age, a word, a way, a gesture
To capture peace, or by-pass desperation.

　　　　　　　　　　　　　　　Be surely wise.

And know that gods denied cannot be banished
Wholly or ever from the lives that bore them, but endure
Even as childhood in unconsciousness.

So long as man-worlds are—remembering,
Mansoul shall glory in old ordered things,
                              Accept our loves.

.   .   .   .

We would return now to our proper station
Between the ancestors and the so bright unborn,
Hold ceremonies suited to these moments
Of brief and partial rightness,—an eternity
Of thought's predicament, desire and pain and death,
                              Be manifest.

And be not strange in the ways of to-morrow
Among the objects of a world's new fancy.
Past hot dog stands, headlined massacres, sectarian churches
Go easily; be patient with the starving intellect,
And youngsters wasting on coffee, doughnuts and cigarettes,
                              Accept all these.

Accept also our contrition. Squandering
Generations born with the so glorious unborn
We learned too late of an entire dilemma.
Facing the truth the worst prevail with lies;
The best, disarmed, find virtue in discretion,
                              Be sceptical.

For the public utterance of men is now an air-raid siren,
And the talk of friends is only reminiscence;
Artists complain, as infants, of small woes,
While clutching churchmen call for sacrifice.
Each one proclaims his own a planet's need,
                              Stay not for these.

Or for the folly that all speech inhabits
And all speakers; but establish a new day
As we must also, bearing to-morrow's burdens,
Yesterday's grief and malice and affliction;
Evil and error called by no proper names,
                              Be with us then.

Be with us on the heights as in the depths,
In shining thought not less than native urge;
Be known and luminous, that understanding
Sufficient for the generation's need may flower
To bear as fruit man's proper amplitude.
                              This be our prayer.

L. A. MACKAY (1901——)

A FEW short, classical elegies, one or two carefully wrought Parnassian sonnets, a handful of love poems full of an angry bitterness, and some brief, witty satires—these comprise the small body of verse published under the pseudonym, "John Smalacombe," by L. A. Mackay, formerly of the University of Toronto and now professor of classics at the University of British Columbia. A brief account of the poet is given in a note with which he prefaced his "Ryerson Chapbook," *Viper's Bugloss* (1938): "John Smalacombe, born Western Ontario, 1901, of English, Scottish, and Irish stock; educated, Toronto and Oxford; married; two children; height, 5 ft. 11 in.; weight 170 lb.; fair; distinguishing marks, none; religion, High Church; politics, High Tory; occupation, teaching; occasional contributor *Saturday Night, Canadian Forum, Canadian Poetry Magazine;* disposition morose, habits retiring." Poems by Mackay appeared in the Canadian number of *Poetry* (Chicago), April, 1941. His occasional reviews and critical articles, particularly a fine series contributed to the *Canadian Forum* (1932–33), reveal him as one of the most intelligent students of Canadian poetry.

ADMONITION FOR SPRING

Look away now from the high lonesome hills
So hard on the hard sky since the swift shower;
See where among the restless daffodils
The hyacinth sets his melancholy tower.

Draw in your heart from vain adventurings;
Float slowly, swimmer, slowly drawing breath.
See, in this wild green foam of growing things
The heavy hyacinth remembering death.

NUNC SCIO, QUID SIT AMOR

I know him now, not now to know demanding.
No goddess-mother bore a child so grim,
So only terrible, though he were standing
Swordless, among the sworded Seraphim.

The hard rock was his mother; he retains
Only her kind, nor answers any sire.
His hand is the black basalt, and his veins
Are rocky veins, ablaze with gold and fire.

HYLAS

Between the blue that burned the swimming bay
And the green welter of the tangled land,
Nosing blood-browed against the grating sand,
The tarred bulk of the mighty Argo lay.
But the tall young Theban thrust his idle way
Through the tough thickets with brown arrogant hand
To where the little river seemed to stand
Dozing, beneath the dead mid-swing of day.
And saw, there kneeling by the shining stream
Through the still depth white slender bodies rise:
On his strong wrist cool fingers wrapt unseen;
Unfathomably in blue quiet eyes
His soul drew down, and he as in a dream
Sank through the still bright water quietly.

I WISH MY TONGUE WERE A QUIVER

I wish my tongue were a quiver the size of a huge cask
Packed and crammed with long black venomous rankling darts.
I'd fling you more full of them, and joy in the task,
Than ever Sebastian was, or Caesar, with thirty-three swords in his
    heart.

I'd make a porcupine out of you, or a pin-cushion, say;
The shafts should stand so thick you'd look like a headless hen
Hung up by the heels, with the long bare red neck stretching, curv-
    ing, and dripping away
From the soiled floppy ball of ruffled feathers standing on end.

You should bristle like those cylindrical brushes they use to scrub
    out bottles,
Not even to reach the kindly earth with the soles of your prickled feet.
And I would stand by and watch you wriggle and writhe, gurgling
    through the barbs in your throttle
Like a woolly caterpillar pinned on its back—man, that would be
    sweet!

BATTLE HYMN OF THE SPANISH
REBELLION

The Church's one foundation
    Is now the Moslem sword,
In meek collaboration
    With flame, and axe, and cord;
While overhead are floating,
    Deep-winged with holy love
The battle-planes of Wotan,
    The bombing-planes of Jove.

A. J. M. SMITH (1902——)

BORN in Montreal in 1902 and educated at McGill University and the University of Edinburgh, A. J. M. Smith is now a professor of English at the Michigan State College, East Lansing. He has contributed criticism and verse to a number of magazines in England, the United States, and Canada, and in 1941 received the Harriet Monroe Memorial Award for a group of poems in the Canadian number of *Poetry*. *News of the Phoenix*, a volume of verse, is to be published in the fall of 1943.

SHADOWS THERE ARE

Shadows there are, but shadows such as these
Are shadows only in the mortal mind,
Blown by the spirit, or the spirit's wind.

Yet shadows I have seen, of me deemed deeper,
That backed on nothing in the horrid air,

And try as try, I cannot limn the form
That some of them assume where I shall pass.
They grow transparent, and as sharp, as glass.

A HYACINTH FOR EDITH

Now that the ashen rain of gummy April
Clacks like a weedy and stain'd mill,

So that all the tall purple trees
Are pied porpoises in swishing seas,

And the yellow horses and milch cows
Come out of their long frosty house

To gape at the straining flags
The brown pompous hill wags,

373

I'll seek within the woods' black plinth
A candy-sweet sleek wooden hyacinth—

And in its creaking naked glaze,
And in the varnish of its blaze,

The bird of ecstasy shall sing again,
The bearded sun shall spring again,

—A new ripe fruit upon the sky's high tree,
A flowery island in the sky's wide sea—

And childish cold ballades, long dead, long mute,
Shall mingle with the gayety of bird and fruit,

And fall like cool and soothing rain
On all the ardour, all the pain

Lurking within this tinsel paradise
Of trams and cinemas and manufactured ice,

Till I am grown again my own lost ghost
Of joy, long lost, long given up for lost,

And walk again the wild and sweet wildwood
Of our lost innocence, our ghostly childhood.

ODE: ON THE DEATH OF W. B. YEATS

An old thorn tree in a stony place
Where the mountain stream has run dry,
Torn in the black wind under the race
Of the icicle-sharp kaleidoscopic white sky,
   Bursts into sudden flower.

Under the central dome of winter and night
A wild swan spreads his fanatic wing.
Ancestralled energy of blood and power
Beats in his sinewy breast. And now the ravening
Soul, fulfilled, his first-last hour
   Upon him, chooses to exult.

Over the edge of shivering Europe,
Over the chalk front of Kent, over Eire,
Dwarfing the crawling waves' amoral savagery,
Daring the hiding clouds' rhetorical tumult,
   The white swan plummets the mountain top.

The stream has suddenly pushed the papery leaves!
It digs a rustling channel of clear water
On the scarred flank of Ben Bulben.
The twisted tree is incandescent with flowers.
The swan leaps singing into the cold air:
    This is a glory not for an hour.

    Over the Galway shore
    The white bird is flying
    Forever, and crying
    To the tumultuous throng
Of the sky his cold and passionate song.

NEWS OF THE PHOENIX

They say the Phoenix is dying, some say dead.
Dead without issue is what one message said,
But that has been suppressed, officially denied.

I think, myself, the man who sent it lied.
In any case, I'm told, he has been shot,
As a precautionary measure, whether he did or not.

THE PLOT AGAINST PROTEUS

This is a theme for muted coronets
To dangle from debilitated heads
Of navigation, kings, or riverbeds
That rot or rise what time the seamew sets
Her course by stars among the smoky tides
Entangled. Old saltencrusted Proteus treads
Once more the watery shore that water weds
While rocking fathom bell rings round and rides.

Now when the blind king of the water thinks
The sharp hail of the salt out of his eyes
To abdicate, run thou, O Prince, and fall
Upon him. This cracked walrus skin that stinks
Of the rank sweat of a mermaid's thighs
Cast off, and nab him; when you have him, call.

THE FACE

The man with the acid face
Under the hammer of glass
Imperils the pure place.
The emotion of the mass,
Inverted, seems to ask
The jack queen king and ace
To do the task.

Wait for a sure thing—
Card into sleeve blown,
Arm out of sling,
Friends posted at phone;
Then when trumps are declared
And partner's strength known
Overpower the guard.

But keep the face mum
Till the right minute come.
Look left and look right:
Whose hand will you bite
With the safest delight?
Whose safe will you crack
With a pat on the back?

*   *   *

Replace the slave state face
With a face of bread:
Each shall choose his place,
Be Dead, or Red.
The cards are no way stacked
And he may live by grace
Who wills to act.

NEIL TRACY (1905———)

NEIL TRACY was born in Sherbrooke, Quebec, in 1905, and was educated at Bishop's University. The poet, who is blind, has published one pamphlet of poems, *The Rain It Raineth* (1938). Charming, gay, lighthearted, conventional in form, but with a directness of approach that sometimes suggests the freshness of medieval poetry, the little book is a rare, if small, achievement. It is introduced by the French-Canadian poet, Alfred Des Rochers, in a Foreword that is almost as appealing as the poems themselves.

I DOUBT A LOVELY THING IS DEAD

I doubt a lovely thing is dead,
    An inward thing, so clear and sweet;
I come at night and lay my head
    Against its breast, and hear no beat;
    I touch its hands, and feel no heat.

Lo! I have slain a lovely thing,
    For I am blind in soul and sight;
If it would live, it needs must sing,
    It could not prosper in the night;
    It waned, and waited for the light.

With loneliness and empty rooms,
    With dust and ashes of the past,
I sat and heard the busy looms
    Work out the warp of First and Last;
    Where night and day the shuttle cast.

A gentle thing, that blooms in love,
    That lies with Beauty in her bed;
How slow for me the counters move
    Through senseless fingers, on their thread;
    Alas for me, that it is dead!

377

PRELUDE

A thing long sought:
Something long held, and lately lost;
Sold for a song, but for a passion bought.

What did its losing cost?
One soul's death, another's shame;
I walk with a ghost; she plays a game.

Nothing shall turn
To dust save Beauty and Youth;
Gold and gems and words do not burn;
Not an oath shall move;
No truth of your swearing shall feed the flame:
I shall keep your vows in a golden urn.

Have I cried in my youth for death?
Did I call upon life for surcease?
They say so and lie, in the heat of their breath.

No: I planted a seed in the ashes of faith,
A germ in the track of the fire:
A thing that shall feed on your peace,
That shall cling like moss to the bones of Desire;
And the brightness of it shall trouble your sleep,
And the beauty of it shall cause you to weep;
Till you call to me from your bed, over the years
    and the lands.
I shall come with my urn in my hands,
To mend our vows over the wreck of the feast,
Over the corpse of the beast;
With a thing long sought.

BALLADE MORALE

Says Auccasain to Nicolette,
"The year is old, the night is wet;
    My door is safe with bar and chain,
    Stout is my roof against the rain;
With song the fire and feast are set;
    The spring will fetch brave days again;
I pray you, do not leave me yet."

Says Nicolette to Auccasain,
"I sought the little leaded pane;
    My starved late-wandering vision met,
    A-gleam with silver and with jet,
A goodly youth who swept the plain:
    While you, with paunch and jowl beset,
Relive dead deeds within the brain."

Says Auccasain to Nicolette,
"Betimes, I walked the parapet;
    I spied a maid amid the grain,
    Singing an old Provençal strain:
Her languid lips and eyes beget
    In me the follies of a swain:
What, Madame, do you tarry yet?"

L'Envoi

Says Nicolette to Auccasain,
    "How am I used? would I forget
    Old glory, for a raw cadet?
Alas, my lord, you give me pain."

ALFRED G. BAILEY (1905——)

ALFRED BAILEY is professor of history at the University of
New Brunswick and a distinguished student of anthropology.
He was born at Quebec in 1905 and educated at the University of
New Brunswick, the University of Toronto, and the London School
of Economics. He published some early verses in 1927 and a "Ryer-
son Chapbook," *Tao*, in 1930. His later poems have appeared in the
Canadian Forum and *Preview*.

VARIATIONS ON A THEME

"I shall wear white flannel trousers, and walk upon the beach."—
The Love Song of J. Alfred Prufrock.

> If Charon drove a hearse along the beach
> in black unhurrying state
> not fearful of arriving here too soon
> nor fearful of too late . . . .
> If it moved up along
> would I be prone to sing a Gascon song?
> Would I emit . . . .
> and suitably attired welcome it?
>
> In the gloom of evening
> as on the Capitol
> the monks were singing
> would I concord in song?
> while Jupiter ramped down
> Olympus' shrieking side.
> If it . . . . would I . . . . about the turn of tide . . . .
> If it . . . . would I . . . . accoutred for the day,
> would I make ready for a ride
> ere this hearse rolled away
> along the beach, along

380

the beach, would I to song
and give my testament, into the hands
of sandy lawyers (who make the beach a brief
for my diffuse inconsequential grief),
concerning purses, mansions, lands,
and doff my cap to let Queen Dido pass,
to give a queen permission,
give the key—
as graciously as was my wont of old—
of cities that have been my care this while?

Would she be pleased to cherish it?
Would she be pleased to smile
and sing a bar or two
and lunch at four?
Would Charon's hearse be waiting at the door
upon the beach with rodents at the wheel,
impatient for the hearse to roll along,
impatient for the meal?
Would I to song
or bleat awhile with my ephemeral queen
and then be gone?

COLONIAL SET

That wolf, shivering by the palisade,
nosed the footprints of a hard winter,
grew thin.
The Indians are fighting drunk.
The Frenchmen keep the squaws.

"How I long to be
in Normandy.
The carriages are waiting at the door.
The ladies lie in laces at the fête,
*Festin à tout manger**
to gobble up
the choicest viands of the *cuisinier*,"
the water murmured,
beating its breasts shapelessly on the shore.

* Term used by the Jesuits with reference to the "eat-all" feasts as practiced
by the Hurons in the seventeenth century.

A cold agony kept pace with the storm,
keeping the temper of the waves leashed,
towering with destination in the northeast,
beating away warm
blood from the heart's core,
checking the arteries,
clogging the burden of the veins,
congealing stagnant lusts in an inland pool.
Animalculae shrivel and die in their sacks.
The beaver cowers in his dam. The caribou
snorts frostily.
Hoofs clatter on the ice-pack.
The rampikes of the forest
attain a brittle silence.

IDEOGRAM

spacialesque trumpets corrode
the haute peaks of the world
with spiral blasts to remember Reason
who gambled with Freedom for a pennyworth of salt,
forsaking the sea, tumbling about the clouds
to rivet without fail, to fail
clutching his bosom with remembrance

nimble feet we had, dancing
to the crisp tune of crustaceans
and so we came to grips with the godhead
deifying the joints, whirling
on a spoke of the sick wheel

UNCROWNED

The ogre leaps with massing hands
and takes the king's head for his football feet,
takes all and what would be a stump of neck
contains no shrivelled seed of future crowns.

Hope dozes in the eye and tongue drips out
as blowpipe hate knots face to score a goal:
and faces fired in the glass of lust
drum hands on arteries of pulsing bone.

The carrion is sharpened for the feast
and butter bursts from eyeballs roasting slow.
Cream-wafered ears where rubies once were set
and vitamins of ghost reward the beast.

The dynasty is swallowed by the panting pump
and no blood-basted armies fish it back.

LEO KENNEDY (1907——)

LEO KENNEDY was born in England in 1907 and came to Canada when he was five years old. He was educated in Montreal and trained in a Catholic tradition, from which he later broke away. He contributed stories and verse to the *McGill Fortnightly Review* and was one of the editors of the short-lived but lively *Canadian Mercury*. In 1933 he published a book of lyrics, *The Shrouding*. Some of the most inescapable influences of the twenties—John Donne, Emily Dickinson, T. S. Eliot, and Sir James Frazer—can be discerned in the cadences and images of many of Kennedy's verses, but when, in his best poems, emotion controls and uses his considerable rhetorical power, we have a poetry as rich and as resonant as any in modern Canadian verse. An advertising man by profession, Kennedy has shown in a number of more recent poems his sympathy with radical movements and the world-wide anti-Fascist resistance which had developed in China and Spain before the outbreak of the second World War.

There is an appreciative essay on Leo Kennedy in W. E. Collin's *The White Savannahs* (1936).

EPITHALAMIUM

This body of my mother, pierced by me,
In grim fulfilment of our destiny,
Now dry and quiet as her fallow womb
Is laid beside the shell of that bridegroom
My father, who with eyes towards the wall
Sleeps evenly; his dust stirs not at all,
No syllable of greeting curls his lips,
As to that shrunken side his leman slips.

Lo! these are two of unabated worth
Who in the shallow bridal bed of earth
Find youth's fecundity, and of their swift

Comminglement of bone and sinew, lift
—A lover's seasonable gift to blood
Made bitter by a parchéd widowhood—
This bloom of tansy from the fertile ground:
My sister, heralded by no moan, no sound.

WORDS FOR A RESURRECTION

Each pale Christ stirring underground
Splits the brown casket of its root,
Wherefrom the rousing soil upthrusts
A narrow, pointed shoot,

And bones long quiet under frost
Rejoice as bells precipitate
The loud, ecstatic sundering,
The hour inviolate.

This Man of April walks again—
Such marvel does the time allow—
With laughter in His blesséd bones,
And lilies on His brow.

MEEK CANDIDATES FOR
GRAVE SPACE

In shrouds distinct, on palls apart
   The latest ones to tire
Arrange their waxen limbs with care
   And piously expire.
A common hope dilates each breast,
   One spark glows in each eye,
A spasm uniform to all
   Provokes the strength to die.
The lips creased deep with pain compose
   A feverish syllable,
The halting tongue revives to phrase
   The name impeccable,
And "God," emits the swooning brain,
   And "Love," taps out the heart,
And "Death," concludes the failing breath,
   To bid corruption start.

MAD BOY'S SONG

The small activity of mice,
The velvet passing of a moth,
And one grey spider's cautious tread
Make thunder in this shed:
Where God has stored his tightened drum—
A mind inside a head!

CAROL COATES

CAROL COATES (CASSIDY) is the youngest daughter of the late Dr. H. H. Coates, Japanese scholar, translator, and authority on Japanese Buddhism. She was born in Tokyo and lived half her life in Japan. She was educated at the University of British Columbia, from which she was graduated with distinction in 1930. She is now on the staff of the Bishop Strachan School, Toronto. She is the author of *Fancy Free*, one of the "Ryerson Chapbooks" published in 1939, and *Poems*, privately produced, 1941. The influence of Japanese poetry is very strongly felt in Mrs. Cassidy's sharply etched, very feminine imagist poems.

FIRST FLIGHT

The day, brittle with ice,
snaps underfoot,
and newly sifted snow
holds the sunlight in a soundless peace.
No motion stirs,
not even a bird cuts its black flight
against the turquoise sky—
not a whisper of wind
shivers the naked trees
or drifts the swans-down snow
across the wide chill sweep of runways
merging the roads of earth and sky.

The hangar doors slide to the touch
and superb in the armor of the skies,
sheathed in immaculate steel,
the scintillating chariot of the air
rolls to the take-off.

Slowly the motor's music
climbs to a crescendo
where speech sinks into pantomime,
and thought shudders into silence.

387

Then, spurning the ground,
up, up, on silver pinions
like a skimming bird topping the trees,
we climb the horizon's arch,
as sovereigns of speed and power
challenge the zenith's goal,
as partners of the winged gods
omnipotent in thought,
pluck the sun from its orbit
or trace the constellations
to their lair.

Sheer precipices of space
greet the falling gaze,
catapulting the eyes down, down,
through islands of spun mist
to the unreal lake below,
to white oil tanks lying like hatboxes
on the shelves of the winter sun,
toy trains shunting matchsticks
on playtime tracks,
narrow ribbons edging the fields
where creeping dots glint like beetles,
and from horizon to horizon
we marvel at a world made in miniature
to meet a table top.

Forgetting our feet tread the ethereal air,
careless of time, of safety,
we soar,
regarding security as some old friend,
till the curve of an unsignalled corner
parches the tongue with terror.
What if the panting engines fail
or the pilot's hand forget the swing
of an aerial arc!
But the perfect pulse of the great bird's heart
and the smooth glide of parallel wings
make trivial the novice fear.

Though oblivious above,
time below demands an end.
We circle,
then down the steps of the sky descend,

deserting the clouds,
beckoning away the trees, the house-tops.
Too soon, in a miracle of poised flight
the waiting wheels spin to the runway's touch
and shorn of wings we taxi the field,
grieving at solidity below.

A diminuendo in the deafening music
signals an end,
the tempo of the propeller's beat
slackens to its rallentando close,
and the blade falls,
like the final note of a symphony
secure and come to rest.

The sensation of feet stabbing the earth
loosens the limbs
and wakens the mind to the nonchalance of a steady
    hand
entering in the log book
the cryptic notations of even flight.

A. M. KLEIN (1909———)

IT IS a somewhat paradoxical fact that the greatest poet living to-day in Canada whose work is a conscious and inspired expression of nationalism is not concerned with Canadian nationalism but with an alien, proud, and ancient nationalism—that of Judea. Ludwig Lewisohn, in his Introduction to Klein's *Hath Not a Jew* . . . . (1940), was correct in discerning that the essential poetic value of Klein's work lies in the completeness of its immersion in Jewish culture and Jewish feeling. "Abraham Klein," wrote Lewisohn, "the most Jewish poet who has ever used the English tongue, is the only Jew who has ever contributed a new note of style, of expression, of creative enlargement to the poetry of that tongue. He is a far better English poet than the Jewish poets who tried to be non-Jewish English poets. In high things and low, honesty is not only the best policy; it is the only policy that makes for life." This is high praise, and, whether or not the comparisons will bear examination, it is undeniable that Klein's poetry has a richness and power, a surging emotional drive, and a dry scholastic (we should say talmudic) wit that assures it a distinguished place, not in Canadian poetry only, but in modern English and American verse generally.

Abraham Moses Klein was born in Montreal in 1909 and educated at McGill University. At the university he contributed some of his earliest poems to the *McGill Fortnightly Review* (1926) and later to the *Canadian Mercury* and the *Canadian Forum*. Two of the best of his early poems, the Eliotish "Soiree of Velvel Kleinberger" and an impassioned rhapsody on Spinoza, "Out of the Pulver and the Polished Lens," appeared in the anthology, *New Provinces* (1936). Meanwhile, a number of his finest Jewish poems were beginning to appear in the *Menorah Journal*.

Although he was trained for the law and is at present a practicing barrister in Montreal, Klein at one time studied for the rabbinate and is a master of the Hebrew language and of Jewish history, theology, and culture. For many years he has been active in the Zionist organization in Canada and is now editor of the *Canadian Jewish Chronicle*.

390

Dr. Leon Edel, in *Poetry: A Magazine of Verse*, April, 1941, has presented a balanced view of Klein's poetry. It springs, he wrote, "from the roots of a consciousness where Hebrew and legal lore have become strangely and exotically intermingled with Shakespeare and T. S. Eliot. . . . . Klein, heir to an authentic Jewish tradition, reflects that tradition in every line he writes. His verses are declamatory because far back the prophets too spoke as from the rooftops and because down the centuries Jews have . . . . lectured to God. His wit is the dry wit of the medieval scholar; his reasoning is legalistic, not because he happens to be a lawyer, but because the talmudists were great reasoners and hair-splitters." The critic objects to the note of resignation characteristic of so many of the poems in *Hath Not a Jew* —for instance, the conclusion of the important "Childe Harold's Pilgrimage"—and expresses the wish that the book were more representative of Klein's gift of eloquent rebellion. It is this note, combined characteristically with resignation and pride, that gives dignity and moral significance to the more recent "*In re* Solomon Warshawer," one of the greatest, though most specialized, "war poems" to have come out of Canada during the second World War. It is necessary to mention the presence in Klein's poetry of other qualities than any that have been named: humor, ranging from the boisterous and broad to the tenderest and most subtle; a lightness and grace of fancy; and a sympathy and love for whatever in humanity is innocent and helpless—children, simpletons, and old people.

IN RE *SOLOMON WARSHAWER*

On Wodin's day, sixth of December, thirty-nine,
I, Friedrich Vercingetorix, attached
to the VIIth Eavesdroppers-behind-the-line,
did cover my beat, when suddenly the crowd I watched
surrounded, in a cobbled lane one can't pass through,
a bearded man, disguised in rags, a Jew.

In the said crowd there were a number of Poles.
Mainly, however, there were Germans there;
blood-brothers of our Reich, true Aryan souls,
breathing at last—in Warsaw—Nordic air.

These were the words the Jew was shouting:
I took them down verbatim:

Whom have I hurt? Against whose silk have I brushed?
On which of your women looked too long?
I tell you I have done no wrong!
Send home your children, lifting hardened dung,
And let your curs be hushed!
For I am beard and breathless, and chased enough.
Leave me in peace, and let me go my way.

At this the good folk laughed. The Jew continued to say
he was no thief, he was a man for hire,
worked for his bread, artist or artisan,
a scribe, if you wished, a vendor or a buyer,
work of all kinds, and anything at all:
paint a mural, scour a latrine,
indite an ode, repair an old machine,
anything, to repeat,
anything at all,
so that he might eat
and have his straw couch in his abandoned stall.

Asked for his papers, he made a great to-do
of going through the holes in his rags, whence he withdrew
a Hebrew pamphlet and a signet ring,
herewith produced, Exhibits 1 and 2.

I said: No documents in a civilized tongue?
He replied:

Produce, O Lord, my wretched fingerprint,
Bring forth, O angel in the heavenly court,
My dossier, full, detailed, both fact and hint,
Felony, misdemeanor, tort!

I refused to be impressed by talk of that sort.

From further cross-examination, it appeared,
immediate history: a beggar in Berlin,
chased as a vagrant from the streets of Prague,
kept as a leper in forced quarantine,
shunned as the pest, avoided like a plague,
he had escaped, mysteriously come
by devious routes, and stolen frontiers, to
the nalewkas of Warsaw's sheenydom.

Pressed to reveal his foul identity,
He lied:
One of the anthropophagi was he,
or, if he wished, a denizen of Mars,
the ghost of my father, Conscience—aye
the spectre of Reason, naked, and with scars;
even became insulting, said he was
Aesop the slave among the animals . . . .
Sir Incognito . . . . Rabbi Alias . . . .
The eldest elder of Zion . . . . said we knew
his numerous varied oriental shapes,
even as we ought to know his present guise—
the man in the jungle, and beset by apes.

It was at this point the S.S. man arrived.
The Jew was interrupted; when he was revived,
He deposed as follows:

At low estate, a beggar, and in flight,
Still do I wear my pride like purple. I
Am undismayed by frenzy or by fright,
And you are the objects of my pitying eye.
For you are not the first that I have met—
O I have known them all
The dwarf dictators, the diminutive dukes,
The heads of straw, the hearts of gall,
Th' imperial plumes of eagles covering rooks!

It is not necessary to name names,
But it may serve anon,
Now to evoke from darkness some dark fames,
Evoke
Armada'd Spain, that gilded jettison;
And Russia's last descended Romanov,
Descending a dark staircase
To a dank cellar at Ekaterinoslov;
Evoke
The glory that was Babylon that now is gloom;
And Egypt, Egypt, scarcely now recalled
By that lone star that sentries Pharaoh's tomb;
And Carthage, founded on sand, by water walled;
And Greece—O broken marble!—
And disinterred unresurrected Rome.

These several dominions hunted me;
They all have wished, and more than wished, me dead;
And now, albeit I walk raggedly,
I walk; and they are echoes to my tread!

Is it by your devices I shall be undone?

Ah, but you are philosophers, and know
That what has been need not continue so;
The sun has risen; and the sun has set;
Risen again, again descended, yet
To-morrow no bright sun may rise to throw
Rays of inductive reason on Judaeophobic foe.

Is there great turmoil in the sparrow's nest
When that bright bird, the Sun, descends the west?
There is no fear, there is no twittering;
At dawn they will again behold his brightly plumaged wing!
Such is the very pattern of the world,
Even the sparrows understand;
And in that scheme of things I am enfurled,
Am part thereof, the whole as it was planned,
With increase and abatement rife,
Subject to sorrow, joined to joy—
Earth, its relenting and recurring life!

Aye, but the signet ring, the signet ring!
Since you must know, barbarian, know you shall!
I who now stand before you, a hunted thing
Pressed and pursued and harried hither and yon,
I was, I am the Emperor Solomon!
O, to and fro upon the face of the earth,
I wandered, crying, "Ani Shlomo," but—
But no one believed my birth.

For he now governs in my place and stead,
He who did fling me from Jerusalem
Four hundred parasangs;
Who stole the crown from off my head,
And robed him in my robes, beneath whose hem
The feet of the cock extend, the tail of the demon hangs!
Asmodeus!

Mistake me not: I am no virtuous saint;
Only a man, and like all men, not godly,
Damned by desire—
But I at least waged war, for holy booty,
Against my human taint;
At least sought wisdom, to discern the good;
Whether of men, or birds, or beasts of the wood;
Spread song, spread justice; ever did aspire—
Howbeit, man among men, I failed—
To lay the plan, and work upon the plan
To build the temple of the more-than-man!

But he, the unspeakable prince of malice!
Usurper of my throne, pretender to the Lord's!
Wicked, demoniac, lycanthropous
Leader of hosts horrific, barbarous hordes,
Master of the worm, pernicious, that cleaves rocks,
The beast that talks,
Asmodeus!

Who has not heard the plight of his domain?
Learning is banished to the hidden cave,
Wisdom decried, a virtue of the slave,
And justice, both eyes seared, goes tapping with a cane.

His counselor is the wolf. He counsels hate.
His sceptre is a claw.
And love is a high crime against the state.
The fury of the forest
Is the law.

Upon his charnel-throne, in bloodied purple,
Hearkening to that music where the sigh
Pauses to greet the groan, the groan the anguished cry,
Asmodeus sits;
And I—

At this point the S.S. men departed.
The Jew was not revived. He was carried and carted,
and to his present gaoler brought;
awaiting higher pleasure.

                And further deponent saith not.

UPON THE HEAVENLY SCARP

I

And on that day, upon the heavenly scarp,
The hosannas ceased, the hallelujahs died,
And music trembled on the silenced harp.
An angel, doffing his seraphic pride,
Wept; and his tears so bitter were, and sharp,
That where they fell, the blossoms shriveled and died.

II

Another with such voice intoned the psalm
It sang forth blasphemy against the Lord.
O that was a very imp in angeldom
Who, thinking evil, said no evil word—
But only pointed, at each *Te Deum*,
Down to the earth, and its unspeakable horde.

III

The Lord looked down, and saw the cattle-cars:
Men ululating to a frozen land.
He saw a man tear at his flogged scars,
And saw a babe look for its blown-off hand.
Scholars, he saw, sniffing their bottled wars,
And doctors who had geniuses unmanned.

IV

The gentle violinist whose fingers played
Such godly music, washing a gutter, with lye,
He saw. He heard the priest who called his aid.
He heard the agnostic's undirected cry.
Unto him came the odor Hunger made,
And the odor of blood before it is quite dry.

V

The angel who wept looked into the eyes of God.
The angel who sang ceased pointing to the earth.
A little cherub who'd spied the earthly sod
Went mad, and flapped his wings in crazy mirth.
And the good Lord said nothing, but with a nod
Summoned the angels of Sodom down to earth.

HEIRLOOM

My father bequeathed me no wide estates;
No keys and ledgers were my heritage;
Only some holy books with *yahrzeit* dates
Writ mournfully upon a blank front page—

Books of the Baal Shem Tov, and of his wonders;
Pamphlets upon the devil and his crew;
Prayers against road demons, witches, thunders;
And sundry other tomes for a good Jew.

Beautiful: though no pictures on them, save
The scorpion crawling on a printed track;
The Virgin floating on a scriptural wave,
Square letters twinkling in the Zodiac.

The snuff left on this page, now brown and old,
The tallow stains of midnight liturgy—
These are my coat of arms, and these unfold
My noble lineage, my proud ancestry!

And my tears, too, have stained this heirloomed ground,
When reading in these treatises some weird
Miracle, I turned a leaf and found
A white hair fallen from my father's beard.

BESTIARY

God breathe a blessing on
His small bones, every one!
The little lad, who stalks
The bible's plains and rocks
To hunt in grammar'd woods
Strange litters and wild broods;
The little lad who seeks
Beast-muzzles and bird-beaks
In cave and den and crypt,
In copse of holy script;
The little lad who looks
For quarry in holy books.

Before his eyes is born
The elusive unicorn;
There, scampering, arrive
The golden mice, the five;

Also, in antic shape,
Gay peacock and glum ape.
He hears a snort of wrath:
The fiery behemoth;
And then on biblic breeze
The crocodile's sneeze.
He sees the lion eat
Straw, and from the teat
Of tigress a young lamb
Suckling, like whelp nigh dam.

Hard by, as fleet as wind
They pass, the roe and hind,
Bravely, and with no risk,
He holds the basilisk,
Pygarg and cockatrice.
And there, most forest-wise
Among the bestiaries
The little hunter eyes
Him crawling at his leisure:
The beast Nebuchadnezzar.

AUTOBIOGRAPHICAL

I

Out of the ghetto streets where a Jewboy
Dreamed pavement into pleasant bible-land,
Out of the Yiddish slums where childhood met
The friendly beard, the loutish Sabbath-goy,
Or followed, proud, the Torah-escorting band
Out of the jargoning city I regret
Rise memories, like sparrows rising from
The gutter-scattered oats,
Like sadness sweet of synagogal hum,
Like Hebrew violins
Sobbing delight upon their eastern notes.

II

Again they ring their little bells, those doors
Deemed by the tender-year'd, magnificent:
Old Ashkenazi's cellar, sharp with spice;
The widow's double-parloured candy-stores
And nuggets sweet bought for one sweaty cent;

The warm fresh-smelling bakery, its pies,
Its cakes, its navel'd bellies of black bread;
The lintels candy-poled
Of barber-shop, bright-bottled, green, blue, red;
And fruit-stall piled, exotic,
And the big synagogue door, with letters of gold.

III

Again my kindergarten home is full—
Saturday night—with kin and compatriot:
My brothers playing Russian card-games; my
Mirroring sisters looking beautiful
Humming the evening's imminent fox-trot;
My uncle Mayer, of blessed memory,
Still murmuring Maariv, counting holy words;
And the two strangers, come
Fiery from Volhynia's murderous hordes—
The cards and humming stop.
And I too swear revenge for that pogrom.

IV

Occasions dear: the four-legged aleph named
And angel pennies dropping on my book;
The rabbi patting a coming scholar-head;
My mother, blessing candles, Sabbath-flamed,
Queenly in her Warsovian perruque;
My father pickabacking me to bed
To tell tall tales about the Baal Shem Tov,
Letting me curl his beard.
O memory of unsurpassing love,
Love leading a brave child
Through childhood's ogred corridors, unfear'd.

V

The week in the country at my brother's (May
He own fat cattle in the fields of heaven!)
Its picking of strawberries from grassy ditch,
Its odour of dogrose and of yellowing hay,—
Dusty, adventurous, sunny days, all seven!—
Still follow me, still warm me, still are rich
With the cow-tinkling peace of pastureland.
The meadow'd memory

Is sodded with its clover, and is spanned
By that same pillow'd sky
A boy on his back one day watched enviously.

VI

And paved again the street; the shouting boys
Oblivious of mothers on the stoops
Playing the robust robbers and police,
The corn-cob battle,—all high-spirited noise
Competitive among the lot-drawn groups.
Another day, of shaken apple-trees
In the rich suburbs, and a furious dog
And guilty boys in flight;
Hazelnut games, and games in the synagogue,
The burrs, the Haman rattle,
The Torah-dance on Simchas-Torah night.

VII

Immortal days of the picture-calendar
Dear to me always with the virgin joy
Of the first flowing of senses five
Discovering birds, or textures, or a star,
Or tastes sweet, sour, acid, those that cloy,
And perfumes. Never was I more alive.
All days thereafter are a dying-off,
A wandering away
From home and the familiar. The years doff
Their innocence.
No other day is ever like that day.

VIII

I am no old man fatuously intent
On memoirs, but in memory I seek
The strength and vividness of nonage days,
Not tranquil recollection of event.
It is a fabled city that I seek;
It stands in space's vapours and Time's haze;
Thence comes my sadness in remembered joy
Constrictive of the throat;
Thence do I hear, as heard by a Jewboy
The Hebrew violins,
Delighting in the sobbed oriental note.

RALPH GUSTAFSON (1909——)

RALPH GUSTAFSON was born near Sherbrooke, Quebec, in 1909, and was educated at Bishop's University, where he had a distinguished academic career, and at Oxford. A first volume of poems, largely traditional in form, *The Golden Chalice* (1935), was given the Quebec Government Literary Award the following year. *Alfred the Great*, a chronicle play in blank verse, was published in England in 1937. A group of poems which appeared in the *Sewannee Review* in 1940 heralded a more adventurous and subtle style. Extremely musical, they combine conciseness with allusiveness and give a characteristically disillusioned expression of the modern sensibility. In 1941 *Epithalamium in Time of War* was privately printed in New York. Here the influence of Gerard Manley Hopkins, which had been noticeable in much of Gustafson's later poetry, has become, in the words of Professor E. K. Brown, "inspired imitation." "But," the critic added, "Mr. Gustafson's own personal stamp is obvious— the lightness of musical and intellectual pace, easily distinguishable from Hopkins's quickness, in a kind of daintiness." The influence, it would seem, of Anglo-Saxon verse, in which the poet immersed himself while writing *Alfred the Great*, is to be found in the numerous lines sharply broken in the middle, but the originality and strength of the poem as a whole cannot be denied. It was published in the *Canadian Forum* during 1942. The same year *Lyrics Unromantic* appeared in a limited edition. Mr. Gustafson is the editor of a compact *Anthology of Canadian Poetry* in the widely circulated "Penguin Books."

DEDICATION

"They shall not die in vain," we said.
"Let us impose, since we forget
The hopeless giant alphabet,
Great stones above the general dead,"
The living said.

401

"They shall not be outdone in stones.
Generously, sculptured grief shall stand
In general over numbered bones
With book and index near at hand
For particular sons.

"And we the living left in peace
Will set aside such legal date
At such and suchlike time or state
Or place as meet and fitting is,
Respecting this."

O boy, locked in the grisly hollow,
You who once idly peeled a willow-
switch, whistling, wondering at the stick
Of willow's whiteness clean and slick,
Do not believe that we shall bury
You with words: aptly carry
Cloth flowers, proxy for love.
O we have done with granite grief
And silk denials: summing you
Within the minutes' silence—two!
More than you had need to target
Hate, against the pitiless bullet's
Calculated greed oppose
Heart's anger: falling, gave to us
What power to lance the pocket of
An easy past, what use of love
Teaching children's laughter loud
On shutters in an evil street,
What edge, O death, of days, delight?
What linch of love, spate of sun?
And shall we with a sedentary noun
Signature receipt, having had read
The catechism of the generous dead?

You who live, see! These,
These were his hills where laughter was
And counted years of longing, grain
And wintry apples scorched in sun,
Of corded hemlock deep in snow.
Here at his seven birches growing
Oblique by the boulder the fence has stopped—
Rusted wire, posts lopped

For staking. To circle love, he said.
And there are other fables made:
Of plough and intricate loom; the broken
Soldier on the sill; and latin
Parchment framed, conferring letters
On hooded death; the axe the motto
Against the wall; abandoned hills.

Fables for stout reading. Tales
Listened to by twice-told death.
Our tongue how silent, muscles lithe
O land, hoist by the lag-end of little
Deeds? What lack of monstrous metal,
Monumental mouths; over
This land what love, wheel, lever
Of God, anchorage, pivot of days,
Remembering?

        Old and certain the sea,
The mountain-tilted sky, old,
Older than words, than you are old,
Boy, who never thought to point the hill
With dawn! Only as these, our telling:
As men labour: as harvest done:
At dusk a joyful walking home.
Of nearer things: how he was young,
And died, a silent writing down.

THIS SPEAKING WERE ENOUGH

This speaking were enough
If words were true—
And every action its own end
That compassed you.

I would not need the grace
Of more than this,
To say "I love"—and then have done
With emphasis.

To tell in other terms
What I have told—
Predict the gold or silver moon
As silver? gold?

I could protest again
And it would be
That I should measure north and south
My apogee.

But I have need, oh I
Have need of more—
Than synonym of love and love,
Before, before,

Who know this traffic false
The telling cheat,
And every word before the saying,
Obsolete.

TOPONYMY

Lens and line
Across the map deploy,
Sight cornerstones
Of man and boy.

Between, where Oder
And the Danube run,
Are acres adequate
For every son—

Soil enough
For geography and death
Who requisitions but
A shoulder's-breadth

For one or more.
He will not leave it less
Who lays a boundary
With bone and flesh—

Boundary bone
Plus loyal loin and lip—
Proof determinate
Of final map.

Have plummet point,
Let civil eye survey
The fatal length of limb
The coign of clay;

Determine where
This loyalty shall lie—
Within, without whatever
Field, what sky.

FINAL SPRING

Of grass, insurgent bud aware,
We in the loop of sudden spring,
Trammelled by tangled green and song
Nostalgic on the ear,
Thrown by the lariat of sun
Are branded with initialled fear.

Between the brazen daffodil
Sprawling headlines through the park
Between the question on the wind,
On lintels of the hill,
And storage in the hollow tree
Joy adds a hasty codicil.

For we are the muscled living, therefore
Make a hasty signature,
Dispossess the urgent root
Certify the heir:
Fear, in the framework of the wind,
This, and the threat of fear, and fear.

EPITHALAMIUM IN TIME OF WAR

For Pauline Gustafson and
Lieutenant Hector Belton
March 22, 1941

Now is the time in valiant days
When break we from the warring heart's
Huge anger. Across the watery ways,
The quadrant of the globe's quick girth—
Though guns in monstrous utterance phrase
Their grim denials—summer starts,
March bursts the answering hawthorn-sprays,
The crocus green from English earth,
Gladdened are simple birds who sing

Remembered joy, tomorrow's mirth,
And all that gentle love shall bring.

Of man's dictation cite the deed
Or writ or reach to clamp a root,
Or lien a leaf, stop sunward weed;
With scarlet wax and taper seal,
With signet hold the hinge of tide—
Manacle morning, make mandrake mute!
On June clap gyves and dungeon seed!
What cumbrous Caesar can repeal
Golgotha's grass? Watch where a wing,
A whorl, make use of wind and wheel
That code and key and clavis bring.

How shall the heart be less than leaf
Whose signature makes mock of mouths?
Of more than grasses man though brief
The bravery of his summer's term.
Will Godhood brook the snaffle of
A straw? O we shall muster deaths
And with the paradox of love
Loose hate, ally the wooing worm:
Precepts borrow from the king
Sucked in a cabbage, with Pharaoh's sperm
Shall found a line of radish. Bring,

Then, bud and bomb before this Foe
And let him contemplate his guts.
But now, where birch and maple grow,
Comes spring to parallel the thorn
And England's pledge in bosky blow
Where Nightingale her honey puts.
The month's last ravelin of snow
Is white in woods; beneath the horn
Of moon the icicle goes; birds sing;
And every fraise and freshet torn
With gash and gold that meltings bring.

Together, a string of ancient crows
Plunge from their limb—roaring, the plane
Takes drunkenly the field and goes
Gale-hardy, skygallant hanger in blue.

In darkened foundries burst hot snows;
Acres harvest heavy grain.
The pampering crane at wharf-edge stows
Its hate. At every chimney, clue
And crest of iron answer cling.
And men, where lately poppies grew,
This, and gentle love shall bring—

For steel and stop, our loves design:
In factories death is packed with palms
Not harsh to bread and blesséd wine.
(Say with what blueprint, ward and wit
Shall fist find faith, where Fear confine,
Hard Charon quit with easy alms?)
Behold, where drums the day's decline,
The Sabbath's seven candles lit.
No cap nor clock nor reckoning,
No fuse but love shall hallow it,
No boulder but its Easter bring.

And so to martial hills and holms
Where Magog holds a town in fee,
Love's hater, index, darling comes.
Out of the monster cannon's seed,
The armoured epoch's gravid wombs
Make paradox, from spike and tree
Glad words, read April palindromes!
Assert the seasons of your need,
For in the compass of this ring
The future's corners are decreed,
God's golden inch, His scaffolding.

Then take this dear this double love
Whose loop and lunge on heaven's bollards
Bind. All love shall Harbour have
Whose silken nets its fathoms find.
Nor fear, O let no lover grieve:
Against the veer and vertical
Of God the world's vast corners cleave,
Our pitch and parallel is lined.
Listen! a thrush declaring spring!
Saint Francis walks among mankind.
One golden round! God's mastering.

Now is the holy time, sweet noon.
Within this chapel's candled dusk
Does love lack loss, place glory on.
Gain gladness! Against these eastward two,
Take angles, sights, high orthogon;
Mortally, measure against, risk,
Arrive at, solve, survey His sun!
God's binder goes. Golden through
His gates they come! Now belfry, ring!
Love, them, each living thing, renew!
To her, to him, His blessings bring!

JAMES WREFORD (1915——)

JAMES WREFORD (WATSON) was born in China in 1915 and educated at George Watson's College, Edinburgh, and the University of Edinburgh. After teaching in Sheffield University he was appointed to the faculty of McMaster University, Hamilton, and came to live in Canada shortly before the war. He has contributed poetry to the *Listener* and to Thomas Moult's anthology, *The Best Poems of 1939*, as well as to the *Canadian Forum*, the *Canadian Poetry Magazine*, and the West Coast poetry magazine, *Contemporary Verse*. Wreford's best work is direct and intense, a record of experience that comes out of the heart of our own times, relevant to the world struggle against reaction, and presented in terms of contemporary speech and image.

EARLY WILLOWS

There is no bargain basement no
last January sale shall get
a cut rate peace, a short cut to
relieve the mounting debt.

The corner drugstore noways can
both diagnose and salve the grief
that winters in the heart of man
despite the swiftly pushing leaf.

Too soon you paint the polder green,
signal the special express of Spring:
the steam's not up can save this year
from the death-dropping wing.

Too soon you flag the faltering hope,
or burnish up the pale desire,
thrust out the clenched fist and too soon
explode the marsh with fire.

Time shall not see you nest the song
or hold the purple eggs of love:
for war has still to glut the beak,
and peace has lost its dove.

Let not another green thing grow
the rivers row or the West Wind blow;
for the polar front has carried down
the latitude of snow.

In this cold sector shall no life
be won but to be waste again:
the rate of increase circles round
to swell the count of pain.

For what have aching root and branch
born this tremendous, tremulous leaf?
Shall not the profiteer produce
his silver from our grief?

And yet your spear-point protest shall
revoke the Chellean man who stands
above the thundering machine
with groping, stone-age hands;

cry irrepressible revolt
against the winter mind that yet
has not an end of winters made,
and in your dying fret

our snow-bound world with shadowed faith,
if with the premature the not less true
green of that far off common earth
at last will credit you.

KIRKLAND LAKE

Under the dark industrial sky
we wonder why we have to die
who living, were valued at a wage
that starved our youth and murdered age?
Or why engage for tyrants here
to end the tyranny of fear,
whose quarrel is with all of those
the heavens of our desire that close?

For justice undertake a cause
that has no justice in its laws,
but claims for unity the right
forbids the citizen unite.
For thirty dollars shall we sell
our happiness to mend their hell,
to save their cuckoos, clear our nest,
redeem by our unrest their rest
and fight for freedom who are not free?
Let freemen die, but why should we
who toil to set the rich on high
three shifts beneath the smoking sky.
Let those who call on us to keep
their freedom safe and safe their sleep
account and pledge us higher for
the wealth and peace our griefs ensure!
a week-end fit for play like theirs
and futures guaranteed from cares,
evenings when not too tired a man
his leisure take and pleasure can,
a chance for more than daily bread—
their daughters for our sons to wed,
so working and in wanting we
may equal them and be as free.
But till that day let them not cry
upon our loyal sons to die,
who with our usual logic see
they die for freedom that are free.

WINTER WEATHER

Wintering time and weather with
the mercury low and locked in wrestling winds
precipitate upon our breath
snows that are not our sin:
so do not blame the frozen face
and eyes whose very tears are ice,
nor the dipping pole has spoked the race
thrown out of gear the wise
and well bred wonder, love,
the mechanised passion and blue-print kisses
and the streamlined marriage that seemed unmov-

ably stable and was not really missed.
For shall he not who backs the wind
and on his left hand feels it know
the storms are near that to the blind
such bitter bleakness sow?
Then not this fanged and fearful frost
green-griming and still balmless blight
but, after all, this putting to rest
and at long last winter quiet;
not the thin blood which God knows He
made for the gardens of Babylon and
moon drenched Cyclades above a tideless sea:
not the environmental and germ-true man,
but blame, if you must, this prime
unreasonable claim against the drift
and masking shadow and the time
turning away from Egypt's cleft
embosoming but embattled love;
the little Shulammite that prized
Solomon above the lilies, and above
the green of Eden, an Eden fossilised.
Blame this, if at all—the dry, unsatiated cry
for lips that yet more red than human are
and for those arms would underlie
eternity, but not this hour.

PATRICK ANDERSON (1915——)

PATRICK ANDERSON was born in England and educated at Oxford University, where he was president of the Union. He now lives in Montreal and is a schoolmaster. He is largely responsible for the founding of the "Preview" group, which is made up of F. R. Scott, P. K. Page, Bruce Ruddick, Neufville Shaw, and Anderson. The ideals of this talented group have been tersely stated in a Foreword to the first issue of their mimeographed bulletin *Preview*, March, 1942:

As the group takes shape, it becomes clear that general agreement exists on several points. Among them are the following. First, we have lived long enough in Montreal to realize the frustrating and inhibiting effects of isolation. All anti-fascists, we feel that the existence of a war between democratic culture and the paralysing forces of dictatorship only intensifies the writer's obligation to work. Now, more than ever, creative and experimental writing must be kept alive and there must be no retreat from the intellectual frontier—certainly no shoddy betrayal, on the lines of Archibald Mac-Leish, Van Wyck Brooks, and others, of those international forces which combine in a Picasso, a Malraux, or a Joyce. Secondly, the poets amongst us look forward, perhaps optimistically, to a possible fusion between the lyric and didactic elements in modern verse, a combination of vivid, arresting imagery and the capacity to "sing" with social content and criticism. Thirdly, we hope to make contact, as a group, with new writing movements in England, the United States and other parts of Canada.

"A combination of vivid, arresting imagery and the capacity to 'sing' with social content . . . . a fusion between the lyric and didactic elements in modern verse . . . ."—this is what has been brilliantly achieved in such poems as "War Dead," "Desert," and "Capital Square."

SUMMER'S JOE

He unlocked an apple first, then lifted the latch
of the ancestral tree,

whistled amongst the tall corn gaily
like a scythe of birds:
on the shore the lion waves lay down on their paws
and above the trodden sand
a storm of gulls made sadness as white
as April does;
he climbed the stalled peak above the hush
of the slimmed sea,
the lark went up on his stalk and the gorse
had a fry of bees—
O sign me into your water, he cried,
to the cool annul,
write me into your smooth bible
he called to the lake,
unwind me on your reel, he said
to the road of go,
slow me into a grey rock!
but the answer was No, Joe.
He called to the hunting morning then
to shoot his blood,
he asked the seamstress of the woods
to stitch his manhood,
he stripped to show his flesh, his flesh
was white as snow—
give me ecstasy of total love!
but the answer was No, Joe.

Then dropped by wind at the starting-point
he was damned by stone,
he was left with the grocer's salt of love
in the place of boards;
swallows passed him and sparrows shot
above his head,
light left in a sail for the farthest south,
eyes fell from a kite;
while the natural lechers in their pool
pulled down the shades,
fireflies with their pouting milk
perplexed the roads—
when night's a journey land's in doubt,
flesh is a traveller,
ho for the lantern of yourself,
ho for the clock!

In the always-easy bed he found
the lazy chart,
in the uncharted land he saw
the heart's riot,
wrestling weak angels then he climbed
gristle and bone
until on top of himself he saw
that he was still alone:
O God from my Italian pride
deliver me now,
and from my terrible steepness!
but the answer was No Joe
the answer was No.

Then sudden in the scope of sea
with the delight of found
he saw his treasure island,
he saw his milkwhite fathom.
To every spar and nerve he set
his orchard sails
and in the fleet of love his eyes
were sea-blue admirals,
while at his telescope of brass
she lulled her palms,
lay level to his pride, lay still
to his rocked rigging . . . .
O secret in that heart of a place
a bird looks out,
pivots the forest on its nest, its eye
the germ of light—
no join was seen between flesh and flesh,
between hair and grass,
loving themselves the world they loved
with a mirror's process;
leaving their fear in another place,
their clock in a pool,
it seemed that the earth had made of them
its capital
for the deputies of leaves and waves
the motes of wit,
a parliament of the water-jet
and a sun-up senate.
He turned towards his love and said,

Love, tell me now
is not our love perpetual?
but she said No Joe.
Is not our ecstasy for life
with a hey-nonny-no?
and she replied from a long way off
and her answer was No.
I call you by our bed of love
couple, roll and hairy-ho!
she answered: While we loved these died,
with no again, a feast of No.

DESERT

Hereabouts is desert, it's a bad country,
grows nothing, nothing to show for, sand has no whereabouts,
goes everywhere and nowhere like a sea:
yes, I said, and noticed the flash of sun on grit
and knew that all the hourglasses in the world had broken
and this was the sum of all the hours of the world.

Did you ever see a man bleed in sand? I
asked him, did you ever see a soldier, a khaki
hero with his life blood blotting entirely and quickly
into the khaki sand? Did you ever see a man drown in
    quicksand
or, let alone a man, a tree or a bedstead?

It's not just that there's so much of it, he said,
nor the bitter heat of it nor its blinding glare
but it's the shiftlessness, that there's no purpose here,
nothing but a blanket warming a blanket, or a sum
multiplying and dividing itself forever, a sum
adding and subtracting itself for ever and ever.

CAPITAL SQUARE

Danger is silent in the bloodless square:
the boxing brute of stone half hides his fist,
the moon in the haunt of weight is a heavy ghost
and the sun is a toastmaster,
the punishing façades disguise their skill
and fountains play before the parliament of standstill.

You may go freely through the paved immense
slowness, the architectural snow;
admire the statues stiffened in the silence
with No upon their lips and the heart at zero,
until having made some circles you understand
you are a pigmy held in a stone hand.

No warmth is here, only an abstract good;
your dead shall never bleed nor your love return;
children ask here no gifts nor the hungry food . . . .
but now and then four walls of added men
swing into symmetry, with a stone noise
harden and echo at a statue's voice.

IN THE HOSPITAL

The white gowned doctor holds the charming arm,
a cut-down blossoming bough in a vase of tears:
soundless it blows in the doctor's eyes
as he peels off his gloves, and sadly goes out of the room—
under her mask the young nurse sighs
and the patient rushes on in his two-armed dream.

WAR DEAD

Always the dead seem unsuccessful:
as though they had spoiled their photos
they smile with second meanings into our pain:
so, after all, it was that they were after.

The day they died a mother added
another arch to her church,
now she will look
on victory as something bright, but secular.

And where in the cleanest landscape we,
hardly known to ourselves, are running
to some excitement like the centre of light—
a child has turned, a hole in his head.

The eyes where we stood are dark
and the low earth, with careful science,
begins to remove all traces
of those in whom we might have been justified.

P . K . PAGE (1917——)

PATRICIA PAGE was born in England in 1917, the daughter of Major General L. F. Page, D.S.O. She was educated at St. Hilda's School, Calgary, and is at present engaged in war work in Montreal. Miss Page has contributed to *Poetry* (Chicago), the *Canadian Forum*, *Saturday Night*, *Contemporary Verse*, *Canadian Poetry Magazine*, and *Preview*. She is one of the leading figures in the group of young writers associated with F. R. Scott and Patrick Anderson, who have banded themselves together to use their writing as a weapon against fascism. Although some of her best poems are quite free of social or political implications, her work has shown a steady development in the direction of a complex and strongly expressed statement of political and personal responsibility.

LANDSCAPE OF LOVE

Where the bog ends, there, where the ground lips, lovely
is love, not lonely.
     Land is
love, round with it, where the hand is;
wide with love, cleared scrubland, grain
on a coin.
Oh, the wheatfield, the rock-bound rubble;
the untouched hills
     as a thigh smooth;
the meadow.
Not only the poor soil lovely, the outworn prairie,
but the green upspringing,
the lark-land,
the promontory.

A lung-born land, this,
a breath spilling,
scanned by the valvular heart,
the field glasses.

THE STENOGRAPHERS

After the brief bivouac of Sunday
their eyes, in the forced march of Monday to Saturday
hoist the white flag, flutter in the snow storm of paper,
haul it down and crack in the midsun of temper.

In the pause between the first draft and the carbon
they glimpse the smooth hours when they were children—
the ride in the ice-cart, the iceman's name,
the end of the route, and the long walk home.

Remember the sea where floats at high tide
were sea marrows growing on the scatter-green vine
or spools of grey toffee, or wasps nests on water;
remember the sand and the leaves of the country.

Bell rings and they go and the voice draws their pencil
like a sledge across snow; when its runners are frozen
rope snaps and the voice then is pulling no burden
but runs like a dog on the winter of paper.

Their climates are winter and summer—no wind
for the kites of their hearts—no wind for a flight;
a breeze at the most, to tumble them over
and leave them like rubbish—the boy-friends of blood.

In the inch of the noon as they move they are stagnant.
The terrible calm of the noon is their anguish;
the lip of the counter, the shape of the straws
like icicles breaking their tongues are invaders.

Their beds are their oceans—salt water of weeping
the waves that they know—the tide before sleep;
and fighting to drown they assemble their sheep
in columns and watch them leap desks for their fences
and stare at them with their own mirror-worn faces.

In the felt of the morning, the calico minded,
sufficiently starched, insert papers, hit keys,
efficient and sure as their adding machines;
yet they weep in the vault, they are taut as net curtains
stretched upon frames. In their eyes I have seen
the pin-men of madness in marathon trim
race round the track of the stadium pupil.

THE MOLE

The mole goes down the slow dark personal passage—
a haberdasher's sample of wet velvet moving
on fine feet through an earth that only
the gardener and the excavator know.

The mole is a specialist and truly
opens his own doors; digs as he needs them
his tubular alleyways; and all his hills
are mountains left behind him.

ISOLATIONIST

When the many move, the man
in the cubicle of content
cowers, suddenly discovered, suddenly rent
by the reality of crowds.
He has trained the climbing vine,
written "roses" on his ledger,
lived like a saint and finds himself a leper.

Immaculate of belief and violent on Mondays,
thinking no evil and thanking no second party
he has leaned in the evenings on the low-lipped
    window
and learned of his saintliness from outlines of
    lovers.

Now lovers leap the sash and the many winnow
his penny bank of wisdom and set it swirling
down the unclogged drain in the hidden scullery.
People take sudden shape and are suddenly human,
smash walls, uproot chairs and juggle cutlery
while he sits with gloved hands in a buttoned
    confusion.

RONALD HAMBLETON (1917———)

RONALD HAMBLETON was born in Preston, England, in 1917 and came to Canada in 1924. He was educated in Vancouver and has worked at a variety of jobs on the Pacific Coast and in Toronto, where he now lives. He has also traveled in England, where he came into contact with some of the younger poets of the modern school. He has contributed to the *Canadian Forum* and the *Partisan Review*. He is one of the best of the younger Canadian poets who are approaching the proletarian theme from an intellectual and metaphysical standpoint.

A LOVER AND HIS LASS

The bright things of the morning
Fanned the temple of sorrow
Beyond this youth's eyes and left
The wing's delight, where forehead
Can grasp, though inclined to bow.

Then: he ventured to assert,
And heard his daring return
Boomerang back to him with her fancies
Giving bias, having gathered wings
And fine embroideries.

He ventured, and within their stasis
Of sculptured, couched love
Was, I heard, contumely and
The bare finger of stripped joy
Pointed with damned knowing aim.

One who had discovered that
There is nothing in Love's acid
That will dissolve the grid

Separating true heart from heart,
Nothing actually bitter enough

To engineer the awful soaring chaos
Of heart within identifying
Heart, that both know everything:
Finds gladness in this impotence,
And the ribs remain locked.

One who had strained, passed
These two sailing upon the grass,
Sweetly venturing their own
Stillness, taking with axis-aim
The core of their environ.

Perhaps they will get up when
It rains; perhaps they will leave
The grass golden when an aeon
Later it painfully tries
To ignore their correction.

LAST NIGHT, WHEN FEVERED MINUTES

Last night, when fevered minutes
    At length lay exhausted,
And the quiet time began its
Deliberate contriving,
Determined on giving
    To the fret it had ousted,
A new sort of living,

I, ambushed within your
    Disguising covert,
Became the reviewer
Of actions and motives,
Feeling assertive
    But secretly covered
And mentally furtive,

As if our Duality
    Had eclipsed my Self,
And by some agility
Kept acres pressed

For our interest
 Into the sweet gulf
Of your lips and breast.

Then, dearest, you were asleep,
 And I was free to become
Faithless, or to weep
At misery, or contemplate,
To murder or create,
 Or even to succumb
To a bourgeois fate.

That is, when we're beyond
 Temptation, we may attempt,
Like the tempted don
Or the self-hanged student,
A new excitant,
 For the moment exempt
From ties, and imprudent.

But the only attractive
 Prospect was outlined
In the perspective
Of our two eyes' vision,
As it brought Reason
 Further inland
To its right position.

That was what I, beneath
 Your web of travelled hair
Over my eyes, and the path
Your hand made down my face,
Thought, as I felt the space
 Widen between what we were
And what will replace.

For in this revolt
 The rebels have fled
Before the assault;
And we stand silent,
Knowing the excellent
 Journey travelled
To a fertile island.

AUTUMN, AND I WOULD GO
BACK TO YOU

Autumn, and I would go back to you.
This mist moves down my sides and shapes again
Forms that a warmth would evaporate.
What mist moves tranced luminous sand
To these shapes washable away?
Washable away by you, beloved,
With your hand in the gap that the parting made.

Though imminent and large beside the form
That bore it,
Like a child being all the mother before birth,
Reveals a mastered familiar
Not unlike not otherwise than us.

SOCKEYE SALMON

Caught in the glib catcher's net
With the fly that wanders, is the wonder fish;
Threshes a moment in the windowed lace
Till the eye is opaque and supremely glazed.
Not projects outward no tangent beam,
Not gets the increase of scenery
Passing to afflict the retina.
Being unfit to negotiate
The invisible livelihood of lungs,
It flails in a harder-to-swim-in sea.
Outward in material lies its wherewithal,
And the gills adjust, discriminate,
But is caught by the introspective air
That moves captor's brain and viscera.

Hung like a murderer with stretched-out neck,
Prepared for dissection, absorption, use,
Subject to putrefactive air,
In gaunt symmetry lies the wonder fish;
The trip from the egg to the waterfall,
Leaping lively or lying sunned,
The spawning, the schooling, the quick increase,
Are value and profit and capital.

No natural course is dissatisfied,
No function corrupted, there is no waste.
Use has been served up with vinegar,
The matter discussed with great dispatch.
In the ribbed lucent shallows is the window clear;
And the eyes' connection established there
All harmony, because all enmity
Has logically come to stay;
Cements by its close attractive gaze;
For man and fish find purest pleasure
In their prostituting mutual sight.

MARGARET AVISON (1918——)

MARGARET AVISON was born in 1918 and lives in Toronto. She is librarian and research assistant at the Institute of International Affairs. She has shown little interest in publishing her poetry, but the intensity of feeling and the originality and sincerity of her reactions to experience give her best poems a high value. Sensitive to the wilder aspects of nature, she is concerned, as in "The Butterfly," to bring order and meaning out of the welter of phenomena and to interpret, as in "Neverness," the mutations of time in terms of something significant in the lives of the human beings who throng Yonge Street at the noon rush hour. Her poetry is metaphysical poetry, passionate, intellectual, and essentially religious.

NEVERNESS

or

THE ONE SHIP BEACHED ON ONE FAR DISTANT SHORE

Old Adam, with his fist-full of plump earth,
His sunbright gaze on his eternal hill
Is not historical:
His tale is never done
For us who know a world no longer bathed
In the harsh splendour of economy.
We millions hold old Adam in our thoughts
A pivot for the future-past, a core
Of the one dream that never goads to action
But stains our entrails with nostalgia
And wrings the sweat of death in ancient eyes.

The one-celled plant is not historical.
Leeuwenhoek peered through his magic window
And in a puddle glimpsed the tiny grain
Of firmament that was before the Adam.

I'd like to pull that squinting Dutchman's sleeve
And ask what were his thoughts, lying at night,
And smelling the sad spring, and thinking out
Across the fulness of night air, smelling
The dark canal, and dusty oat-bag, cheese,
And wet straw-splintered wood, and rust-seamed leather
And pearly grass and silent deeps of sky
Honey-combed with its million years' of light
And prune-sweet earth
Honey-combed with the silent worms of dark.
Old Leeuwenhoek must have had ribby thoughts
To hoop the hollow pounding of his heart
Those nights of spring in 1600-odd.
It would be done if he could tell it us.

The tissue of our metaphysic cells
No magic window yet has dared reveal.
Our bleared world welters on
Far past the one-cell Instant. Points are spread
And privacy is unadmitted prison.

Why, now I know the lust of omnipresence!
You thousands merging lost,
    I call to you
Down the stone corridors that wall me in.

I am inside these days, snug in a job
In one of many varnished offices
Bleak with the wash of daylight
And us, the human pencils wearing blunt.
Soon I'll be out with you,
Another in the lonely unshut world
Where sun blinks hard on yellow brick and glazed,
On ads in sticky posterpaint
    And fuzzy
        At midday intersections.
The milk is washed down corded throats at noon
Along a thousands counters, and the hands

That count the nickel from a greasy palm
Have never felt an udder.
　　The windy dark
That thrums high among towers and nightspun branches
Whirs through our temples with a dry confusion.
We sprawl abandoned into disbelief
And feel the pivot-picture of old Adam
On the first hill that ever was, alone,
And see the hard earth seeded with sharp snow
And dream that history is done.

　　　　　*　　*　　*

And if that be the dream that whortles out
Into unending night
Then must the pivot Adam be denied
And the whole cycle ravelled and flung loose.
Is this the Epoch when the age-old Serpent
Must writhe and loosen, slacking out
To a new pool of Time's eternal sun?
O Adam, will your single outline blur
At this long last when slow mist wells
Fuming from all the valleys of the earth?
Or will our unfixed vision rather blind
Through agony to the last gelid stare
And none be left to witness the blank mist?

MARIA MINOR

I conceived. And Sorrow
Stirred within the womb.
My loins were pushed asunder
To make Adam room.

We met on the blonde uplands
That overlook the sea
And swift did Adam's navel
Blot out my agony.

The East is far and weary.
The thrush's young are fed.
I go down among the leaf mould
To mash my head.

OLD ADAM

The simple horizontal
Is a lie dull eyes create
And only in a glut of grief
Seems earth prostrate.

Light-years are grim-embrasive,
Elliptical they flow;
Vivid but pearl-deep jewel
This life of days we know.

I see not cruciform but just
One bead of blood from thence,
The heart essential prisoned
In a circumference.

THE BUTTERFLY

An uproar,
a spruce-green sky, bound in iron,
the murky sea running a sulphur scum,
I saw a butterfly, suddenly.
It clung between the ribs of the storm, wavering,
and flung against the battering bone-wind.
I remember it, glued to the grit of that rain-strewn beach
that glowered around it, swallowed its startled design
in the larger irridescence of unstrung dark.

That wild, sour air, those miles of crouching forest, that moth
when all enveloping space
is a thin glass globe, swirling with storm
tempt us to stare, and seize analogies.
The Voice that stilled the sea of Galilee
overtoned by the new peace, the fierce subhuman peace
of such an east sky, blanched like Eternity.

The meaning of the moth, even the smashed moth, the
meaning of the moth—
can't we stab that one angle into the curve of space
that sweeps so unrelenting, far above,
towards the subhuman swamp of under-dark?

BIBLIOGRAPHY

BIBLIOGRAPHY

I. SPECIAL COLLECTIONS IN CANADIAN LIBRARIES

Special collections in Canadian libraries of interest to the student of Canadian poetry are listed in the *Ontario Library Review and Canadian Periodical Index*, August, 1940. The most important are the following:

Anthropology.—The Father Morice Collection, University of Ottawa Library.

Wilfred Campbell.—Queen's University Library, Kingston. Twenty-seven volumes, manuscripts, photographs.

Canadian literature.—Queen's University Library, Lorne Pierce Collection. About three thousand volumes: first editions, manuscripts, photographs. Rich in Carman items.

Victoria University Library, Toronto, C. C. James Canadian Poetry Collection. An invaluable work of reference for poetry before 1900 is C. C. James, *A Bibliography of Canadian Poetry* (Toronto, 1899).

Canadiana.—Toronto Public Library. See Frances M. Staton and Marie Tremaine, *A Bibliography of Canadiana* (Toronto, 1934), and Toronto Public Library, *Landmarks of Canada: What Art Has Done for Canadian History: A Guide to the J. Ross Robertson Historical Collection* (2 vols.; Toronto, 1917–21).

Folk songs.—Mount Allison University Library, Sackville, Nova Scotia. Mary Mellish Archibald Memorial Library. About eleven thousand items and nine hundred and fifty phonograph records. See "Mary Mellish Archibald Memorial Library, 1905–1937: A Guide for Students" (Sackville, 1937). (Mimeographed.)

Charles Mair.—Queen's University Library. The Charles Mair Collection of about two thousand books, papers, manuscripts, etc.

II. ANTHOLOGIES OF CANADIAN POETRY

(The arrangement in this section is chronological.)

DEWART, EDWARD HARTLEY. *Selections from Canadian Poets; with Occasional Critical and Biographical Notes, and an Introductory Essay on Canadian Poetry.* Montreal, 1864.

SERANUS (MRS. S. FRANCES HARRISON). *The Canadian Birthday Book, with Poetical Selections for Every Day in the Year from Canadian Writers, English and French.* Toronto, 1887.

433

LIGHTHALL, WILLIAM DOUW. *Songs of the Great Dominion: Voices from the Forests and Waters, the Settlements and Cities of Canada.* London, 1889.

———. *Canadian Poems and Lays: Selections of Native Verse, Reflecting the Seasons, Legends, and Life of the Dominion.* London, n.d.

An edition of *Songs of the Great Dominion,* slightly shortened, in the "Canterbury Poets Series."

ROBERTS, GOODRIDGE BLISS. "Younger Canadian Poets." An appendix to *Younger American Poets,* ed. DOUGLAS SLADEN. New York, 1891.

WETHERELL, J. E. *Later Canadian Poems.* Toronto, 1893.

Contains selections from Cameron, Campbell, Carman, Lampman, Roberts, D. C. Scott, and F. G. Scott (with portraits); also an appendix of poems by Pauline Johnson, S. Frances Harrison, Agnes Maule Machar, Ethelwyn Wetherald, Sara Jeannette Duncan, and Isabella Valancy Crawford.

STEDMAN, EDMUND CLARENCE. *A Victorian Anthology, 1837–1895.* Boston and New York, 1896.

Pages 633–76 are an excellent brief anthology of nineteenth-century Canadian poetry. The poets included are Mrs. Moodie, Shanly, Heavysege, Duvar, Mair, Logan, George Murray, Cameron, Crawford, W. D. Lighthall, Roberts, Campbell, G. F. Scott, Elizabeth Roberts, Lampman, Carman, Mrs. Harrison, D. C. Scott, Gilbert Parker, Pauline Johnson, Arthur Weir, and Ethelwyn Wetherald.

RAND, THEODORE H. *A Treasury of Canadian Verse, with Brief Biographical Notes.* Toronto and London, 1900.

CASWELL, EDWARD S. *Canadian Singers and Their Songs.* Toronto, 1902. New ed., 1919.

A collection of portraits and autograph poems.

HARDY, E. A. *Selections from Canadian Poets.* Toronto, 1906.

BURPEE, LAWRENCE J. *Flowers from a Canadian Garden.* Toronto, 1909.

———. *A Century of Canadian Sonnets.* Toronto, 1910.

WHYTE-EDGAR, MRS. C. M. *A Wreath of Canadian Songs, Containing Biographical Sketches and Numerous Selections from Deceased Canadian Poets.* Toronto, 1910.

A good deal of mediocre poetry but some useful bibliographical information on the pre-Confederation period.

CAMPBELL, WILFRED. *The Oxford Book of Canadian Verse.* Oxford and Toronto, 1913.

GARVIN, JOHN W. *Canadian Poets.* Toronto, 1916. Revised and enlarged, 1926.

BROADUS, E. K. and E. H. *A Book of Canadian Prose and Verse.* Toronto, 1923. Revised and enlarged, 1934.

STEPHEN, A. M. *The Golden Treasury of Canadian Verse.* Toronto, 1928.

BENSON, NATHANIEL A. *Modern Canadian Poetry.* Ottawa, 1930.

RITCHIE, ELIZA. *Songs of the Maritimes.* Toronto, 1931.

CARMAN, BLISS, and PIERCE, LORNE. *Our Canadian Literature, Representative Verse, English and French.* Rev. ed. Toronto, 1935.

BROOKER, BERTRAM. *Yearbook of the Arts in Canada, 1936.* Toronto, 1936.
An anthology of contemporary prose and verse.

GARVIN, JOHN W. *Cap and Bells: An Anthology of Light Verse by Canadian Poets.* Foreword by LORNE PIERCE. Toronto, 1936.

New Provinces: Poems of Several Authors [*Robert Finch, Leo Kennedy, A. M. Klein, E. J. Pratt, F. R. Scott, A. J. M. Smith*]. Toronto, 1936.

BENNETT, ETHEL HUME. *New Harvesting: Contemporary Canadian Poetry, 1918–1938.* Toronto, 1938.

CREIGHTON, ALAN, and RIDLEY, HILDA M. *A New Canadian Anthology.* Toronto, 1938.

Voices of Victory: Representative Poetry of Canada in Wartime. Toronto, 1941.

GUSTAFSON, RALPH. *Anthology of Canadian Poetry* (*English*). Harmondsworth, England; Toronto; and New York, 1942.

For critical analyses of most of these anthologies see J. D. Logan and Donald G. French, *Highways of Canadian Literature,* chap. xxix; W. A. Deacon, "A Guide to the Anthologies," in his *Poteen;* and A. J. M. Smith, "Canadian Anthologies, New and Old" in *University of Toronto Quarterly,* July, 1942.

III. CANADIAN LITERATURE

ARCHER, WILLIAM. *Poets of the Younger Generation.* London, 1902.
Contains appreciative essays on Carman, Roberts, and Duncan Campbell Scott.

BAKER, RAY PALMER. *A History of English-Canadian Literature to the Confederation: Its Relation to the Literature of Great Britain and the United States.* Cambridge, Mass., 1920.
One of the few scholarly treatments of Canadian literature. Indispensable for the period covered.

BROWN, E. K. 'Canadian Nature Poetry," *Think,* VII (1941), 9.

———. "The Development of Poetry in Canada, 1880–1940," *Poetry: A Magazine of Verse,* April, 1941.
The best brief introduction, intelligent and sound.

———. "Poetry," in "Letters in Canada," *University of Toronto Quarterly.* Annually, since 1936, in the April number.
A useful survey of the year's work in Canadian poetry, bibliographical and critical.

BURPEE, LAWRENCE J. *A Little Book of Canadian Essays.* Toronto, 1909.
Essays on Cameron, Crawford, Duvar, Heavysege, Lampman, Lanigan, and others. Sketchy, but contains information not easily found elsewhere.

COLLIN, W. E. "Poetry," in *Canadian Literature To-day,* ed. E. K. BROWN. Toronto, 1938.
A series of broadcasts sponsored by the Canadian Broadcasting Company.

———. *The White Savannahs.* Toronto, 1936
A collection of essays on Canadian literature, provocative and alert. Particularly important are the essays on Lampman, Pickthall, Pratt, and Klein.

COOPER, JOHN A. "Canadian Poetry," *National Review*, May, 1897.

DEACON, WILLIAM ARTHUR. *Poteen*. Ottawa, 1930.
Literary journalism, often stimulating, sometimes uncritical.

EDGAR, PELHAM. "English-Canadian Literature," *Cambridge History of English Literature*, Vol. XIV. London and Cambridge, 1916.
A sympathetic and scholarly interpretation by the finest of the older critics.

HARTE, W. BLACKBURN. "Some Canadian Writers of To-day," *New England Magazine*, September, 1890.

KENNEDY, LEO. "Direction for Canadian Poets," *New Frontier*, June, 1936.
A call to Canadian poets to embrace the social theme.

KERR, J. "Some Canadian Poets," *Empire Review*, July, 1937.

LOGAN, J. D., and FRENCH, DONALD G. *Highways of Canadian Literature*. Toronto, 1924.
An ambitious and comprehensive textbook, uncritical and badly written.

McCRACKEN, M. S. "Tradition of Pre-Confederation English-Canadian Literature," *Revue de l'Université d'Ottawa*, October–December, 1937.

MACMECHAN, ARCHIBALD. *Head-Waters of Canadian Literature*. Toronto, 1924.
A gracefully written and sympathetic sketch, conservative and correct.

MACMURCHY, ARCHIBALD. *Handbook of Canadian Literature*. Toronto, 1906.
A useful compendium of facts.

MARQUIS, T. G. "A History of English-Canadian Literature," *Canada and Its Provinces*, Vol. XII. Toronto, 1914.
A biographical survey, somewhat capricious in judgment but well worth reading.

MORGAN, HENRY J. *Bibliotheca Canadensis, or A Manual of Canadian Literature*. Ottawa, 1867.
A large biographical encyclopedia; an indispensable guide to the study of Canadian literature before the Confederation.

PIERCE, LORNE. *An Outline of Canadian Literature (French and English)*. Toronto, 1927.
Contains much useful information; an appreciative criticism of the Romantic poets.

———. "Literature—English-Canadian," *Encyclopedia of Canada*, Vol. IV. Toronto, 1935–37.

PRATT, E. J. "Canadian Poetry—Past and Present," *University of Toronto Quarterly*, October, 1938.
Catholicity of taste is revealed in this essay by the leading Canadian poet of today.

RHODENIZER, V. B. *A Handbook of Canadian Literature*. Ottawa, 1930.
On the whole, the best book of its kind, although Canadian poets tend to be praised according to the nearness of their approach to the styles of Keats or Shelley.

ROBERTS, SIR CHARLES G. D. "Some Reminiscences of Bliss Carman in New York," *Canadian Poetry Magazine*, December, 1940.

ROBERTS, GOODRIDGE BLISS. "The Canadian Poets," *King's College Record*, December, 1886.

SCOTT, DUNCAN CAMPBELL. "Poetry and Progress: Presidential Address to the Royal Society of Canada, May 17, 1922," *Proceedings and Transactions of the Royal Society of Canada*, Vol. XVI (3d ser., 1922).

SHOOLMAN, R. "Is There a Canadian Literature?" *Story*, March, 1937.

SMITH, A. J. M. "Canadian Anthologies, New and Old," *University of Toronto Quarterly*, July, 1942.

————. "Canadian Literature," *London Times*, May 15, 1939.

————. "Canadian Poetry—a Minority Report," *University of Toronto Quarterly*, January, 1939.

————. "'Our Poets'—a Sketch of Canadian Poetry in the Nineteenth Century," *ibid.*, October, 1942.

————. "Wanted—Canadian Criticism," *Canadian Forum*, April, 1928.

STEPHEN, A. M. "Canadian Poets and Critics," *New Frontier*, September, 1936.

STEVENSON, LIONEL. *Appraisals of Canadian Literature*. Toronto, 1926.

WALDRON, GORDON. "Canadian Poetry, a Criticism," *Canadian Magazine*, December, 1896.
Important as an early recognition of the limitations and weaknesses of the school of Roberts.

IV. STUDIES OF INDIVIDUAL AUTHORS

Only the most important items and those with general implications are listed here. Other references will be found in the biographical introductions.

AYRE, ROBERT. "Pauline Johnson," *Canadian Forum*, October, 1933.

BROCKINGTON, LEONARD W. "Duncan Campbell Scott's Eightieth Birthday," *Saturday Night*, August 1, 1942.

BROWN, E. K. "Duncan Campbell Scott, Individual Poet," *Manitoba Arts Review*, spring, 1941.

BURPEE, LAWRENCE J. "Charles Heavysege," *Transactions of the Royal Society of Canada*, Vol. VII (2d ser., 1901–2).

CAPPON, JAMES. *Bliss Carman*. Toronto, 1930.

————. *Roberts and the Influences of His Time*. Toronto, 1905.

————. *Charles G. D. Roberts*. "Makers of Canadian Literature." Toronto, n.d. (1925).

CONNOR, CARL Y. *Archibald Lampman, Canadian Poet of Nature*. Foreword by RAY PALMER BAKER. Montreal, 1929.

DEWART, EDWARD HARTLEY. "Charles Sangster," *Canadian Magazine*, May, 1896.

EDEL, LEON. "Abraham M. Klein," *Canadian Forum*, May, 1932.

EDGAR, PELHAM. "Duncan Campbell Scott," *Dalhousie Review*, Vol. VII (1927–28).

GREENSHIELDS, E. B. "A Forgotten Poet [Heavysege]," *University Magazine* (Montreal), October, 1908.

HALE, KATHERINE. *Isabella Valancy Crawford*. "Makers of Canadian Literature." Toronto, n.d.

HATHAWAY, E. J. "Isabella Valancy Crawford," *Canadian Magazine*, October, 1895.

KENNEDY, LEO. "Raymond Knister," *Canadian Forum*, September, 1932.

KLINCK, CARL F. *Wilfred Campbell: A Study in Late Provincial Victorianism.* New York and Toronto, 1942.

LAURISTON, VICTOR. *Arthur Stringer, Son of the North.* "Makers of Canadian Literature." Toronto, 1941.

LEE, H. D. C. *Bliss Carman: A Study in Canadian Poetry.* Buxton, 1912.

McCAIG, D. "Alexander McLachlan," *Canadian Magazine*, November, 1897.

MacDONALD, J. F. *William Henry Drummond.* "Makers of Canadian Literature." Toronto, n.d.

MACKAY, L. A. "W. W. Campbell," *Canadian Forum*, November, 1933.

————. "Bliss Carman," *ibid.*, February, 1933.

————. 'Wilson MacDonald," *ibid.*, April, 1933.

MARQUIS, T. G. "C. G. D. Roberts," *Canadian Magazine*, September, 1893.

MILLER, MURIEL. *Bliss Carman: A Portrait.* Toronto, 1935.

MUNROE, DAVID. "Joseph Howe as Man of Letters," *Dalhousie Review*, January, 1941.

PIERCE, LORNE. *Three Fredericton Poets [Carman, Roberts, and Sherman].* Toronto, 1933.

————. *Marjorie Pickthall: A Book of Remembrance.* Toronto, 1925.

POMEROY, ELSIE. *Sir Charles G. D. Roberts: A Biography.* With an Introduction by LORNE PIERCE. Toronto, 1943.

PRATT, E. J. "Marjorie Pickthall," *Canadian Forum*, June, 1933.

SHEPHERD, ODELL. *Bliss Carman.* Boston, 1924.

STRINGER, ARTHUR. "Archibald Lampman," *Canadian Magazine*, April, 1894.

————. "Wild Poets I've Known" [Carman, Drummond, Lampman, Pickthall], *Saturday Night*, March 1, April 26, May 24, June 14, 1941.

SUTHERLAND, BRUCE. "The Writing of Patrick Anderson," *First Statement*, May 14, 1943.

SYKES, W. J. "The Poetry of Duncan Campbell Scott," *Queen's Quarterly*, spring, 1939.

'Two Canadian Poets: Fréchette and Drummond," *Edinburgh Review*, April, 1909.

V. HISTORICAL AND CULTURAL BACKGROUND

BRADY, ALEXANDER. *Canada.* Toronto, 1932.

BOURINOT, J. G. *Our Intellectual Strength and Weakness: A Short Historical and Critical Review of Literature, Art and Education in Canada.* Montreal and London, 1893.
An expansion of the presidential address delivered to the Royal Society of Canada, May, 1893. An extremely valuable work.

BURPEE, LAWRENCE J. *The Oxford Encyclopedia of Canadian History.* "Makers of Canada Series," Vol. XII. Toronto and London, 1926.

BURT, ALFRED LEROY. *A Short History of Canada for Americans.* New York and Toronto, 1942.

CHAMBERLIN, W. H. *Canada Today and Tomorrow.* Boston and Toronto, 1942.

CREIGHTON, D. G. *The Commercial Empire of the St. Lawrence, 1760–1850.* New Haven, 1937.
This significant work explores implications beyond the field indicated in the title.

GIBBON, JOHN MURRAY. *Canadian Mosaic: The Making of a Northern Nation.* Toronto, 1938.

GRANT, W. L. (ed.). *The Makers of Canada.* New ed. 12 vols. Oxford and Toronto, 1926.

HUTCHISON, BRUCE *The Unknown Country.* New York and Toronto, 1942.

LONG, MORDEN H. *A History of the Canadian People,* Vol. I: *New France.* Toronto, 1942.

MACCORMAC, JOHN. *Canada, America's Problem.* New York, 1940.

MACFARLANE, R. O. "What Is a Canadian?" *Manitoba Arts Review*, spring, 1938.

MCINNES, EDGAR W. *The Unguarded Frontier.* New York and Toronto, 1942.

MACLENNAN, HUGH. "Culture, Canadian Style," *Saturday Review of Literature*, March 28, 1942.

MORGAN, HENRY J. *Sketches of Celebrated Canadians, and Persons Connected with Canada from the Earliest Period in the History of the Province down to the Present Time.* Montreal, 1865.
Preserves information about Canadian worthies unobtainable elsewhere.

ROBERTS, CHARLES G. D. *A History of Canada.* Boston, London, Toronto, 1897. Rev. ed. 1909.

Rose, J. Holland; Newton, A. P.; and Benians, E. A. *The Cambridge History of the British Empire*, Vol. VI: *Canada and Newfoundland*. Cambridge, 1930.

Scott, F. R. *Canada Today*. Toronto, 1938.

Shortt, Adam, and Doughty, Arthur (eds.). *Canada and Its Provinces*. 22 vols. Toronto, 1914.

Siegfried, André. *Canada*. London, 1937.

Trotter, R. G. "Has Canada a National Culture?" *Queen's Quarterly*, summer, 1937.

[Various Authors.] *Canada*. Reprinted from the *Times*, May 15, 1939. London, 1939.

Wallace, W. Stewart. *The Growth of Canadian National Feeling*. Toronto, 1927.

Wallace, W. Stewart (ed.). *The Encyclopedia of Canada*. 6 vols. Toronto, 1935–37.

Wittke, Carl. *History of Canada*. 3d ed. rev. New York, 1941.

Wrong, George M. *The Canadians: The Story of a People*. Toronto, 1938.

Wrong, George M., and Laughton, H. H. (eds.). *The Chronicles of Canada*. 32 vols. Toronto, 1914–16.

INDEXES

INDEX OF AUTHORS

INDEX OF FIRST LINES

447

448   THE BOOK OF CANADIAN POETRY

Date Due